T0385207

Sharing My Love of Cricket

HENRY BLOFELD

Sharing My Love of Cricket

Playing the Game and Spreading the Word

**HODDER &
STOUGHTON**

First published in Great Britain in 2024 by Hodder & Stoughton Limited
An Hachette UK company

The authorised representative in the EEA is Hachette Ireland, 8 Castlecourt
Centre, Dublin 15, D15 XTP3, Ireland (email: info@hbgi.ie)

4

A CIP catalogue record for this title is available from the British Library

Hardback ISBN 9781399733250
ebook ISBN 9781399733274

Typeset in Adobe Caslon by Hewer Text UK Ltd, Edinburgh
Printed and bound in Great Britain by Clays Ltd, Elcograf S.p.A.

Hodder & Stoughton policy is to use papers that are natural, renewable
and recyclable products and made from wood grown in sustainable
forests. The logging and manufacturing processes are expected to
conform to the environmental regulations of the country of origin.

Hodder & Stoughton Limited
Carmelite House
50 Victoria Embankment
London EC4Y 0DZ

www.hodder.co.uk

Huge thanks to my wife, Valeria, and her daughter, Tanya, for their great help with internet tantrums, and to my daughter, Suki, for her inspiring enquiries.

And a big thank you to Roddy Bloomfield, who came up with the title and who, with great friendship and understanding, has helped mastermind ten of my books.

CONTENTS

Introduction   1

1 Marvellous Characters Everywhere   7

2 The Commentator's Chair   21

3 Modus Operandi   39

4 Four Byes in Rio   49

5 Rest Days   59

6 To India by Rolls   71

7 A Street Corner in Kandahar   85

8 Our Brave New World   101

9 Is Bazball the Saviour?   111

10 Groucho Laps up Bazball   121

11 A Miracle Denied   135

12 Painted with a Broad Brush   155

13 The Hundred and Beyond   163

14 New Kids on the Block   181

15 Friendly Banter   195

16 The Mixture is Rich   207

17 An Unexpected Lifeline   223

Picture Acknowledgements   231

Index   233

INTRODUCTION

THE two halves of this book are the bookends of my life with cricket. It all began for me in 1947, when Denis Compton and Bill Edrich made 3,816 and 3,539 first-class runs for Middlesex and England and I was hooked. The public flocked to see them, a relentless sun beat down on their orgy of runs and the players were paid small change for their efforts. In the immediate post-war years, the fare was County Championship and Test cricket, and it was all conducted in an atmosphere of peaceful happiness and contentment. Cricket in England then seemed a structure as permanent, unshakable and tranquil as the Pavilion at Lord's.

In the first half, I have tried to give an idea of the life we were able to lead in the days when I learnt the game and paddled briefly in the shallow end of first-class cricket, before entering first the press and then the commentary box. The press box was a different place then, and I have attempted to put flesh and blood back into some of the engaging, disparate figures who, sitting at the bare and rather spartan desks around the county grounds, brought the news of each day's play to their readers. The commentary box was a different place too, full of ripe characters led by those two brilliant broadcasters John Arlott and Brian Johnston and shaped by the deft hand of our producer, Peter Baxter, who was in control for thirty-four years and never received the credit he should have done for turning *Test Match Special* into such a unique programme.

I have to admit to being self-indulgent and taking readers on two extraordinary journeys of a kind made possible by the more relaxed fixture list in those far-distant days. In 1976, John Woodcock, the famous cricket correspondent of *The Times*, and I drove with three others in a 1921 Rolls-Royce from London to Bombay to watch Tony Greig's England side in India that winter. Four years later, I went to six South American countries while helping to manage a side of young first-class cricketers put together by the businessman Derrick Robins. Both were remarkable adventures which could hardly be fitted into today's hectic cricketing schedule.

Fast-forward to 2022 and a ferociously different world. Cricket, for so long the uncomplaining poor relation of major sports, was now gripped by money, and when that happens, greed is never far behind. Limited-over cricket was fast taking over. India had seized hold of the Twenty20 game and, with brilliant marketing, was turning it into a round-the-world, money-controlled franchise fiesta. As a result, Test cricket was fighting for a place in the calendar, if not for its very existence. It was at this point that the two splendid New Zealanders who effectively control England's cricket – Brendon McCullum, the head coach, and his chief lieutenant, the amazing Ben Stokes, the captain – came together to transform Test match cricket with Bazball. This may have been McCullum's invention, but it could never have worked without Stokes's inspirational support. Suddenly Test cricket was being played at an exciting new tempo. Attack was the aim of the game and draws, for so long the bugbear of Test cricket, were eliminated – unless the weather intervened. Test cricket became far more user-friendly as a result, and in 2023 the extraordinary Ashes series in England was played in front of twenty-four full-house crowds.

For all that, a drawn Test match is not always a bore, and I have to say that the most exciting Test match I ever watched ended in a draw. England played the fifth and final Test against the West Indies at Bourda in Georgetown, Guyana, in 1967–68. At the end of the sixth day – if the series had not already been decided, the final Test had an extra day – England's last man, Jeff Jones, hemmed in by close catchers, somehow survived the final over, bowled by that wonderful off-spinner, Lance Gibbs. The draw gave England the series.

Despite the arrival of Bazball, there is now less and less room for Test cricket in the annual calendar, with new T20 franchise tournaments springing up not only in the cricket-playing world, but also far beyond its traditional boundaries, and one such is Major League Cricket (MLC) in the USA.

First-class cricket was played in the United States before 1914, when the game there was put firmly in its place by its ugly cousin, baseball. After that, the American attitude to cricket became nothing if not contemptuous. This was admirably summed up by Groucho Marx in 1954 when he made an unlikely visit to Lord's to see a day's Test cricket. He had watched most of the morning session when someone asked him what he thought of it. 'So when is it going to start?' was his disarming reply. He would have been surprised to learn that in 2024, MLC, inspired by the Indian Premier League and financed largely by expatriate Indians, would be embarking on its second season. Not only that, but the T20 World Cup in 2024 would be jointly hosted by the West Indies and the United States, with international cricket even coming to New York.

I thought Groucho ought to have another crack at the game, so I arranged for his ghost to go along to Edgbaston to watch the first Ashes Test in 2023, just to see what the great man would make of Bazball. He so enjoyed that game that he insisted on staying on to watch the second Test at Lord's, where he had the time of his life.

Another surprising Indian-inspired initiative prompted the setting-up of a big T20 competition in Saudi Arabia for 2024. The Saudis are keen to make this the most eye-catching of all the T20 franchises. These two new tournaments, in the US and Saudi Arabia, will not only make it even harder to fit Test matches into the cricketing year, they may well prevent England's own T20 gig, the Blast and its half-brother, The Hundred, from attracting the world's best players – for these two tournaments will not be able to afford them.

Is it possible to bring some sort of order to all of this? In the glaring absence of any help from the ICC, the game's governing body, the MCC have bravely organised a meeting of the leading protagonists of the T20 franchise world and those doing their best to preserve Test cricket, at Lord's on 5 July 2024. It is extremely unlikely that any far-reaching decisions will have been taken then, for no one will have had the authority to do so, but important promises of serious intent will, I hope, have been made which will lead to the franchise lot being more concerned about the future of Test cricket. Or have we already gone too far down the present track for there to be a real chance of anyone being willing to pull back? As it was, it appeared that those involved, especially on the franchise side, were more concerned with the money side of the modern game than the intrinsic values of the sport. But at least this was a start in the struggle to reorganise the game.

While all this has been going on, England's cricket has been hit by another serious problem. In March 2021, the ECB set up the Independent Commission for Equity in Cricket (ICEC) to look into the state of the game in England. Originally inspired by the death of George Floyd, the importance of this was emphasised by the complaints made by Pakistan-born Azeem Rafiq about the racist treatment he had received while playing for Yorkshire. In June 2023, the ICEC delivered a most damning report which said that cricket in England was institutionally racist, sexist, classist and misogynist. The ECB have already said that much must be done to make cricket in England a game with a level playing field for everyone. They have yet to come up with their promised plan of action.

The world in which I began my life in cricket could hardly be further away from the world of cricket today. In the second half of this book, I have attempted to discuss some of the problems that grip the modern game. It is extraordinary that those in charge appear to have been so blind to what has been going on and to have made so little attempt to influence the way things have developed. Who knows where we will end up, but because cricket is such a wonderful game that has always stood for the best in life, I am buoyed by the great belief that common sense will in the end prevail, and that Test cricket and the T20 franchise world will be able to live side by side in peace. Then, there will still be something for everyone. If two-innings cricket ever disappears and the one-day game allows the balance between bat and ball to become hopelessly distorted in favour of the bat, the game could degenerate into an unwatchable farce.

I would like to end this introduction with a lovely example of how things happened when I was a boy and which I am sure would never be allowed today. In May 1956, when I was in the Eton Eleven, we played a game against a Forty Club side which had been put together by Walter Robins, who had captained England briefly in the thirties. He brought down eleven old Middlesex players. The one who was not so old was Denis Compton, my all-time hero, who was then thirty-eight. During the previous winter he had had his right kneecap removed as the result of an injury while playing football for Arsenal. This was his first cricket since the operation.

He could hardly move and when he bowled his left-arm spinners, he stood with one foot on either side of the bowling crease and simply brought his arm over. When he batted later on, his right foot, now the back foot, was anchored in the crease (see the photograph on page 1 of the picture section) and he was able to come forward with the left. He made some cautious runs and was good company at lunch, but there was surely no chance of him ever playing serious cricket again. However, the knee improved amazingly quickly and in July he was back in the Middlesex side and batting well enough to be chosen to play in the fifth Test against Australia, at The Oval. England were 2–1 up in the series and, even if they had lost this match, would have retained the Ashes, which may have helped the selectors decide to take a chance with Compton. He made 94 in England's first innings of 247 and Don Bradman, from his seat in the press box, described it as the best innings of the series.

I don't think this sequence of events could have happened today. After such an operation, would a star like Denis Compton have been allowed to try to rebuild his career in this rather haphazard way? There was not a single journalist there that day at Eton, just a lone photographer. Although Compton then went on to score a lot of runs for Middlesex, I can't see modern Test selectors taking a chance like that in the final Test, especially with a thirty-eight-year-old after such serious surgery, and then going on to pick him for the tour of South Africa the following winter. What passed muster in 1956 is most unlikely to have been even considered almost seventy years later.

Another difference between then and now is that the modern world does not throw up the characters that were once a part of every team. Limited-over cricket has meant there is no room for the oldies, the knowledgeable old pros who show the youngsters the way. The supreme example of this was Wilfred Rhodes, who was almost forty-nine when, taking six wickets in the match, he helped England to victory against Australia at The Oval in 1926. He went on to play in all four Tests in the West Indies in 1929–30 when he was fifty-two. We live in a different world today.

1

MARVELLOUS CHARACTERS EVERYWHERE

'Up for almost anything'

I N a world that has changed as fast as this one has over the last few decades, it is almost inevitable that the elderly will often be accused of looking back longingly at much that went on in the 'good old days'. With all the extraordinary things happening with such alarming rapidity, especially in the shortened forms of the game, this applies as much to cricket, which resisted significant change for such a long time, as it does to anything else in this helter-skelter world. At this stage of the book, I shall not only go along with that accusation, I shall stand guilty as charged and take full advantage!

When I was first taken over by cricket, there were individuals involved who reflected the character of the game they were playing or watching. It may not have been until much later, when hindsight came into play, that they were fully appreciated. At the time, they were the norm, and it is only when compared with the present day that they stand out as icons of a world that has gone for good. Let us have a look at some of them.

It was in 1947 that cricket first grabbed me. In May, I began a five-year stint at Sunningdale School near Ascot. I was taught to play cricket at the age of about seven and a half by the formidable

Miss Paterson, a lady who clicked her fingers and took no prisoners. She seemed old then – almost everyone did – but was probably only forty-ish. She bowled a lively underarm and stood no nonsense. Somehow, and I am not certain how or why, she instilled within me an immense love for the game. I have always been in her debt. Miss Paterson, who presumably had a first name although I don't think I ever came across it, was a figure of her time. I am not at all sure what she would have made of the 'reverse sweep' or the 'ramp' or anything similarly unchristian, had it come her way. The joy of cricket as taught by her was swiftly rubbed in during the following summer holidays, when my father and mother took me across the old park at home to watch our village team in action.

The villages of Hoveton and Wroxham in Norfolk, separated by a rather elderly bridge over the river Bure, forgot their differences when it came to cricket and played happily together on the lovely ground at Hoveton, which sadly is no more. In my mind, I can still see many of the players, but the one I shall remember the most was Colonel Ingram-Johnson. He had been for many years, I am sure, a redoubtable soldier who, as his name somehow suggests, had spent most of his career helping to preserve the peace in India. He was now a trifle portly with a bit of a swagger and the customary officer's moustache. He still kept wicket well enough, was never short of an opinion or an appeal, he made useful runs in the middle order, and ran between the wickets with a middle-aged sense of entitlement. Colonel Ingram-Johnson was a man seldom troubled by self-doubt. He was called Inky by those in the know; otherwise he answered to 'Colonel'. He had a thin, rather gloomy wife who spoke with the deepest of voices. She never had a cigarette out of her hand and had a cough to match, and sat dutifully on a brown rug with a glass within reach.

Another character, if in a lower key, was the aptly named Arthur Tink – at least I thought his name fitted him well, for it seemed to imply a severe lack of frivolity. He looked almost frail and was not given to talking much, seldom smiled and bowled with astonishing accuracy at a gentle medium pace off a seven-pace run-up. If anyone tried to slog him, the ball almost always ended up in the hands of mid on. Arthur had an outstandingly beautiful wife, Mona, who had long dark hair and a lovely smile which on a good day was on the verge of being seductive. I never knew what Arthur did for a living, and there was something more than faintly mysterious about him. He was certainly not broke either, just extremely careful. I wondered what hidden depths he had needed to acquire the spectacular Mona.

My parents took me in 1948 for the first time to Lakenham Cricket Ground in Norwich, where Norfolk played most of their home games in the Minor Counties Championship. I well remember my first few visits, for I was mesmerised by every ball. There were wonderful characters everywhere, starting with Norfolk's tall, handsome captain, Wilfrid Thompson, in his forties then, with black, swept-back, gleaming hair. He set his field in a loud, commanding voice, bowled fast and smote soaring sixes – I found them unbelievably exciting – onto the bowling green at the Pavilion End. I was captivated, too, by the three Rought-Rought brothers, Rodney, Basil and Desmond, who wore excitingly colourful club caps of the sort Fred Trueman was later to describe, with disdainful emphasis, as 'jazz 'ats'. Two of the Rought-Roughts had played first-class cricket, which, for me, was the ultimate qualification for hero worship.

The characters on the other side of the boundary were led by Mike Falcon, shooting stick in hand, grey-haired, with a cheerful voice and a happy chuckling laugh. Taking eight wickets at just above medium pace, he had helped to bowl Warwick Armstrong's unbeaten Australian side to defeat by Archie MacLaren's XI at Eastbourne at the end of their tour in 1921. Falcon had first captained Norfolk in 1911 and did not surrender the post until the end of the 1946 season. He was an outstanding bowler who batted more than just a bit. He had never wanted to play first-class cricket, although his friend Pelham Warner had tried unsuccessfully to make him change his mind and join Middlesex. Falcon once told me he had no wish to play county cricket six days a week, and that anyway he was not qualified to play for Middlesex. He paused here for a moment, before saying with a chuckle, 'But these days, I suppose anyone who pumps ship in Charing Cross Station is qualified to play for Middlesex.' He would talk about Sydney Barnes, one of the two or three greatest bowlers of all time, coming to Lakenham in the twenties to bowl at medium pace for Staffordshire – Barnes played most of his cricket for Staffordshire. 'At the end of a Norfolk innings of any length,' Falcon told me, 'there would be a bare patch on a good length about the size of an orange where Barnes had relentlessly pitched the ball for hour after hour. He would not allow his captain to take him off.'

Another great Norfolk character I was lucky enough to play with for several seasons in the county side was the remarkable Bill Edrich. He returned to captain his home county in 1959 when his days with Middlesex and his even better-known partner-in-arms, Denis Compton, were over. Bill knew a huge amount about the game and he stood at first slip, where he talked about his cricketing life almost non-stop. He made lots of runs for us, mostly on the leg side, held on to quite a few catches, was always keen to win and wonderfully quick to spot an opponent who was trying to get one over him. There was Maurice Crouch, for instance, a prosperous farmer and long-serving captain of Cambridgeshire who could be an unlovable rogue on the field. He and Bill had some great moments, especially when, at Lakenham, I caught Crouch behind the wicket for his second nought of the match. It was the first time he had made a pair of spectacles, and when the umpire gave him out he refused to go. Bill made a rousing speech from beside me at first slip, and for once an almost speechless Crouch, who had several times tried in vain to interrupt, was forced to drag himself off, muttering every step of the way. It was a memorable verbal joust. Bill was a fine captain and led us to the top of the Minor Counties table in 1960 but, to his dismay, we lost the challenge match to Lancashire Second XI by quite a margin. Bill kept on with Norfolk until his late fifties. They don't make 'em like him any more.

In the years I spent growing up with the game and before my whole life turned professionally and irrevocably to cricket, I met many unforgettable characters. When I went to Eton, I learned a great deal from Claude Taylor, who was in charge of Lower Sixpenny (the under-15s). He loved the beauty and artistry of cricket and was a brilliant coach, able to communicate the joys and skills of the game in a delightfully digestible form. CHT (Eton masters, called 'beaks', were known by their initials) had once made on behalf of Oxford the slowest hundred ever scored in the Varsity Match at Lord's. Now the gentlest of men, he taught Classics, played the oboe with scholarly precision and was married to the sister of Ian Peebles, a Scotsman who had bowled leg-breaks and googlies for England in the thirties.

I left school in unusual circumstances, having bicycled into a bus which was moving fast enough for me to spend a long time unconscious with a broken skull, before resuming life and going straight up to Cambridge. The huge leap from school to university was perfectly illustrated by the comparison between the names of past teams on their respective walls in the pavilions on Agar's Plough at Eton and at Fenner's, the venerable old university ground. Fenner's boasted such names as, among many others, K.S. Ranjitsinhji, G.L. Jessop, A.P.F. Chapman, P.B.H. May and E.R. Dexter, with which Agar's Plough was unable to compete, although there were a couple of England captains, Gubby Allen and George Mann. I had been captain of the Eton XI in 1957, but a few months later the captain I was playing under at Cambridge was no less a player than the supreme batsman and future England captain Ted Dexter. Our opponents were Kent, led by Colin Cowdrey, another England captain, and it was a first-class match – quite a step up. My first catch behind the wicket in a first-class match was Cowdrey c Blofeld b Dexter. Not a bad start, although I made a duck in my first first-class innings.

Dexter was an extraordinary character both on and off the field. I played a handful of games under his captaincy in 1958 and I don't think I ever had a conversation with him. Sometimes he was friendly, but most of the time he was far distant, seemingly unaware of the rest of us and in a world of his own. On the field, his character was classically summed up in the next match, against Lancashire. On the second morning we walked out to bat together in silence at the start at 11.30. I shall never forget how the umpires and I then kept leaping out of the way of his furious but perfect straight drives off none other than Brian Statham, who spent much of his time opening the bowling for England with Fred Trueman. Ken Higgs, who also went on to open the bowling for England, was playing in that game and received similar treatment. Dexter's strokeplay was extraordinary, and watching him bat from the other end was a remarkable experience.

Somehow I stayed in until lunch and afterwards we walked out again, for the third time, and once more it was in complete silence. Not a single word was spoken on any of the journeys. Dexter made a remarkable hundred while I just failed to reach an edgy fifty. Talking of extraordinary characters I came across that year at Cambridge, Dai Davies was one of the umpires for the match against the New Zealand touring side at Fenner's. In the first evening after the close of play, Davies, a Test match umpire who had played for Glamorgan for many years, stood on the bar and sang 'Land of My Fathers' in his vibrantly powerful Welsh voice – it was his birthday.

In my second year, I scraped into a more moderate Cambridge side as an opening batsman. The two most notable characters I met that year were both opponents with unique cricketing qualifications. We played Nottinghamshire at Trent Bridge and their captain, Reg Simpson, had persuaded that great Australian all-rounder Keith Miller to come up from London and play for Nottinghamshire. He opened the bowling and sent down a leg-break in the first over of the match. I know because I faced the over. Miller then made a hundred by kind permission of me: when he was 65 I dropped him from a skyer at deep midwicket.

A few weeks later we played the MCC at Lord's and Denis Compton was in the home side in one of his last first-class matches. A trifle portly, he made an inimitably improvised 71 in their first innings. I somehow managed to make 138 in our second, my only first-class hundred. When I reached three figures the great man himself walked forward from slip and shook me by the hand. It doesn't get much better than that. (If you'll forgive a little name-dropping, I had the other great moment of my life on my first honeymoon, in Jamaica. After an introduction by Ian Fleming, we went to dinner with Noël Coward at his house, Firefly Hill. After dinner, our host pushed back his chair, sat down at the Bechstein grand in his dining room and played and sang 'Mad Dogs and Englishmen', 'Don't Put Your Daughter on the Stage, Mrs Worthington' and 'The Stately Homes of England'. Another mind-boggling memory from more than sixty years ago.)

It is fair to say that, after Cambridge, I was initially driven back to cricket as a means of employment following nearly three years as a disenchanted trainee merchant banker in the City of London. I was thrust on behalf of *The Times* into a strange new world when I found myself in the press tent at the Bat and Ball Ground at Gravesend in late May 1962. Kent were playing Somerset and by a lot of curious chances the job of reporting the match had come my way at about eight o'clock the previous evening. This was thanks to one of the greatest characters I have ever known, who was to become probably the best friend I ever had. His name was John Woodcock and he was the *Times* cricket correspondent for thirty-three years, from 1954 to 1987. You will hear more of him in the pages to come.

Illness had caused *The Times* to need a supernumerary at the very last minute to cover this match. Woodcock, whom I had met for the first time a couple of days earlier, knew I was keen to try my hand at writing about cricket and, unseen, the sports editor of *The Times* was persuaded to give me a go.

My five hundred words on each of those two days at Gravesend just about got me a pass mark. After doing three more games, when on each occasion I told my City employers I was ill, I let them know, to their immense relief, that they had seen the last of me. I left the City and entered press boxes intermittently for *The Times* for the rest of that summer.

Being the newest of new boys, I tiptoed nervously into each press box I was sent to and tried to be as unnoticeable as possible. As I was an inveterate devourer of cricket reports, I knew the names of many of those on the chairs around me. In the old press box at The Oval, which had an inescapable smell of Dickensian mustiness, I soon found myself shaking hands with John Clarke of the *Evening Standard*: dishevelled dark hair, middle-aged, often smoking a pipe and usually cheerful, sometimes wearing a brown homburg, when he was the spitting image of Rupert Davies playing Inspector Maigret. In the other corner, so to speak, was the thin, bespectacled, dark-haired Evelyn ('Lyn') Wellings of the *Evening News*, the other London evening paper. Generally speaking, he preferred to write with vitriol rather than ink and never minced his words about anything. He hated the game's establishment and the feeling was mutual. He could be extremely rude, often had rows in the box and disagreed with most things said to him. His copy will have kept his paper's lawyers on their toes. He had once bowled at medium-fast for Oxford University and Surrey, and was never the flavour of the month in either place. Having said all that, he was always extremely kind to me, maybe because I was no sort of perceived threat. His large wife, who I always found charming, ran the family travel agency just off New Bond Street, for which Lyn was always trying to drum up business. I often wondered how Mr and Mrs Wellings got on at home – which was none of my business.

I had a slight built-in advantage when I first entered the press box. At Eton, I had met the famous E.W. ('Jim') Swanton, and when I departed from Cambridge after two years he had made me a member of the cricket club he had founded in the thirties, the Arabs. Soon, I was even more in his good books because I scored a hundred in my first game for them. Swanton may have been known as 'Pomponius Ego' by some of his friends and liked things to be done his way, but he was decent enough to me, although he disapproved of a lot of the things I later said on air. My second outing for *TMS*, at Edgbaston in 1972 for a limited-over international against Australia, was a case in point. During the day I had a conversation on air with Jack Fingleton, the old Australian batsman, then a journalist. We were talking about what causes a cricket ball to swing, without coming up with a definite answer as there are as many contributing factors as there are opinions. We were about to move on when I said, 'All I can say is that, having been an opening batsman, I know the ball does swing.' Swanton arrived in the box near the end of the game to be ready for his close-of-play summary. He came straight up to me and in an indignant voice said, 'How dare you talk about your own cricket in this company. I shall never expect to hear you do that again.' Until then, I thought the day had gone better for me than I had feared. I was horrified, and whenever our paths crossed in the next few weeks he made a point of bringing it up again. Even now, I am not sure what he was getting at, except that maybe he felt I was trying to put my batting on a level with Fingleton's. I apologised to Fingleton when I saw him about a week later. He smiled. 'That's Swanton for you,' he said. 'Don't worry about it, you did well.' Which helped.

Swanton was a large man and once, on the ship taking the England players to South Africa for the 1956–57 tour, he went to see the team's physiotherapist, who proceeded to give him a good going-over on the massage table. As he was finishing, he said to Swanton, 'The trouble with you, Mr Swanton, is that your body is too big for your legs.' It was a remark that Jim never quite knew how to take. Swanton used his size to emphasise his presence, which was impressive if sometimes a little overdone. He had a deep authoritative voice, could not cope with fools, was heavily religious and a serious snob – if the two are compatible. If Swanton saw a duke or a bishop in the room, there was no holding him. He was a most able writer about cricket, although not in the same class as Woodcock, and a capable broadcaster, especially when doing those wonderful close-of-play summaries.

Cricket has never had a much better friend than Swanton, the self-appointed king of the England press box. On tour Jim and his wife, Ann, who was also a snob, would move round whichever country it was, as if they were not so minor members of the royal family. Swanton was an institution, although I dare say we laughed at him as much as we did with him. He did not mind his leg being pulled – as long as it was done by God, the Duke of Norfolk or the extraordinary Colin Ingleby-Mackenzie, who famously captained Hampshire.

It took me longer to get to know the trio I always thought of as the Three Musketeers. Charlie Bray had once captained Essex and was now the *Daily Herald*'s cricket man; Brian Chapman, a fine writer and highly successful journalist, looked after the *Daily Mirror*'s cricketing requirements; while Crawford White was similarly employed by Lord Beaverbrook at the *Daily Express*. They were a formidable threesome and they liked to hunt as a pack.

Bray, who would have been the oldest, had by then acquired a noticeable girth and was not far from retiring, something he had in common with his newspaper which, in a remarkable transformation, was to turn into *The Sun*. Bray had the misfortune to stand in for the official captain of Essex when they played Yorkshire at Leyton in 1932. Yorkshire won the toss and Percy

Holmes and Herbert Sutcliffe put on 555 for the first wicket, beating the previous world first-class record of 554. As it happened, the scoreboard had got ahead of itself and had posted 555, at which point, the record broken, Sutcliffe got himself out. A recount found that the score was in fact only 554 and a hastily 'discovered' no-ball ensured the new record was in place.

Chapman was the brightest of the three and the most delightful man. Under grey hair, part tousled, part crimpy, he smiled easily, did not know a huge amount about cricket, but had a terrific way with words and wrote his two competitors off the page. He was the most genial of companions and was at his best in the bar at the end of the day. If asked what he would like to drink, his invariable reply was 'A large gin and Dubonnet, please'. There was a dicey moment once when the reply came swiftly back, 'Brian, I asked you to nominate the drink. I will nominate the amount.' I am glad to say he took it in his stride, kept smiling, and in due course was rewarded with his double. He had been the Manchester editor of the *Daily Express* before turning his hand to cricket at the *Daily Mirror*.

Crawford White, from Lancashire, the youngest of the Three Musketeers, was good-looking in a mildly David Niven-ish sort of way, but the least confident performer of the three. Known by everyone as Chalky, he was always up for a party, but was never relaxed about the story he had dictated to his office earlier that evening. He found writing difficult and would hum tunelessly in the hope of finding inspiration. His progress thereafter was usually punctuated by a succession of anguished telephone calls to his office. He had an eye for a pretty girl and was anxious that his wife, Doris, who was no fool, should not find out. When he retired from the *Express*, Cornhill Insurance, who were by then sponsoring England's cricket, employed him to look after the needs of the press box during Test matches. He thus became an enthusiastic and avuncular purveyor of Rosé d'Anjou.

The Three Musketeers usually turned up at the ground a little late and were then the life and soul of the party until soon after lunch, when they would go into their first huddle. Its purpose was to begin to think about the angle they would take for that night's story. Bray was the main source of ideas, while Chapman listened thoughtfully in silence. When the final decision had been made, White, the leg man, went off and asked the appropriate questions in or around the players' dressing rooms and got the obligatory quotes. Glass in hand, Bray and Chapman awaited his return. When he reappeared with the goods, they set about writing their stories. Ironically, Chapman, who had done nothing throughout but listen, now proceeded to write by far the best story. What fun they were.

And then there was Johnny Woodcock. Small, dark-haired and eternally cheerful. He shuffled along with a limp caused by an accident and then an infection which had led to innumerable new hips, few of which worked as well as the surgeons had hoped. A good games player when he was young, he spent a lot of his life in dreadful pain, not that he ever let on, for he was as brave as they come. Just occasionally on a long aeroplane journey you would see him wince as he changed position. He was extremely quick-witted, always the greatest of fun to be with, and he was up for almost anything. After an initial show of mild reluctance, he enjoyed a properly made dry martini as much as I did. Noël Coward's way of making the best dry martini touched a mutual chord. 'You pour an awful lot of gin into a glass and then wave it in the general direction of Italy' was how it went. Wooders, as we always called him thanks to Brian Johnston's infectious use of nicknames, certainly knew where to find Italy.

I had many splendid adventures with Wooders as we went on numerous cricket tours together. I have never met anyone who was a better or more thorough watcher of a day's cricket. He wrote beautiful English, no one understood the game better, and in his writing he never thumped the table or tried to force anything down your throat. He was far and away the best writer, day in, day out, in my time. It would also have been impossible to find a nicer person than Wooders, unless Kerry Packer and his World Series Cricket was up for discussion, when the red mist would descend. It was Alan Gibson, another brilliant writer, and broadcaster too, who, in *The Times*, happily described Wooders as 'The Sage of Longparish', which was where he lived in Hampshire.

These few inhabitants of the press box all that time ago are illustrative of a gentler, less combative and cut-throat world than today. There was more time to enjoy and reflect on life. Yes, it was life before the invention of the helter-skelter limited-over world which dictates so much of the game as we know it today, and the fast tempo of life that surrounds it. It was a different, more relaxed world, and one it would be foolish to think we will ever see again. I was lucky to have been a part of it.

2

THE COMMENTATOR'S CHAIR

'Almost worthy of a nightclub'

WHEN I first stepped into the commentary box at the top of the Lord's Pavilion, there was something comfortingly familiar about it. A little cramped, with two narrow wooden posts going up to the ceiling, presumably to hold the roof in place, it was happily higgledy-piggledy, with a warm and exciting atmosphere. We were sitting almost behind the bowler's arm and could put up with a bit of discomfort for that. Several men, mostly middle-aged and wearing jackets, collars and the obligatory *Test Match Special* tie on the first day, were using microphones and other equipment similarly blessed with long-service medals to bring the story of the cricket to the outside world. The box itself was a new home for *TMS*, as we had just been moved from our old home at the top of the neighbouring Warner Stand, where we had been perched over the head of fine leg, not the best position from which to commentate. There wasn't room in the Warner Stand for both the television and the radio boxes, so we had been shifted to the Pavilion. The commentator, the summariser and the scorer sat like tolerably well-behaved schoolchildren in class, at a long, narrow wooden desk covered with green baize which ran across the front of the box.

Three or four people – they were constantly coming and going – stood behind talking intermittently in voices which should have been not much above a whisper. In the far corner at the back of the box, sitting on a slightly raised stool that would just about have done duty in a bar, was our producer, Peter Baxter, with headphones clamped to his ears, a collection of stopwatches, a small clock, a notebook, several pencils, a pile of papers on a small desk in front of him and a worried look on his face. One of his main, and hardest, tasks was trying to persuade the talkers at the back of the box to keep their voices down. He was also trying to ensure the commentators kept to the straight and narrow, as well as organising the many added extras which fitted into the programme each day.

Then, suddenly, what had been a reasonably contented interest on his part became more intensely involved. There was a movement from near the door and the cheerful face of Brian Johnston, with his enormous ears, pushed his way towards the commentator's chair. It was ten to twelve and time for the first commentary change of the day. A large man in a dark jacket wearing a black tie said in a familiar, almost exaggerated Hampshire burr, 'And after another word from you, Trevor, it will be Brian Johnston.'

There was a slight squeak as John Arlott pushed back his chair. Johnners gave a nimble twist almost worthy of a nightclub to provide him with a little more room for manoeuvre. Then he slipped into the empty seat, with Trevor Bailey on his right. On the other side, a bearded man with free-range tousled dark hair was guarding the papers around him from inadvertent assault by the new commentator. This was our scorer, Bill Frindall, who Johnston had christened 'the Bearded Wonder'.

'Good morning, Brian,' came next in Trevor's carefully modulated tones. 'Morning, Boil,' was Johnners's cheerful reply. And he was off. Arlott walked straight out of the box. 'Where's he gone?' I whispered to Baxter. 'To have a glass of wine, I expect.' We were up and running.

The next arrivals who poked their noses rather hesitantly round the door were one of the England Test selectors accompanied by an MCC committee member. We were at the end of the top balcony of the Pavilion, two floors up from the visitors' dressing room. It was not too far for some of the great and good from the committee room to come and visit us. John Arlott, whose best days of climbing four flights of stairs were nearing an end and now included much puffing, described the climb up to the commentary box as 'the ascent of Everest'.

Another early visitor was Nancy, who oversaw the players' and the committee dining rooms. She became an important figure in the Pavilion and, during Test matches, made the lamb sandwiches Brian insisted on having every day for lunch. She or one of her girls brought them up on a tray during the first half-hour's play. Johnners was a bit of a fusspot about his food, and for years Nancy came to his rescue. She had been in charge of this august kitchen for many years, and before she retired she was awarded the British Empire Medal – and not only for making Johnners's sandwiches.

When I joined *Test Match Special*, it was still in the grip of a strong amateur influence. Brian Johnston, who personified the amateur take on life perhaps more than anyone, was actually on the staff of the BBC, as was the retiring cricket producer, Michael Tuke-Hastings, and his successor, Peter Baxter. Otherwise, it was an amateur production, professionally amateur if you like. I have no idea what John Arlott's arrangements were with the BBC. Christopher Martin-Jenkins was another who worked full-time for them, but the rest of us were freelancers, including summarisers like Trevor Bailey and Fred Trueman. I sometimes felt that *TMS* was viewed with suspicion by the professionals who ran the sports room in Broadcasting House, simply because the programme was successful more in spite of them than because of them.

My own arrival at *TMS*, in 1972, was unusual even for those days. I had been writing about cricket for various newspapers since 1962, which may have happened initially because I had the luck to play a handful of first-class matches and presumably knew a little about the game. Six years later, one of my journalistic colleagues asked me in a press box if I had ever thought about commentating. I had not, and said so. Then, thinking I might have been missing out, I asked him what I should do to be given the chance of having a go. He told me to write to the head of outside broadcasts at the BBC and ask if I could have a trial. His name was Robert Hudson, a considerable broadcaster himself. I wrote to him and he replied, asking me if I could go along to The Oval in two weeks, where Brian Johnston would be commenting on a Surrey match. In between Brian's commentary spells, Hudson wanted me to go into the box and do two twenty-minute spells of commentary which they would record down the line in Broadcasting House. I went to The Oval, a bagful of nerves, and did the two spells, with Brian introducing me each time. I did not think I had been at all good. Soon afterwards I was asked to go to Broadcasting House to meet with the assistant head of outside broadcasts and listen to the two recordings.

His name was Henry Riddell. He was a huge man and must have been at least six foot six inches tall. He had been a great friend of the immortal Lord Reith, the founding father of the BBC. Riddell was charming. We listened to the tapes, and afterwards he told me he liked how I 'painted the picture', and was then critical about some other things I had not done so well. After about an hour of this, he astounded me by saying, 'Yes, we like it, and we are adding your name to our list of cricket commentators, although there may not be many opportunities for you.'

I simply could not believe it, and my last ten-pound note took me out to a celebratory dinner that night, although he was right about the opportunities. That meeting was in July 1968 and when we had arrived at the end of August 1971 the telephone had still not rung. That winter I was going as a journalist to the West Indies to cover New Zealand's first ever tour of the Caribbean. In the West Indies, there are two radio networks in each island and both covered the cricket. One employed the New Zealand commentator Alan Richards and the other also needed an overseas commentator. When asked, I lied and assured them I had done a lot of commentary in England. To my surprise, I got the job and in the Test series that followed I was able to cut my teeth in a way few would now get the chance to do.

I had listened to cricket commentary for a long time and thought I knew what to do. It did not go as badly as all that and I heard no complaints. Word must have got back to Robert Hudson, because when I returned home I found a letter from him asking me to cover a county match for the BBC at Chelmsford over the old Whitsun weekend. I didn't put my foot in it there either, and the following Thursday I received another letter from Hudson asking me to join the *TMS* commentary team for two limited-over internationals at the end of the summer against Australia, at Lord's and Edgbaston. It had happened quickly and it is hard to imagine something like this occurring today, but that was exactly how my commentary career began for me.

The two lynchpins of *Test Match Special* at that time were John Arlott and Brian Johnston. These two more than anyone else turned *TMS* into the unique programme it has become. They had only come together on the programme in 1970, two years before I began, because although Arlott had joined the main radio team in 1947, Johnners had been with BBC television from 1946 until 1969, when he was sacked because they considered him to be too funny – if you can believe it. *TMS* snapped him up, and he and Arlott made a wonderful contrast. When they came together the listenership figures shot up. Writing about them both now, it is difficult to know where to start, for so much has been written already. They could hardly have been more different. To start with,

Arlott drank more wine than most, while Johnners was not far short of being a teetotaller. He had an occasional glass of champagne and, after Arlott's impressive tuition, was prepared to enjoy the odd glass of white burgundy.

Arlott had two great loves in life: one was cricket and the other was wine, and I would hate to have to say which came first. He was a man of great warmth and emotion, and was also a poet of some renown. His descriptive powers and command of the English language were magnificent. He never made a cricketer look foolish or said anything unkind about a player. He was aware of and appreciated the sense of joy which came with success on the field, just as he more than understood the disappointment and sometimes the despair of players at their bleakest moments. He had an excellent, but leisurely, sense of humour, and a good story by Arlott at dinner would usually last for more than one glass. He always wore a black tie in memory of his oldest son, who died in a road accident. He hated pomposity and was contemptuous of the game's establishment and establishments everywhere. When he retired, the MCC offered him honorary life membership, which he turned down. He did not mellow with old age.

The little story that stays with me happened at dinner in our hotel the night before my first Test match with *TMS*, against India at Old Trafford in 1974. Five of us dined together and the wine waiter was late on parade. When eventually he appeared, he asked Arlott, at the head of the table, if any drinks were required. Arlott replied quickly and with emphasis, 'Yes, we'll have five of the red and two of the white to start with.' 'You mean glasses, sir?' the wine waiter asked, having no idea who he was talking to. 'Glasses?' Arlott exclaimed with querulous indignation. 'No, silly man, bottles.'

Whether he would now be able to express his attachment to wine as openly as he did in those days must be in doubt, not least because the commentary box is teetotal during the hours of play. But then how would Arlott's wonderful voice and the reflective nature of his commentary have fitted into the commentary box at the present time? His voice, to say nothing of his measured and mesmerising delivery, would have been pushed to the limit by a Bazball Test match, and a T20 cliffhanger might have been a step too far. Actually, I think professional pride would have made him get his tongue round Bazball, which he would have hugely enjoyed, but he would have found the pace of the T20 shenanigans more of a struggle. T20 would not have been his thing, as it lacks the beauty and rhythm of two-innings cricket, which was important to him and on which his commentary was founded. But being the pro he was, he would have coped and we would have loved it.

With Brian Johnston it was all upfront. Johnners burst upon you. The cheerful voice, the nose, the ears, the huge lobes below those ears, the slightly cheeky face, the co-respondent two-tone shoes and the jovial walk. Johnners would have coped with the T20 high jinks because he would have enjoyed it more than Arlott.

It was a quarter past ten on the second day of a Test match at Lord's when Johnners came through the door of the box.

'Morning, Blowers. Ten men under one umbrella and none of them got wet.'

'Good morning, Johnners. Why didn't any of them get wet?'

'Because it wasn't raining.'

This was a typical start to any day in the commentary box in England.

Now, the lobes of both ears were so long that he could tuck them into his ears and they stayed there, something I have never seen anyone else able to do. At times, he used this to provoke humour in the box or to enliven a particularly dreary interview. It was impossible to watch him tuck them in and keep a straight face, especially when he then raised both eyebrows and they popped out like a couple of corks. Johnners was irrepressible. Like Arlott, he was a consummate broadcaster; no matter the subject, he would have done it brilliantly. He, too, was a supreme communicator with a sense of humour which was second to none. He could see the funny side of anything and he loved to make puns. His quick mind enabled him to come up with a constant stream of jokes. At times, he was difficult to work with because he was always sending those around him into fits of giggles.

Some people thought that many of his jokes were prepared, but if they had been, he also would have had to prepare the context, which would have been impossible. When he said something hugely funny, no one collapsed with laughter more than he did himself. If you use a prepared joke you are already so familiar with it that you usually deliver it with a poker face. Johnners would also dissolve with laughter at other people's jokes, as anyone will know who has ever heard the famous 'leg over' moment set up by Jonathan Agnew at The Oval in 1991. The only problem I had with Johnners's sense of humour was that it often left me in no fit state to carry on.

Johnners loved cricket and had been an enthusiastic wicket-keeper in club cricket and enjoyed telling the story of when he once stumped someone off Richie Benaud in a charity match. Those who listened to him always felt he was talking to them personally, and everyone loved him. His humour was well known on radio long before he joined *TMS*. Soon after he joined the BBC, he became the central figure in *In Town Tonight*, a radio programme in which he got up to all sorts of crazy things. On one occasion they dug a small, shallow trench between the railway lines the Flying Scotsman used on the way north. Johnners lay down in the trench on his back, microphone at the ready. The Flying Scotsman roared over him as he commentated. He soon interrupted himself and exclaimed, 'Goodness me, I think some-one's just gone to the lavatory.' On another day, they somehow squeezed him into a red pillar box on a street corner. An old lady came along to post a letter and as she stuck the envelope into the slit, Johnners pulled it from her fingers, said, 'Thank you very much,' and she fainted.

*   *   *

It was Arlott and Johnston who together steered *TMS* down the memorable path it now follows. The rest of us may have tweaked it here and there, but they were the main architects. Another stalwart figure who was an important part of the fabric of *TMS* was Christopher Martin-Jenkins (CMJ). He had the perfect *TMS* voice – crisp and beautifully clear, and given its emphasis by his own view of what was happening before him. Tall with fair crimpy hair, CMJ was a joy to listen to and was in all senses but one a Mr Reliable. He joined *TMS* in 1972, thus fulfilling a great ambition, and brought with him a happy turn of phrase, great enthusiasm and an excellent knowledge of the game. He was another with a good sense of humour and he was a brilliant mimic. CMJ was deeply devoted to the Christian faith and also to the game of cricket and *TMS*. It was his profound devotion to the game which perhaps prevented him from ever quite revealing the full extent of his humour on air. With CMJ, cricket deserved to be taken seriously. He was a gifted after-dinner speaker who told wonderful stories but seldom let himself go in the same way when commentating. He was a superb commentator to listen to because he always told you exactly what had happened. You could rely on him one hundred per cent. It is fair to say that, unlike one or two others in the box, he lived life with his bat and pad pretty close together and seldom let his hair down to any great extent. He was a prodigiously hard worker, and in addition to his broadcasting and other commitments, he was also the cricket correspondent of the *Daily Telegraph* and then *The Times*. It is a big ask to write a thousand-word report after a full day's commentary. No wonder CMJ occasionally looked a trifle harassed in the closing stages of the day.

The one unreliable aspect of CMJ's life was his punctuality, or rather the lack of it. Before he sadly died in 2013, he was already known as 'the late CMJ', which rather strangely seemed to mystify him. Producers knew that if they put him down for the early-morning *Today* programme, Garry Richardson would probably have to fill the slot on his own. Then there was the opening half hour on the ground before the start of play, which was also a problem for him. A keen golfer, CMJ loved to play an early-morning nine holes and would find the tenth and probably the eleventh utterly irresistible. He would arrive breathless after the programme had begun with tales of traffic jams no one else had encountered. Other appointments throughout the day could be a bit hit-or-miss too. Whether CMJ was bewildered by his lateness and unable to understand how it had happened or surprised that anyone should mind if he were late was unclear, but he never changed his ways. It was awful that cancer should have gripped such a splendid man, who did everything he could to stay fit, in the awful way that it did.

Don Mosey was nothing if not a tetchy Yorkshireman, and he joined *TMS* at about the same time as CMJ and me. Actually, the correct order of arrival was CMJ, me and then Mosey, although Mosey liked to think he got there first. He was on the short side, with spiky grey hair and middle-aged with a mildly strutting walk. When Brian Johnston first met him he thought he looked just like an alderman, and thanks to Johnners he became known by most people as 'the Alderman'. His north-country tones were an important addition to the *TMS* team. I think he felt he was balancing out not only a southern influence in the team, but also the public-school contingent, something he felt strongly about.

I rated him a good friend, but there was no doubt that there was a bit of a north/south divide in the box. When I had been up at Cambridge, I had played cricket on the verge of the university side with his brother, Stuart, an able fast bowler. In the box, the Alderman was close to Brian Johnston and they endlessly played a word game against each other, which involved giving each other alternate letters and trying to form words. Johnners had a home-spun technique and, more often than not, was the winner. This wordy relationship fell apart when the Alderman wrote a book entitled *The Best Job in the World* and spent a great many pages pointing out that all the rest of us were just about the biggest bunch of rotters he had ever come across. After that, the word game went into immediate retirement.

The Alderman told me more than once that he was a bowler's and not a batsman's commentator like the rest of us. I sort of saw the difference when he said that to me, but when I listened to him I was not entirely sure how he was able to make the distinction. To me, it all sounded much the same as everyone else.

Undoubtedly the Alderman was good for our commentary box and its output. My strongest memories of him come from a tour of Pakistan by Mike Brearley's England side in 1977–78. The last game before the third and final Test match in Karachi was an unimportant one-day match against Sind at the Gymkhana Club, also in Karachi. During the course of it, Brearley's arm was broken by a short ball from a bowler called Sikander Bakht, of whom Brian Johnston memorably once said, 'Sikander's Bakht is worse than his Bite.' (I told you he was good at puns.)

The press were staying at the Midway House Hotel near the airport and the England captain breaking his arm was hot news, not least because his vice-captain, Geoffrey Boycott, took on the captain's job. The information had to be sent back urgently to the BBC. There were no telephones or other press facilities at the Gymkhana Club, so the Alderman instantly took a taxi back to the Midway House, an hour away. When he arrived he asked the receptionist to put through a transfer charge call to the BBC in London, for in those days that was the only way direct contact could be achieved. He was told the call would take two to four hours to come through. The Alderman began the long wait as patiently as he could. When I got back after the end of the match, he was still pacing up and down in his room, in between making impatient half-hourly visits to the reception desk. The first receptionist came to the end of her spell and handed over to someone whose English was not so fluent. She and the Alderman did not fully understand each other. When the call eventually came, more than four hours had elapsed since it had been put through. The new incumbent at the reception desk was unsure what to do, and it was some time before she realised she must go and fetch the Alderman. She knocked tepidly on his door, saying, 'Telephone, Mr Mosey,' and was amazed when the door burst open and the Alderman left the room as if he was Usain Bolt in a hurry. He almost knocked her over and raced to the reception desk, snatched up the telephone and yelled into the receiver, 'Don Mosey!' The lady operator at the BBC said very politely, 'I am afraid Mr Mosey is in Pakistan,' and hung up.

These were the essential human ingredients of the commentary box when I was first allowed in. Others flitted in and out, as I did in my first years, when I was much more out than in. There was also another essential ingredient that played an important part in oiling the cogs of the wheels that kept us going. In those days, far from being discouraged, bottles of wine were a constant. Listeners kept sending us champagne or wine, and although Peter Baxter was anxious to keep references to booze to a minimum, alcoholic sustenance was far from forbidden. At about midday, or at any rate not long afterwards, listeners would hear the reassuringly robust noise of the cork leaving its bottle of champagne for the first time. This was undoubtedly a moment of discomfort for our producer until 'the Boil' (Trevor Bailey) came up with a not entirely unsatisfactory explanation, which perhaps took some of the sting out of it: 'Ah,' he would say in his authoritative tones, 'the medicine'.

There was a wonderful occasion at Lord's not all that long after I had joined *TMS* when a box was delivered to us by one of the MCC staff working at the Pavilion entrance. It contained an impressive-looking chocolate cake which more than tickled Johnners's fancy. Arlott, who was not a cake eater, sat in the commentator's chair and looked round in mock disgust, 'Why can't our listeners send us something useful like champagne?' he growled. Within little over an hour, a porter from Fortnum & Mason in Piccadilly, wearing the company's livery, had turned up at the commentary box with a case of half a dozen bottles of champagne. After that, we tried talking about the joy of eating caviar, but sadly that fell on deaf ears. The champagne was hastily chilled in Nancy's fridge, and when the last hour of the day began we put a bottle to good use. We were allowed to get away with it then, but discipline today would have been understandably tighter – even if we did, helpfully for the listeners, give the score rather more often in those far-distant days.

Cakes of all shapes and sizes were a constant part of *TMS* life then, and remain so. They were mostly sent to Johnners, and in my early days the majority were chocolate cakes, which were his often-stated preference. People came to visit us in the box throughout the day, which was lovely, but occasionally they became too adhesive and we had to find ways of moving them on. Those who lingered often did so because they enjoyed tucking into our supply of cakes, so we became more careful who we offered them to. One year, there was a national competition to discover the village cricket club that provided the best cricket teas. There had been competitions in different parts of the country and the winners came to one of the Test matches and spread out their teas, and we had to decide on the best. Lots of ladies fluttered about in lovely colourful dresses and aprons, and after sampling their wares we made our decision. It was so much fun.

In the old days, the Trent Bridge Test was difficult to beat. We stayed at the unique Langar Hall Hotel, where we were looked after in great comfort and style by Imogen Skirving, whose family home it had once been. Our commentary box was on the first floor of the Trent Bridge pavilion, and the club's chairman always gave our commentary team the freedom of the committee room during a Test match. The hospitality therein was a big bonus. It also meant that if we wanted to interview someone important, it was only a quick step upstairs for them. The commentary box itself was tiny and uncomfortable, but we were so close to the action I almost used to think I was fielding at fine leg. I remember having to get out of the box in a hurry one day by climbing over the figure of one of our summarisers, Colin Milburn, the dearest of men, but a considerable physical obstacle. When the stand at the Radcliffe Road End was rebuilt, we had to move to what was undoubtedly the best commentary box in the country, but it meant no more committee room. For all its spacious excellence, my antiquated heart remained in the pavilion. All the commentary boxes had their own character, and none more so than the old box in the rugby stand at Headingley, where the deep step down to the front row was a veritable death trap. We had a lot of fun trying to move Arlott into position for his next spell, as his best days of mountaineering were far behind him.

Those people who visited us in our commentary boxes almost invariably remarked on what they saw as our seemingly relaxed approach to the job. It was as if they came in expecting to find a strictly disciplined atmosphere, rather like the formality of a church service. As it was, they felt they were coming to a party. They were surprised to be offered a piece of cake or a glass of wine and to hear the sotto voce chatter and laughter in the box behind the commentator. I think, too, they expected to see the next commentator sitting on his own, mentally preparing himself – in those days commentary was an entirely male occupation, although ladies often came into the box to see us in action. At all times the commentary box has faithfully reflected the tempo, the style, the speed and the character of the game being described. Also, the box's output always seemed to reflect the crowd's mood: if they are on their feet, so are we, metaphorically at any rate. At the time I began, even though the fun sixties had flown by, life was still changing slowly compared to what was to come, and the cricket too. But whatever the circumstances, the atmosphere in the commentary boxes I inhabited was one of mostly controlled high good humour. I am sure it remains the same today, even if I would miss 'the medicine'.

I would like to end this chapter on a personal note. When I was in the commentary box I always tried to 'paint the picture'. At Lord's, when our post was at the top of the Pavilion, a constant stream of red double-decker buses went up and down the Wellington Road at the Nursery End, and at The Oval the Harleyford Road was usually full of them too. At the same time, at Headingley, the Kirkstall Lane made sure the buses in the south did not have it all their own way. The best bus ground of all was the Test ground in India at Delhi, where to the right of the far sightscreen from where we were sitting was a huge bus station. For five days it provided me with a non-stop source of enjoyment. There were also the pigeons at The Oval and Lord's. Seagulls often came along too, and in bulk to Cardiff's Sophia Gardens, and on a good many grounds overseas as well.

It was in Cardiff that I got my comeuppance from the seagull community. Not long before I retired, England were playing an Ashes Test there and for the first two days I was mesmerised by the mass of seagulls, and talked much about their acrobatic activities. On the second day, I even went so far as to say when several of them flew low across the front of our commentary box that I was pretty sure I saw at least half a dozen wink at me. Our bond was strong, or so I thought. At the end of each day I had a twenty-five-minute walk back to our hotel and on the second evening, as I walked down the High Street, a florist had washed down the area on which her plants had been standing and there was a big pool of water at the side of the road which was full of seagulls. As I approached, a car drove furiously through the water and the seagulls scattered before forming a tight formation and flying back over me. I hoped they were saying thank you for all the nice things I had been saying about them. Not a bit of it: as they flew over me they bombed me with whatever they needed to get rid of, and there must have been at least a dozen direct hits. Talk about sheer, naked ingratitude. My relationship with Cardiff seagulls still has a long way to go if it is ever to get back to where it was.

Aeroplanes and helicopters also had their moments, particularly in London. The early-evening Concorde from New York enlivened the last hour of many a day at The Oval. There were occasions, too, when cabbage white butterflies fluttered about the place. Johnners once accused me when I was on the air at Headingley of talking about a butterfly with a limp. I greatly enjoyed seeing all these added extras and giving them a mention, but not at a moment of action. However, I am sure many diehard cricket supporters, mainly living in Yorkshire, will have accused me of preferring a Boeing to the fall of a wicket. But many listeners enjoyed hearing about all these other extraneous bits and pieces. Oh yes, I had almost forgotten, in my later years I developed a great fondness for cranes, which were sticking up all over the place as new buildings were going up in the distance behind the pavilion or wherever.

Now, my excuse for these excesses goes back to when I did those two trial commentaries in 1968 and Henry Riddell had stressed the importance of giving your listeners the full scene in front of you. We were sitting in a small office in Broadcasting House and on the wall at the side of his desk was a picture of two horses. They were standing on the grass in a field which backed onto a wood and there was also a little bit of sky overhead.

'When anyone looks at that picture,' he said, turning to it, 'they obviously concentrate on the horses, which are the main object of the picture, but if it were not for the grass, the sky and the trees, and then the mount and the frame, it would not be a composite picture. When commentating, it is the composite picture of the cricket match you must try and paint for the listener.' He told me the greatest compliment a listener could ever pay to a radio commentator was to say, 'You made me feel I was there.' He went on, 'To do this, you must let listeners know exactly where you are sitting at the ground and what you can see. Then, their imaginations can take over.'

So the stands, the buildings you can see in the distance, the Pennines and the passing trains at Old Trafford, and even the lady wearing the gorgeous red dress in the stand at square leg, are all part of this. I will still not convince that diehard Yorkshire cricket fan, who will be satisfied today because I don't think too many of these things get a mention any more. This is not a criticism, far from it; it is a reflection of a world which has changed so dramatically. We are now watching this new world unfold in front of us at a Test match, just as we are experiencing this change in every aspect of our lives. Life today is much more like a T20 game than a five-day Test match, even though Bazball has brought the two of them closer together.

3

MODUS OPERANDI

'The Duckworth Lewis Method and Henry Blow . . .'

As the product changes, so inevitably does the description of it. Of course, *Test Match Special* has evolved considerably between the time I first joined and the present day. The previous chapter gives an idea of how the atmosphere in and around the commentary box has altered during those fifty years – it would have been surprising if it had stayed the same. I would now like to take a look at how the modus operandi of the box has changed.

The most significant change has been the introduction of women's voices into the mix. As far as *TMS* was concerned, this first happened in 1997–98 when England were playing in the West Indies and Donna Symmonds, who comes from Barbados, joined the team. She had been commentating in the Caribbean since the eighties, and during this series both Donna and Tony Cozier worked for *TMS*. While her presence may have raised a number of crusty old eyebrows in the UK, she was an excellent addition and her presence pointed to the eventual way forward. Her family had always loved the game and had been close friends of Sir Frank Worrell, the first black man to captain the West Indies on a permanent basis. He was one of that great triumvirate of Bajan (Barbados) players, the three Ws: Sir Everton Weekes, Sir Clyde Walcott and Sir Frank Worrell.

Donna was a lawyer by trade and because of her success in that field was unable to find the time to continue more than occasionally as a commentator. She knew the game well, had a good, strong voice, a lively West Indian sense of humour, and told the story of the day's play in a pleasant style that was easy to listen to. She sounded relaxed and never made the mistake of trying too hard. When she came to commentary – her first Test match was against Pakistan in 1988 – it was a strongly male preserve and she pioneered a tricky course with tact and skill. She had a fine legal mind which will have helped her to spot and avoid most pitfalls. It helped that she was an independent character and very much her own woman. With her, cricket commentary would always be the second string to her bow. She was perhaps the ideal person to break this extremely thick piece of ice. It was not until the West Indies came to England two years later, in 2000, and she joined *TMS* once again, that she was seen and accepted in the UK as a permanent fixture rather than a West Indian-inspired one-off. For a time, Donna's commentary became a part of West Indies cricket, until she was pulled back into the courtroom for good.

Several years passed before another lady joined us in the *TMS* box. In 2007, after thirty-four years in the producer's chair, Peter Baxter passed the baton on to Adam Mountford. Being much younger, Adam quite rightly wanted to introduce a more contemporary style to the commentary box. That same year, Alison Mitchell joined *TMS* as the first woman the BBC had themselves put forward as a commentator. Alison, who had no real cricketing background except for her great love for the game, was given the difficult job of trying to establish herself in the commentary box while being perceived as a token woman who was being used in a male preserve to satisfy the demands of political correctness. She did exceptionally well, showing clever footwork and quick thinking when handling poorly disguised barbs from one or two others in the box. Women cricketers, for example, will never quite know what it is to have a cricket ball whizz past their noses at more than 90 mph. On one occasion, when a batsman had difficulty avoiding such a delivery, the question came: 'Alison, how would you have played that one?' It was a question which I am sure was aimed below the belt. Alison ducked with great agility. I don't think the well-used phrases of cricket commentary had come to her that easily at first, but she more than held her own, was quick to learn and did a fine job.

Alison, who has strong connections in Australia, has made a name for herself there on television. In the UK, she was later given excellent support by Ebony Rainford-Brent, a most able lady who had played for England and really knew the game. She has an outstanding voice and a pleasant style of commentary. It was not long before Ebony was scooped up by television, as was Isa Guha, another former England player who had become a *TMS* commentator. Isa played in two World Cups and nowadays, like Ebony, is much in demand on television and radio. Although her commentary voice may not have had quite the same authority as Ebony's, she played a big part in ensuring that women now have a permanent position with *TMS*. This is well deserved, not least because the greatly increasing quality and importance of women's cricket has produced a much stronger female interest in the game.

Another important change to the output of the commentary box has been the use of the summarisers. When I joined *TMS*, the summarisers were there to help the commentators. The first summarisers I worked with, at Lord's in 1972 in a limited-over game against Australia, were Norman Yardley and Freddie Brown, both terrific characters who had captained England after the war. Their job was to talk between overs, when a wicket fell or something else momentous occurred, and if the commentator wanted something to be explained. Otherwise, the commentator was on his own.

This allowed the commentators to describe the ground, tell listeners what he could see, and in Henry Riddell's words, the opportunity to 'paint the picture'. In my case, as we have seen, this included my love of aerial activities – birds, aeroplanes, cranes and helicopters – as well as buses going about their business at ground level. The endless gaps between the moments of actual combat needed to be filled and gave the commentators the chance to be discursive and descriptive in any way they liked. This as much as anything had given the programme its unique character. No one was better at filling these moments than John Arlott, with his wonderful Hampshire tones, which became increasingly marinated and enriched by substantial amounts of excellent red wine as the years went by.

Arlott joined the BBC immediately after the Second World War as the Literary Producer of the Eastern Service. In 1946, he had followed the visiting Indian side around England doing daily reports for transmission to India. They had made a big impression and during the following winter Arlott was summoned by the head of outside broadcasts, who was formidably named Seymour de Lotbiniere but mercifully answered to the happy abbreviation of 'Lobby'. He wanted Arlott to join the team which commentated for the BBC in the UK. Lobby asked Arlott to sit down in his office and began by saying, 'You have a vulgar voice, but an interesting mind.' I heard Arlott tell that story several times – and without ill-feeling either. By then, he had become the greatest cricket commentator there has ever been, and I think he may have felt that he was giving Lobby a well-earned two-finger salute.

Commentators and summarisers had these distinct roles until an evolutionary process began to roll. The number of summarisers increased and those with strong opinions were always in favour, especially if they had the celebrity status which will have appealed to the selection committee. They understandably grabbed the chance to speak when they could, and the management will not have been unhappy that big-name ex-cricketers on robust contracts should be heard as frequently as possible. Suddenly the summariser's role shifted, and his voice was heard much more. It has reached the point that the summariser now comes in after just about every ball and the commentary itself is carried on almost as a conversation between the commentator and the summariser.

This inevitably clips the wings of the commentators, who are deprived of the chance to describe what is all around them and to go off on flights of fancy, which is what Arlott did so well, as did Alan Gibson, a brilliant commentator who was in the team for a short time around the late sixties and early seventies. Brian Johnston was also descriptive in his own humorous and irrepressibly cheerful way. This change has undoubtedly altered the overall style of commentary and has cut out most of those reflective moments which had once been so much a part of it. Has this been pushed forward by the ever more frenetic cricket on display these days? Or is it simply a reflection of the way the general tempo of society has been moving in recent times? Whatever the reason, it has changed the character of *TMS*, disappointingly perhaps for us oldies, but excitingly, I'm sure, for the bulk of the audience.

Then we come to one vital ingredient of the box which I have not yet touched upon: our scorers. For most of my life with the programme, Bill Frindall was the incumbent. He was turned into a larger-than-life character, primarily by Brian Johnston when he began to call him 'the Bearded Wonder'. It is fair to say that no one believed in his own publicity more than Bill, who liked to think *Test Match Special* had been created around him.

He was a brilliant scorer who came to the box after the two previous scorers, Arthur Wrigley and Roy Webber, had both died while holding the post. Bill had perfect copperplate handwriting and his finished scoresheet of every innings was a work of art. He was also a bit of a tyrant in his own world. He presided over us all from his well-organised nest of scoresheets, reference books, computers, briefcases, a collection of many coloured pens and pencils, the odd rubber and his lunchbox containing his half bottle of wine (delivered to him late in the morning by his current handmaiden, not always the same one two days running). His fruity voice could often be heard issuing instructions and showing his displeasure if his progress was interrupted or his method and its results were queried. Just occasionally he got something wrong and was not allowed to forget it. Finally, there was his noisy way of snorting if anything funny, silly or even faintly suggestive was uttered by the commentator.

But, for all Bill's foibles, he was an unforgettable *TMS* character. It took him a while to settle in with any newcomers to the box, and he was never worried about drawing attention to himself. Bill inherited a new system of scoring put together by his two predecessors, tweaked it and claimed it as his own. His neatness as a scorer was remarkable and he published several books featuring these works of art. He was an enthusiastic cricketer, who put together his own team, as well as playing many games as a seamer for the Lord's Taverners. It was on a tour to Dubai with the Taverners in 2009 that he contracted legionnaires' disease, and he died on his return to England.

Bill's immediate successor was Malcolm Ashton, a large and most genial, bespectacled Lancastrian who had been on hand for some years if ever there had been an emergency. He always did a good job. He now had the misfortune to be scoring during the Test match against Australia at Trent Bridge in 2013. That summer, the Duckworth Lewis Method pop group released their second album, *Sticky Wickets*. When they recorded the song 'It's Just Not Cricket', they asked me to do a sort of mini rap three or four times during the recording. The band consisted of two delightful Irishmen and they were invited by *TMS* to the Test at Trent Bridge to fill the 'View from the Boundary' slot during the lunch interval on the Saturday. The two, Neil Hannon and Tom Walsh, sang the song and I did my bit of rapping, and it was chaos in the box. When play restarted I was on the air with Phil Tufnell. Mitchell Starc bowled the first over of the afternoon, and during the course of what was a maiden I did my best to explain the lunchtime chaos to listeners. It took most of the over, and when I had finished going over it all, to draw a line under it, I said, 'Yes, the Duckworth Lewis Method and Henry Blofeld.'

Tuffers, on my right, gasped loudly and dissolved into tears of laughter. On the other side of me, Malcolm threw his pencil down, put his head on his scoresheet and also shook with laughter. He went so red that I thought he was going to burst. I had no idea what had happened and asked them if I had said something funny. I got no reply. Both were doubled up with laughter and Adam Mountford, our producer sitting behind, was giving a passable imitation of a hyena at the peak of its form. I was sure I knew what I had said and could not see anything remotely funny. I then commentated through the next over with the box shaking with laughter all round me. At the end of the over Tuffers was unable to speak, so I kept going and after a few more overs handed over to Jim Maxwell. As I got out of my chair, Henry Moeran, our assistant producer, asked me if I knew what I had said. He handed me a pair of headphones and told me I ought to listen. I told him there was no need, for I knew exactly what I had said. He insisted, so I put on the headphones and listened. It all went exactly as I had expected – until the very end. I then heard myself say, 'Yes, the Duckworth Lewis Method and Blowjob.' I couldn't believe it, but there it was, loud and clear, and I had no clue where it came from or how it got there. Oh dear!

For some reason, Malcolm's tenure as the Bearded Wonder's successor did not last all that long. In 2014 he was succeeded by the South African Andrew Samson, who had already been scoring for *TMS* when England were playing overseas. Samson was the best scorer I ever worked with, for he not only knew exactly where to find the answers to the difficult questions, but he also had an extraordinary knowledge of the game himself and was able to answer many seemingly impossible questions without having to look up the answers.

I must give you one extraordinary example of Samson's skill. England were in South Africa in 2015–16 and I was asked to join *TMS* for the last two Tests. The first of these was in Johannesburg and England won thanks to a remarkable piece of bowling by Stuart Broad. For this match, South Africa had brought in Hardus Viljoen, a seam bowler who could bat a bit. South Africa batted first and when Viljoen came in towards the end of the innings he hit his first ball for four. Later, he came on to bowl after England had got off to a reasonable start, and with his first ball in Test cricket he had Alastair Cook caught behind the wicket. Before Cook had left the playing area Samson was telling listeners that the last man to have hit his first ball in Test cricket for four and taken a wicket with his own first ball was the New Zealander Matthew Henderson, in the first official Test New Zealand had ever played, against England at Christchurch in 1929–30. When New Zealand went in, Henderson, their number eleven, hit his first ball for four in what turned out to be his only Test match. Goodness knows where Andrew had plucked that one from. The only slight problem with his scoring was his handwriting. A drunken spider would have been ashamed of it, and I had as much fun pointing this out as I had difficulty deciphering what he had written.

By an extraordinary coincidence, when I played a show in the Octagon Theatre in Bolton in March 2023, both Andrew, who had moved with his family from Johannesburg to Chester, and Malcolm Ashton were in the audience. 'A Tippex of scorers' was Malcolm's excellent suggestion as a collective noun.

When I packed it in as a commentator in September 2017, Andrew Samson was still in the scorer's chair for Test matches, while the comedian Andy Zaltzman, a passionate and highly knowledgeable cricket lover, had been helping out with the limited-over games. It was not long before he took over the Tests from Samson, and at first the listeners will have felt they had touched a live electric cable. The statistical details on *TMS* now leapt in one outrageous bound from the solemnity of a church service to the extravagant world of showbiz. Heavens, what a shock, but it was super fun, and Zaltzman has been brilliant. His knowledge of the game, his sense of fun and his timing are splendid, while his ability to know where to find the answers to all those impossible questions is Samson-like and maybe his handwriting is more legible. The production team, led by Adam Mountford, had picked a winner. The atmosphere in the box changed with Zaltzman. The story was still told, but with bells and whistles in attendance. This was how the programme was going, and who was to say it was wrong, apart maybe from the now neglected pigeons and the seagulls?

Of course, there is a great contrast between the *Test Match Special* box as it is today and as it was over fifty years ago when I first stepped through the door. It would be amazing if this were not so, for the world has become a vastly different place. There is nothing more irritating than having to put up with an old commentator complaining that 'Fings ain't what they used to be'. Having said that, I would like to make a heartfelt plea to all radio commentators to remember the importance of telling the story that is unfolding in front of them in the present tense. Every over has six sacred moments when anything can happen. It is for the commentators to build up the suspense, and they can only do this in the present tense, such as 'And Anderson is up to the stumps and he bowls'. It is a moment of complete suspense: anything can happen. If that moment is talked about in the past tense, there can never be any real surprise, for the moment has already gone. If commentators instead break off from what they are saying and give us 'And Root turned that one to square leg', we already know the answer, and in any case the crowd's reaction would have told us if anything dramatic had happened ahead of the commentator. Not good commentary. Moan over, and I won't do it again, I promise.

4

FOUR BYES IN RIO

'A naked not-outer'

Two splendid adventures in my life stand out most of all and which the more leisurely world of international cricket allowed me to fit into my life. One was the drive with Wooders from London to Bombay in a 1921 Rolls-Royce. The other, as we will see in this chapter, was a tour in 1979 of six South American countries – Venezuela, Ecuador, Peru, Chile, Argentina and Brazil – by a team of young county cricketers put together and paid for by Derrick Robins, a shrewd and successful businessman from the Midlands who also once owned Coventry City FC.

I cannot see either of these adventures happening in today's world. Even if the urge to do the journey had been there, politics would be likely to play a big part in preventing the drive to India, for neither the ayatollahs in Iran nor the Taliban in Afghanistan would be exactly welcoming to the old Rolls and its crew, even if Turkey might tolerate us. It must be doubtful whether the England and Wales Cricket Board (ECB) would have welcomed a tour to South America as warmly as the old Test and County Cricket Board (TCCB) did nearly fifty years ago, when the MCC still occasionally dispatched sides to less important cricketing countries like Canada and Argentina where the game still had a solid base.

Both of these two adventures fitted in well with the spirit of the game, the way it was played and regarded, and what it stood for, in what now can only be called 'the good old days'. In this modern,

T20 era, would the MCC committee that was recently eager to tread on its history and cancel the two oldest fixtures at Lord's – the Eton and Harrow match (first played in 1805 on Thomas Lord's original ground) and the Varsity Match between Oxford and Cambridge (1827) – without consulting its members, agree to pay for and send a party of first-class cricketers on a flag-waving exercise to South America? If they refused, would they allow a contemporary benefactor like Derrick Robins to foot the bill and do it for them?

In any case, I suspect a modern sponsor would want more and better for his money, but Derrick Robins loved sport, especially cricket and football. In 1978, he had invited me down to Eastbourne, as his guest to watch his eponymous XI play New Zealand. During that game he asked me if I would like to come to South America with his side the following year as part assistant manager and part social secretary. It was an offer I could hardly refuse.

It was a delightful party managed by the former England bats-man Peter Parfitt, a good friend of mine from Norfolk. The famous old England wicketkeeper-batsman Les Ames, a friend of Robins, came along too, and was the most genial companion and éminence grise. Our medical adviser, Kelly Seymour, was also a former Test cricketer, having bowled his off-breaks in seven Test matches for South Africa in the sixties. Chris Cowdrey captained the side, and he and six other members of our young team went on to play Test cricket.

We flew out of Heathrow in the early spring the following year, changed aeroplanes in Madrid and landed in Caracas the next day. The cricket throughout the tour was sadly one-sided, although the opposition put up a better fight in Buenos Aires, which has a long cricket tradition. There was a vibrant cricket community in Venezuela, where we began the tour, because of the strong West Indian influence. We flew on from Caracas to Quito, the capital

of Ecuador – the tour was a magnificent geography lesson for all
of us – where we stayed mostly with expats. I had the luck to be
billeted with the British ambassador, who looked after Derrick
Robins, Kelly Seymour and me in style.

The only problem was getting into and out of his residence.
Kidnapping ambassadors had become something of a local
pastime, so in order to prevent this, leaving and arriving at our
billet was a trifle complicated. There was a drive-in garage at the
side of the house and a small entrance had been burrowed through
from the garage into the house, so that once safely in the garage
we did not have to risk going out again into the open. When the
car had been driven into the garage and the self-locking door had
come down behind us, we were allowed to clamber out of our
seats and feel our way to the passage at the back of the garage.
Then, head bowed, we would sneak out through a narrow, makeshift entrance which brought us into the house by the stairs, feeling rather as if we were making the film of *The Thirty-Nine Steps*.
I remember Derrick once losing his footing and swearing loudly
enough to put every kidnapper in Quito under starter's orders, but
happily they were not listening.

In Peru, the old British Tennis and Cricket Club in Lima
looked after us well, but sadly we were not there long enough to
visit the Inca ruins at Machu Picchu. In any case, I picked up
some bug that was going around and was not well enough to go
on with the main party to Santiago, the capital of Chile, our next
port of call. Peter Whiteley, our tall, young off-spinner from
Yorkshire, picked up the same thing, and we flew down a day or
two later. I must have spent only four or five nights in Lima,
enough for me to have always wanted to go back. My sadness at
leaving lasted only until we arrived in Santiago. We found we
were staying at the Prince of Wales Country Club in the distant
shadow of the Andes, with one of the loveliest cricket grounds
almost in front of my bedroom window. Once more the cricket
was hardly testing, and I was able to enjoy for the first time, I

should think, the delights of a good number of Chilean red wines. They set a dangerous precedent.

We had been in each of the first four cities just long enough to know that we longed to return to them, but now Buenos Aires, where we were staying for just over a week, promised something slightly different. Cricket had been played in the Argentine for many years, and the standard was good enough for the MCC to send those sides out there from time to time. Our visit was really a continuation of that, and the MCC will have been glad they did not have to pay for it. The British influence in Argentina was strong – this was before the Falklands War.

I had an interesting experience almost before we had arrived in the country. At the airport, the customs officers made what seemed to be not much more than a token examination of our cases, and in my hand luggage I had some cassette tapes which I played on my Walkman. One of them was of that brilliant musical *Evita* produced by Andrew Lloyd Webber and Tim Rice. The officer who found the tape behaved as if he had discovered the Crown Jewels in my grip bag. *Evita* was all about the extraordinary Eva Perón, the former president's wife, and it was felt by the government in Argentina that the country had not come too well out of it and recordings of the show were banned. My tape was confiscated and for a few minutes the customs officers regarded me with the deepest suspicion, going through my main case with great care. In the end, I think they realised the tape was for my own pleasure and I was not part of a spy ring, nor was I trying to overthrow the government or start a rebellion. It all ended with smiles and handshakes. I hope the customs officers then had a really good party, listening to all those wonderful songs.

On this visit I found that in Buenos Aires there was still a megastore – not perhaps quite as mega as they can be today – called Harrods, a blood relative of the store in the Brompton Road in Knightsbridge. Not only that, but we all stayed at the Hurlingham Club, a close relation of the Hurlingham Club near

Putney Bridge in south-west London. The Buenos Aires Hurlingham had its own golf course, polo and cricket grounds, and every other sporting facility you could wish for. There were any number of expatriate Brits living in the country, many of them within easy reach of the Hurlingham, where they propped up the bar in style and made us feel wonderfully welcome.

I was thrilled to be there because I had a long-standing connection with Argentina and its cricket. When I was lucky enough to play in the Eleven at Eton at the age of fifteen, our captain was Clem Gibson, whose family lived and farmed in Argentina, and still do to this day. His father, also Clem, was a considerable cricketer playing for Eton, Cambridge University and Sussex. Like Mike Falcon, he played for Archie MacLaren's XI in that remarkable game against Warwick Armstrong's Australians at Eastbourne in 1921. Father Gibson did not take a wicket in the Australian first innings, but took 6–64 in their second. He went back permanently to the Argentine in the twenties and then took a great many more wickets for them. I met a number of by then old men who talked about old Clem in the most reverential tones. When I played under young Clem at Eton, old Clem would come and watch and talked a lot of good sense about the game, but, modest to a fault, never about his own bowling.

We had one of the more amusing moments of the tour during our eight days at the Hurlingham. There were two consecutive rest days and in that time we had our own in-house golf tournament in which Derrick Robins himself insisted on playing. He always did everything he could to make sure he was one of the winning pair by picking the best player in the party as his partner. When the original pairings went up, Derrick had chosen to play with Bill Athey, the Yorkshire, and later England, opening batsman. The first day was for practice, and to Derrick's horror, the Yorkshire bowler Graham Stevenson hit the ball off the tee at least thirty yards further than anyone else, and straight down the fairway too. This did not suit Derrick at all, and his Machiavellian mind was soon up to its usual tricks. In his room that evening he reconsidered the pairings. The next morning, bright, breezy and brazen as ever, and without even attempting to make some twisted excuse, he simply announced that he had reconsidered the original pairings and pinned up the notice. We now saw that D.H. Robins was paired with G. Stevenson. There was nothing to be done about it, and for the next hour Derrick chortled away even more than usual.

I cannot remember who went off first, but then the great moment arrived. Stevenson got ready for his first shot off the tee and it was difficult to stop Derrick gloating. Back went Stevenson's club, then it began its powerful descent and he hit the ball with a fearful crack. It flew off at great speed, miles away to the right over cover point's head, as it were. Derrick spluttered and must have been on the point of trying to change partners again, while Stevenson looked puzzled but cheerful and fiddled happily with his club. Peter Parfitt put his hand up to his mouth and like the rest of us had quite a job to stop laughing too. And on it went, with Stevenson hitting the ball further and further over cover point's head, and Derrick offering a torrent of not overly gracious advice. Derrick did not appreciate having to live that one down – and for quite a long time too. At the end of the day, he and Stevenson were well down the list.

The national cricket coach in Argentina that year was Brian Ward, who had opened the batting for Essex, and although there was not too much talent at his disposal he did as good a job as he could. On the cricket pitch, Stevenson was altogether straighter than he had been off the tee the day before, and the Argentine side was duly dispatched with time to spare. The next game was against Belgrano, a club which played its cricket on a charming ground in the middle of Buenos Aires with tall, stately office blocks all around, which drew instant comparison with the Honourable Artillery Company's ground by Finsbury Circus in the City of London. We were then due to move on to another ground more than an hour's drive out of the city, but I was detained in Buenos Aires by Derrick Robins for a lunch at which he and his wife were entertaining important Argentinian guests. It was a feast made memorable by my first encounter with a formidable Argentinian red and one of the biggest and best steaks I have ever eaten.

On the days when there was no cricket, we were kept extremely busy by Derrick's vigorous organisational ability, which never allowed any of us more than the occasional twenty-five minutes when nothing had been arranged. I badly wanted to go to Harrods, to at least say I had been there. We drove past it a couple of times, which was as near as I got. I can say that the hectically busy street outside was much more rough-and-tumble than the Brompton Road, which was eminently stately by comparison.

Buenos Aires was a splendid build-up for the joys of Rio. None of the players had put a foot wrong so far, but they had been licking their lips at the prospect of the Copacabana, which they were regarding as the icing on the cake. But first we had to negotiate São Paulo, a city which did not allow Rio to have things all its own way. I was soon to discover this in a mildly disconcerting manner. We were playing only one day's cricket there, against opposition that would not be too testing. Our three evenings in the city could therefore be fully exploited.

On the first evening, I set off with a number of the players to see what São Paulo had to offer. The answer was: plenty. Derrick Robins had told me to keep an eye on the boys as best I could; Kelly Seymour warned them of some of the medical pitfalls that might lie ahead in this free-range city; and Peter Parfitt simply said, 'Good luck, old bean.' We set off with a great sense of anticipation, although we had no idea what we were letting ourselves in for.

The first bar we found was full of outrageously beautiful girls. There were six of us when we entered that bar. Within moments

I was on my own. I bought a very large glass of wine and wondered what to do next. Every so often, one of my charges would re-appear and assure me that everything was going well. I did not know whether to be glad or appalled. After a bit, I thought it was time I started to fend for myself and I began to chat up a tall, heavily suntanned beauty in a green dress. I was in the process of buying her a third extremely expensive drink when she started to wave enthusiastically at a swarthy-looking man on my right before burrowing her way through the crowd and smothering him with kisses. I still had to pay for that third glass, which I had to swallow myself. As the evening went on, one or two of my lot decided they might be more successful on their own and when we got to our final venue, the darkest and sleaziest of nightclubs, only two members of the original squad remained with me. By then, we had had a fair amount to drink and as we peered round the dark sprawling room we could not believe it. We thought we had seen some beautiful ladies already that night, but they were nothing compared with what we saw now. We were thrilled to bits by the enthusiasm these ladies showed for us and we began to play a few slightly clumsy strokes. For a while, everything went according to plan. Then, we all got a bit closer and it was not long before I made the disconcerting discovery that not everything was exactly as I had expected it to be. Our speed of retreat will have been close to the record.

São Paulo was a good practice run for Rio, where we spent our last five days in this fascinating part of the world within touching distance of the famous Copacabana. Getting to the cricket ground at Niterói involved a considerable journey over what must have been the longest bridge in the world, which wound its way for several miles over the many waterways around Rio. The ground was a shallow bowl with banks full of highly colourful flowering shrubs, more than faintly reminiscent of the Nevill Ground and the rhododendrons at Tunbridge Wells. We took on the full might of Brazil in a two-day game. Brazil batted first and they were bowled out for nine, four of the runs coming when our wicket-keeper let one through for four byes. It was hardly important, but our boss was a bully when it came to winning. He was always delighted when we crushed the weak sides we played, but he was now seriously angry about the four byes. It was too ridiculous, but this was Derrick Robins, who occasionally had a massive sense of humour failure.

He had another the next day, which was, I suppose, slightly more justified. Brazil bowled better than they batted and we were still batting at the end of the first day. That evening one of the not-out batsmen went to the Copacabana on a voyage of discovery which would almost certainly have first involved a few drinks before he sighted the girl of his dreams in one of the many bars. They quickly struck up a relationship and found an hotel in which to continue their liaison.

The not-out lothario woke up in the morning to find not only that he was alone, but also that every single garment he had been wearing had gone missing. He found a towel, wrapped it around himself and advanced upon the reception desk in search of his clothes. The chap there listened attentively to his story and eventually opened the door behind him which led into an office. All the not-outer's clothes were laid out in full view. When our not-outer, hugely relieved, moved towards the door, it was shut and locked and he was told he would have to pay something like $500 if he wanted them back.

Our not-out friend, knowing he was some way from the team hotel, which was more than an hour away from Niterói, and that he was scheduled to face the first ball of the day, looked at the clock and realised he was in a bit of a hole. He did some quick thinking and remembered a friend who lived in Rio. It was a great piece of luck that he was able to find his name and number in the telephone book, and luckier still that he was at home to answer the call. He was more than happy to help as best he could and our naked not-outer sat on his bed until his friend arrived nearly an hour later. The dollars were handed over, he got dressed, and they then had to go back to his hotel for him to change into his cricket clothes.

When they arrived at the ground the game had been in progress for nearly an hour and Derrick Robins was beside himself with anger and had plenty to say. His wrath embraced me too, for not making sure that both not-out batsmen were locked into their rooms by nine o'clock the night before. He chuntered away, walking up and down the ground for much of that day, even though we beat Brazil by an innings and plenty. Robins was a hard taskmaster, which was probably why his company, Banbury Buildings, prospered and Coventry City rose from the Third to the First Division, although Jimmy Hill also had a bit to do with that.

Touring nowadays is so streamlined. Nothing is left to chance, and there isn't the time to see so much and meet so many amusing people, or to indulge in a praiseworthy thirst for knowledge. My time in South America was an experience that has become more and more amusing as the years have gone by. What fun it was to have been there in the midst of it all. I hope I am wrong, but I cannot see anything like this tour happening today, especially not with such a capable group of players, several of whom went on to play for England.

5

REST DAYS

'Wild boar hunting with Imran Khan's cousin'

EVER since its invention, cricket has been thought of as a gracious game both on the field and off. It was born all those years ago in England with aristocratic genes. It was played by the nobility, with important help from the other ranks. The clothes players wore reflected its status and gave it even in its earliest days an elegance and a perceived superiority. Moving forward, there was a balletic beauty about the best players going about their business in white flannels. Off the field, the game of cricket stood for all that was right in life and became the yardstick by which good and civilised behaviour was judged. 'It's not cricket' was not a meaningless rebuke. This was the game my generation was brought up to play.

As time went on and society changed, 'It's not cricket' lost some of its impact. It was watered down as some of the things that used to be condemned were now considered if not acceptable, at least not as deplorable as they once were. Society was taking a more relaxed view of morals, and cricket followed suit. Take the business of 'walking'. In the old days, if a batsman snicked the ball and was caught by the wicketkeeper, he was honour-bound to walk the moment an appeal was made. For a batsman who knew he had hit the ball to stay at the crease when the fielding side appealed was most certainly 'not cricket', and when it did happen, friendships could be badly affected.

One of the most important and extraordinary pieces of 'It's not cricket' happened during the first Test match played in Australia after the Second World War. It also destroyed a friendship, though one which may already have been coming to an end. It was an incident which surprisingly seems to have been submerged by the mists of time. In 1946–47, England, whose cricket had been badly mauled by the war, visited Australia under the rather remote post-war captaincy of the forty-three-year-old Walter Hammond. Australia were led by Don Bradman, who had to be coaxed back into action after the six-year lay-off. He was thirty-eight and had suffered a nasty shoulder injury which had been slow to mend. He must by then have felt he had proved everything that he had ever been asked to prove, and part of him was reluctant to have to start all over again. In the end, he gave in and agreed to lead the Australian side out in Brisbane at the end of November.

Australia won the toss and Alec Bedser had Arthur Morris caught at first slip when the score was nine. With the eyes of the world upon him, Bradman took his place and for a time did not find it easy. He had reached 28 and was facing Bill Voce, who had been Harold Larwood's main accomplice in the infamous Bodyline series in 1932–33. Voce was a shadow of the bowler he had been fourteen years earlier and his pace was barely fast-medium. He now over-pitched a ball outside the off stump to Bradman, who went to slash it away on the off side. The ball appeared to hit the top edge of the bat and flew at chest height to Jack Ikin, who held the catch at second slip. Bradman did not move and, seeing this, the England players, who had not appealed, thinking it was a clear catch, belatedly did so and umpire George Borwick immediately gave Bradman not out, saying later he had hit the ball into the ground.

As he walked past Bradman, Hammond said to him, 'What a f------ way to start the series,' and that was the level at which their relationship continued for the rest of it. The consensus of opinion was that it was out, and it is impossible to believe that Bradman himself did not know this. He went on to make 187.

If he had been out for 28, those close to him felt that he would have retired after the match. Instead of which, he not only played in all that series but against India the following year, before calling it a day at the end of Australia's tour of England in 1948. Small, single-minded, self-contained and self-controlled, Bradman would never have been accused of being a saint.

As a postscript to this extraordinary incident, when I played in the early sixties in a Minor Counties match for Norfolk against Staffordshire in Norwich, not only had both captains, Bill Edrich of Norfolk and Jack Ikin of Staffordshire, been on the field that day in Brisbane, but it was Ikin who had held the 'catch'. Around the bar in The Bell after the first day's play in Norwich, conversation soon turned to Bradman's non-dismissal. Both Edrich and Ikin said that you could not have wished to see a clearer catch.

There were a number of people, including some of the others in the Australian side, who said that in tight situations Bradman would almost always put his own interests first. While, by staying at the crease, he had done a great immediate service both to himself and Australia, the incident was one in the eye for the game of cricket and one of its most cherished traditions. By then, there were a growing number of batsmen who did not walk when they knew they had hit the ball. They were not popular. But as the years have gone by, fewer and fewer batsmen have continued to do the decent thing in these circumstances by giving themselves out. For a long time, cricket was synonymous with fair play, but although 'It's not cricket' is still a part of the language, it no longer works as it did, and umpires are put under increasing pressure by today's winner-takes-all approach to the game.

In the old days, when winning was important without being all-important, the professionals were paid a relative pittance whether they won or lost. When life began again after the Second World War, the public flocked to watch top-class cricket in England. By the time the sixties arrived, this post-war enthusiasm had died and the game needed to be reinvented. This was the cue for the launching of limited-over cricket, in the hope that a game which produced a result in one day would appeal more to the public, while the sponsors' money would ensure the enthusiasm of the players. The Gillette Cup began in 1963 and brought with it its own financial rewards for winning and picking up the more minor awards from each match. It was a modest beginning, yet the team that won the competition had a reasonable sum to share between the members of the side. The Gillette Cup started life as a 65-over competition and was an immediate success with the public, as it was for the sponsors. In the end, after eighteen years' sponsorship, Gillette passed on the baton, maybe feeling their company was becoming better known for cricket than for razor blades – perhaps the definition of a perfect sponsorship.

Then, in the seventies, limited-over cricket took off at every level of the game. In January 1971, the Boxing Day Test match between Australia and England in Melbourne was washed out and as compensation to the public the two countries agreed to play the first ever limited-over international. The idea soon caught on and the following year saw the first international limited-over series in England, when Australia were the opponents, and it was for two of these matches that I first joined *Test Match Special*.

At the domestic county level in England the John Player League arrived in 1969, a 40-over competition played on Sundays. It was inspired partly by the success of a series of 40-over exhibition matches put together by Bagenal Harvey, one of the first sports agents, which had been played on Sundays and shown on television. Three years later saw the launch of the Benson & Hedges Cup, a 55-over competition, and in 1975 the first World Cup, sponsored by the Prudential Insurance Company, was played in England as a 60-over competition. In the final at Lord's, the West Indies beat Australia in a game which did not end until after nine o'clock in the evening – and there were no floodlights in those days.

Limited-over cricket may have made a gradual start in the sixties, but ten years later it had become an accepted part of a game which was changing fast. Limited-over games were beginning to be played at club and village level too, although even then I don't think anyone had any idea of where it was all going to lead. The cricket world was about to receive a shock from an accident waiting to happen. Without knowing it, the game found itself being kicked into the modern world.

In 1976, the Australian media mogul Kerry Packer tried to buy exclusive rights to televise international cricket in Australia for his Channel Nine television network. In his attempt to buy these rights he was blocked first by the Australian Cricket Board, even though he was offering them a great deal more money than they were currently receiving from the Australian Broadcasting Corporation for precisely the same package. The established authorities in all the other cricket-playing countries came to the support of their Australian friends and Packer found himself fighting a battle against the worldwide cricketing establishment. However, his pockets were deep enough and his determination was unbreakable. His response was to launch World Series Cricket (WSC) in 1977, buying up the world's best players and starting his own Supertests and limited-over competitions in Australia, whilst paying the participants unheard-of sums of money.

For many years cricket's administrators had been outrageously maintaining their own version of the feudal system. Change was anathema to them. They owned the players and paid them ridiculously little when you consider their great and increasing market value for both sponsors and spectators, but in the committee rooms at Lord's, Melbourne and elsewhere they could not understand it and were deeply affronted. The players and the game itself were itching to break free from these old-fashioned shackles.

Kerry Packer, an immensely rich bully who looked like everyone's idea of a gangster, was not greatly liked but was admired for his fearless and successful business acumen. He may have found himself at the head of this army by chance, but he was the perfect man to lead the charge. He took on a dramatic fight against self-righteous opponents, principally in Australia and England, who regarded Packer as the devil incarnate and will have probably felt they had God, if not justice, on their side. But Packer was not going to let go.

He bought up the Australian and West Indies sides and then put together a Rest of the World XI captained by Tony Greig, the current England captain, who had always been a somewhat contentious figure. Greig became close to Packer and one of his most vociferous and active supporters. Always plausible, Greig was an important figure in this revolution. Another significant Packer employee was Richie Benaud, who before joining WSC was very much an establishment figure. His support helped give Packer cricketing respectability. When Packer went to Lord's to state his case in the committee room, he came through the Grace Gates like a dreadnought with a potent gunboat at his side in the person of Benaud, whom some never forgave for seeming to change sides. When the game's establishment tried to ban their players from joining WSC, Packer took them to the High Court in London, claiming this to be restraint of trade, and won a resounding victory. After that, nothing was going to stop him. It was another irony that Packer's leading counsel, Bob Alexander, was later to become President of the MCC.

World Series was not at first allowed to use the main grounds in Australia and in 1977 played in stadiums used for Australian Rules football, on the Royal Sydney Agricultural Showground and in the centre of a trotting track in Perth, on drop-in turf pitches. Their first game was played at the VFL Park Aussie Rules ground in Waverley, a suburb of Melbourne. I was one of several English journalists who flew to Melbourne to watch this encounter between Packer's Australians and Packer's West Indians.

From the moment I landed in Melbourne it was a battleground of them and us. At that time, I was very much a part of the establishment anti-Packer brigade, and taking a taxi out to VFL Park for the first game felt a bit like a journey into enemy territory. I had with me an extremely heavy BBC tape recorder, a Uher, on which I was going to record commentary on the first over of the first Packer game. I sat in the front row of a press box which I suspect had never before seen such a massive journalistic turnout. The tape has long since disappeared, but I described Andy Roberts bowling the first over to Australia's Rick McCosker. The cricket was high class, but with both sides owned by the same man, the biting edge of competition was missing. The press box was close to the VIP seating and presiding over that was the massive figure of Kerry Packer himself, sitting there like a belligerent yet smug human version of Mount Everest, not to say King Kong.

World Series Cricket was up and running and Packer, knowing the press box contained several committed opponents of WSC, could not resist the chance to gloat. It was not long before he pushed his way into the box with that thick-lipped grin of his, which was even more self-satisfied than usual. The first journalist he spoke to was John Woodcock, a dedicated opponent who, like me, had travelled to Melbourne on a rather circuitous route to Pakistan, where England were about to start a tour. Packer had some strong words with Woodcock, who always refused to tell me what had actually passed between them. Packer did say to the box in general, 'I see quite a few of you have jumped over the fence this morning,' and laughed, by which I suppose he was implying that our presence at VFL Park indicated a new-found support. He was wrong in that, but he had every right to smile for, at great cost, he had got what he wanted and had begun to open the flood-gates to what cricket was to become over the next fifty years. A game run by what he perceived as old-fashioned duffers with their antiquated and reprehensible ideas was now up for grabs in a modern commercial world.

That morning at VFL Park marked an irrevocable change which no amount of huffing and puffing in the committee room at Lord's or elsewhere was going to stop. On offer were coloured clothes, white balls, black sightscreens, umpires dressed in black, glaring advertising signs (even painted onto the outfield), loud rock music, a dancing girl or two in tight tops and the shortest of short skirts, as well as more television cameras than ever before, on-field interviews and a slick new television coverage master-minded by the genius of David Hill, who was in charge of Channel Nine's cricket. It was not quite the Houston Astrodome and base-ball showbiz, but it was still quite a sight. That morning at VFL Park, cricket began to move in that direction as for the first time money began to dictate.

In spite of the strong feelings of the authorities in England, just about every one of the WSC innovations was immediately adopted by the English game, even if the dancing girls were a step too far. The television coverage faithfully reproduced all the new inventions of David Hill. In November 1978 the WSC Australians played the WSC West Indians under the new floodlights at the Sydney Cricket Ground. By then, WSC had been granted the freedom of traditional Australian venues. This was a match I also watched; it was a terrific success and day/night cricket was another WSC invention which caught on fast and before long came to Test cricket as well as limited-over matches. Floodlit cricket greatly increased the game's advertising potential, so, while Kerry Packer may for a time have rocked the very foundations of the game, he certainly pointed the way forward to cricket's present state of prosperity.

Before we move on from Kerry Packer, I want to try and show how in those days the job of following international cricket around the world as a journalist or a broadcaster may have been a more satisfying and sometimes more dramatic way of life than it is today.

Tours nowadays are all about airports, hotels, packing and unpacking, buses or taxis to the ground and back, and out to the airport, with an occasional round of golf squeezed in. I have always enjoyed finding out what is going on around me, and when I first went on tour, to India in 1963–64, there was time to spend the odd night away with friends, to visit the Taj Mahal – almost compulsory – or simply to drive out of town and see a bit of the country, to go to a polo tournament or, in Calcutta, as it was known then, to Alipore racecourse at one end of the Maidan, where one of the stewards was Pearson Surita, an All India Radio cricket commentator who several times joined *TMS* when India were touring England. We would visit him in his large and heavily draped and curtained Victorian apartment on Chowringhee, or go and spend the day at the Tollygunge Country Club in the south of the city. In Madras you could spend the day visiting the lovely old French town of Pondicherry. Every Indian city was full of fascinating things to see if your schedule gave you the chance, as it did in the old days.

Then there were the good restaurants to go to for lunch or dinner and, unlike Brian Johnston, I love Indian food. At that time, we had the joy of a rest day after three days of every Test match, when the day was yours to enjoy. Peter Doyle's seafood restaurant in Sydney, the visit to the Hill-Smith winery at Yalumba, a day at Portsea when in Melbourne and delicious mud crabs in a restaurant outside Brisbane were the traditional rest-day treats in Australia. The disappearance of rest days was a sad if understandable move. There were no rest days in the Packer Supertests, and the main reason for this would have been to prevent the large number of cameras and all the other television equipment lying around unproductively for a whole day when they might be gainfully employed elsewhere; and, anyway, perhaps in a modern world rest days were becoming an anachronism. By the mid-eighties rest days had completely disappeared, although just occasionally there has been a rest day in England when the Sunday of a Test match has coincided with a final at Wimbledon.

The first Packer match at VFL Park was the start of an

extraordinary six months for me. I flew off the next day to Pakistan to commentate with Don Mosey on the three Test matches England were playing there, and Pakistan was always quite an adventure. I went out very early one morning to go wild boar hunting with Imran Khan's cousin. In the first Test in Lahore, we had two days of riots caused by supporters of the former prime minister Zulfikar Ali Bhutto, Benazir's father, who had been bundled into prison. This was also the series when Mike Brearley broke his arm and Geoffrey Boycott took over the captaincy for the third Test and the following tour of New Zealand.

While the England party went on to Auckland, I flew to Perth and at the Gloucester Park trotting track I watched two days of a WSC Supertest when Gordon Greenidge and Viv Richards put together a huge and most exciting partnership. I then went on to Adelaide, where on the last day India got within a measurable distance of scoring 493 in the fourth innings to beat the official Australian Cricket Board's Test side in the fifth Test of the series. Meanwhile, England had lost the first Test in Wellington and I flew in for the second, which was about to start in Christchurch. England won convincingly, but it was made memorable when, in their second innings, they had set off in search of quick runs so they could declare, but Geoffrey Boycott went along at his own leisurely pace. Ian Botham, on his first tour, was now sent in at the fall of the second wicket with the specific instructions to run out his captain, which he did quickly and efficiently, to most people's great amusement. Boycott's face as he walked off was a picture. After that, I had time to visit a great friend in Wellington, who led me first to a dozen wonderful Bluff oysters and then to a plateful of New Zealand's own incomparable whitebait, which are unlike any other whitebait I have ever eaten, before watching a boring draw in the final Test at Auckland.

I now flew across the Pacific and down to the West Indies to watch the series between Bobby Simpson's non-Packer Australians and Clive Lloyd's (mostly) Packer-employed West Indians. In the first two Tests, the Australians were no match for the full might of the West Indies. This started a major row because the Australians had been led to believe they would be playing against the non-Packer West Indians. I joined the tour in Georgetown while negotiations went on furiously, and it was beginning to look as if the tour might be abandoned. There were rumours of Packer's imminent arrival and, as it happened, Austin Robertson, a large and cheerful former Australian Rules footballer who lived in Perth and was one of Packer's two right-hand men, flew in to try and help find a solution. They were a breathless few weeks, but huge fun.

During the two days before the third Test it was like living in the middle of an Agatha Christie novel, as rumours abounded and important people kept dashing in and out of the Pegasus Hotel lift in Georgetown. Prime Minister Forbes Burnham's solicitor, Sir Lionel Luckhoo, a small man with an incorrigible smile, who was curiously twice knighted by the late Queen, made a stealthy, confident entrance before disappearing at the double through a door and up a flight of stairs. This was almost the cue for the arrival of Berkeley Gaskin ('Ghastly Backspin' was his nickname), a redoubtable Guyanese who had bowled fast-ish for the West Indies soon after the war and who spoke the purest Queen's English with the most impeccable accent and emphasis. He never stopped talking and insisted on continually quoting Shakespeare, which was not really a great help. We were now told that Forbes Burnham himself, who lived just round the corner, would appear, but I think he had full confidence in his solicitor and stayed at home, although his security chaps scurried about all over the place.

Then Clive Lloyd unexpectedly stepped out of the lift and, in that lugubrious, Paddington Bear-like way of his, told us that the Packer West Indians had decided to take no further part in the series – I daresay after a lengthy telephone call to Sydney's Bellevue Hill, where Kerry Packer lived. At the time this seemed rather an anticlimax and those of us who did not have deadlines hovering over them beat it for the bar and had a good laugh.

I hope I am wrong but I cannot see anything like those few months happening in today's world when everything is so stream-lined and nothing is left to chance, but what fun it was to have been there in the midst of it all, and to have had the time to see so much and meet so many interesting people. And, for the record, in this six-month period, I watched ten Test matches and only two limited-over games. Yes, it was a long time ago.

6

TO INDIA BY ROLLS

'Alongside the Saadabad Palace'

I N December 1975, I was staying at the Weld Club in Perth while watching Australia play the West Indies in the second Test match of the series. John Woodcock was there and towards the end of our usual oyster-inspired dinner I said to him, 'With any luck this time next year we will be in India watching England.'

'The last time we went to India,' he replied, 'Johnners [Brian Johnston], Mellers [Michael Melford of the *Daily Telegraph*] and I were going to drive there.'

'Why didn't you?' I asked him.

'Because the wives didn't think it was a good idea.'

'Well,' I said, 'right now, you and I have no such encumbrances. Why don't we do it this time?'

And that was exactly how it began, and before we had drained our last glass of wine, we had chosen our first travelling companion. One evening in Sydney the year before I had met a highly glamorous lady in Woollahra and before I knew it she was standing irresistibly on the roof of my friend's rather swish car, having mercifully discarded her high heels. Wooders had met her soon afterwards and agreed that Judy Casey had really selected herself.

When we returned to England, Wooders ran into a jovial farming friend in Hampshire who owned a considerable stable of vintage cars. He suggested to him that he should choose one of them and come with us to Bombay. He thought, 'What fun; why not?', and that accounted for the selection of Adrian Liddell and his magnificent claret-coloured 1921 Rolls-Royce. We thought we probably needed a second car, because four people and their luggage was going to be rather too tight a fit. It was soon after this that I came across a friend with whom I sometimes drank in my club. I told him what we planned to do and his immediate reaction as he drained his glass of whisky, was 'I'll buy a car and come too', and Michael Bennett, horn-rimmed half-moon glasses perched towards the tip of an impressive nose, and the Yellow Peril, a new, gleaming yellow three-litre Rover, completed the party. Five robust individuals with strong views on almost everything in a confined space without too much idea of what lay ahead promised some interesting discussions, to say the least.

There was now a great deal of organisation to be done. We had to decide which way we were going and, having agreed on that, we needed detailed maps of the precise route. Somehow we had to find enough petrol stations to satisfy the huge thirst of the 'Old Gal', as Ady insisted on calling the Rolls. There were the visa requirements of the countries we were driving through, the documents for the cars, and then we decided we should see if we could get ourselves sponsored. It was a time when perhaps there was something slightly caddish about being sponsored, but, unashamed, we picked up our telephones and tried to twist the arms of friends whose businesses might help us. In the end, we put together a mildly incongruous group of three sponsors. I think Esso Petroleum, through a friend of Wooders, was the first to sign up. We persuaded Air India to put their hands in their pockets, and then our third backer, who assumed an increasingly more important role as the journey went on because they supplied us in kind as well as cash, was Long John Scotch Whisky. There was a case or two of forty-ounce bottles and also some cases of beguiling-looking flasks, which held about a third of a bottle. They became invaluable, as we shall see, when it came to persuading customs and immigration officers at awkward frontier posts to wave us through.

*   *   *

Ady always intended to drive the Rolls every inch of the way himself and found that he had me sitting beside him in an uncomfortable passenger seat, once the preserve of the assistant chauffeur. Wooders sprawled comfortably on the ample back seat as if he was the aristocratic owner. There was a glass window which he was able to wind up and down at will, presumably so that the family sitting in the back were not overheard by the chauffeurs. It was a car designed in an age when democracy was not on the tip of everyone's tongue.

The Rover was driven by Michael and occasionally by Judy who, before a clutch was let out for the first time, had sensibly decided that the Rover was the more comfortable means of transport. We had had to alter our original route to fit in with our sponsors' needs. We headed to Paris on behalf of Long John and then, to satisfy the needs of Air India, we nipped across to Frankfurt by way of the best dinner of the trip at a hostelry in the Champagne part of France called Sept Saules, which boasted a well-deserved Michelin Star, and then it was down to Salzburg, also for more sponsorship duties. This put us on the road that led to Yugoslavia and then on to Thessaloniki and across the top of Greece to Istanbul, where we had more sponsorship chores to carry out. On the way to Istanbul we spent two days in the delightful fishing village of Komatini so that Ady, in smart blue dungarees, was able to give the 'Old Gal' her first full service since leaving England.

It was at about this point, as we were approaching Istanbul, the Bosphorus and Asia, that the difference in the approach of the two cars to what lay ahead began to surface. Michael had just retired from the City and understandably wanted to see as much as he could of a part of the world he was most unlikely to see again, and this went for Judy too. On the other hand, Ady, a car freak to his eyebrows, was only interested in driving and looking after the 'Old Gal' so that she could get us to Bombay on time. He concentrated on the road ahead, looking neither to the right nor to the left.

We stayed at the Park Hotel in Istanbul, where the 'Old Gal' made a big impression parked in its own stately manner outside the front entrance and rapidly attracted a large gathering of tourists. We paid a visit to the incredible Blue Mosque and then, after a last dinner in Europe, we set off the next morning across the Golden Horn and into the startlingly different atmosphere of Asia. The three of us in the Rolls almost never got there. We were taking the bridge in our stride when, halfway across, Ady needed to take both hands off the wheel and asked me to steer for a brief moment. No sooner had I got my hands on the wheel than the car gave a lurch to the right towards the framework of the bridge which was taking us over the Bosporus. Seeing what was happening, Ady gave a not-so-stifled yelp, seized the wheel before we made contact with the bridge and toppled over the edge. I don't think Wooders, in the back, was aware of what had happened, but I was off Ady's Christmas card list, certainly for the next day or so.

We were planning to spend that night in Ankara and we had not worried about booking an hotel, for there would surely be no problem finding a suitable billet in the capital city. The Automobile Association had supplied us with elaborate maps and we also had a number of guidebooks. When we stopped for lunch we thought we had better do something about finding some accommodation. To our horror, we discovered that every hotel appeared to be fully booked because each of the political parties in Turkey were holding their annual conferences in Ankara. When Michael Bennett became anxious, he would continually catch hold of his waistband and pull up his trousers, which was anyway necessary because he had never acquired the skill of putting on a belt. This now became a constant tug.

We had pretty well accepted by now that we would have to spend the night in the cars, but we hadn't given up yet. There is quite a network of contacts on these trunk roads, for one is forever meeting up with the same drivers, of lorries and cars doing similar journeys, as well as those travelling fearlessly on motorbikes. At all the many stopping places and filling stations we now asked if anyone could steer us towards a hotel which might not be full. We were met with blank stares.

It was early evening by the time we arrived in the outskirts of Ankara and soon we saw a big and rather imposing petrol station. Although we carried some two-gallon cans on the running board in case of emergency, Ady never liked to miss the chance of filling his tank. We were never quite sure if the filling stations the AA map had promised us would still be there and if they were, would they be out of petrol? We pulled into this station and Ady went up to the filling attendant and said in his usual piercing way, 'I am afraid I have no Turkish.' Which, as the attendant clearly had no English, did not get us much further forward. While this was going on, two or three excited youngsters who had just filled their jalopies gathered with much interest around the 'Old Gal'. Ady immediately went into his party routine and opened the bonnet and gave a running commentary. As luck would have it, the young men did have a bit of English and it became a noisy meeting of great minds. After a while, Wooders suggested to Ady that he should ask them if they knew of an hotel that might have a room or two. The boys said they did, but a couple of telephone calls from inside the filling station confirmed that there was not a bed to be had in Ankara.

Then one of them said, 'I know, you must come and stay at home.' I suppose this was an offer one might normally have been a little cautious about accepting, but the situation was grave and they were obviously such good chaps that we all agreed it was a brilliant idea.

'My parents live in a big apartment over there,' he exclaimed, pointing over his shoulder. 'There are four bedrooms and they would love to have you.'

Judy and Michael were waiting in the Rover parked in the road just outside. I beckoned them over and Michael uncoiled himself from the driver's seat, got out, gave his trousers an imperial hitch up and strutted over in his mildly formidable way. He was delighted at the offer, and so our young friend now disappeared into the filling station to ring up his parents. In no time at all he was back with us, grinning from ear to ear, and in his spluttering but highly enthusiastic English almost shouted, 'It's all fixed up. We're going to get something to eat and by the time we get home they'll be ready for us.'

There was now a procession of four cars and after a tricky journey, when traffic lights kept turning to red with two cars still to get through, we found the Ankara equivalent of a hamburger bar, it may even have been a McDonald's. When we sat down we found that the one whose parents were going to put us up spoke the best English and had spent six months near Oxford. We were all still a bit apprehensive about going to stay with the mother and father of a young man we had met only an hour before, and we asked him about his parents. To our amazement we discovered, after a few interpretational difficulties, that his father was none other than the Turkish Judge Advocate General, the principal military judicial officer for the Turkish army. While this was impressive, I think we felt a little embarrassed that we had blarneyed our way into spending the night with such an important man. We set against this the important fact that there was going to be a secure garage for the 'Old Gal', which was vulnerable to thieves, with boxes on the running board and on the roof too.

We were very much on our best behaviour when we arrived at an impressive apartment block. The cars went into the underground car park and then we were led through the front door of a smart apartment by the son of the owners shouting in excited Turkish to his parents. We were shown into a sizeable drawing room with all the trimmings, including a grand piano. The parents were middle-aged, urbane, charming and extremely welcoming. Three of the group, Ady, Michael and Judy, got bedrooms, while Wooders and I had to make do with three-star sleeping bags on a plush pile carpet. All this after we had significantly dented the

Turkish Judge Advocate General's supply of Scotch whisky. Talk about falling on your feet. Breakfast the next morning was a mixture of the delicious and the interesting as Europe and Asia met somewhere in the middle of the dining-room table. The coffee was as good as any I have ever drunk and I enjoyed all the spicy bits and pieces, certainly more than Ady, who had probably been hoping for porridge. He was not an adventurous eater.

That day we were aiming for Sivas, a city halfway between Ankara and the Iranian border, and the next evening could hardly have been a greater contrast to the one we had just enjoyed. Michael Bennett had been prompting discussions about the way we should go once we were in Asia and had finished our immediate sponsorship duties, while Ady was sticking resolutely to his determination to get the 'Old Gal' to Bombay as quickly as he could. Obviously Michael and Judy had been discussing this impasse in the Rover, just as Wooders and I had been listening to Ady and, having been responsible for Ady joining the party, Wooders was prepared to see it from his point of view.

Sivas, as I remember it, was a sprawling city with some impressive medieval monuments which we were only able to drive past in the dark. The Judge Advocate did not himself know of an hotel in Sivas, but a friend of his had once mentioned a hostelry in the city centre, although without any great enthusiasm. The next morning we set off full of hope, having restocked the Judge Advocate's shelves with some of the whisky Long John had given us. In the evenings, after a long day on the road, our Long John not only went down a treat but it also disappeared increasingly quickly. It had been an unbelievably dusty and bumpy journey on roads that had seen better days. It was hot too, and in that part of the world the sun can be unpleasantly relentless as it glares down on you from a cloudless sky. Ady continually stopped the Rolls to make sure there was enough water in the radiator, but the 'Old Gal' did him proud. We had had a blowout in Greece on the way down to Thessaloniki and another tyre had been damaged, which had prompted Ady to arrange for some spares to be flown out to meet us in Tehran, where we planned to spend the best part of a week staying with a prosperous legal friend of Ady's.

We arrived in Sivas in the late afternoon and found that the hotel which had been rather tepidly recommended was unable to fit us in, but we found another nearby, which would not have found a place in a *Guide Michelin* but produced five bedrooms with plumbing arrangements that were both perplexing and at times incredibly noisy. We were now well into what I called 'squatting country'. We saw our last sit-upon European loo in the Judge Advocate's apartment. After that, we were confronted by what I was assured were called Alaturka loos. There two big clay footprints on which you stood and behind you there was what was effectively a hole in the ground. On the first occasion, it takes a moment or two to work out the safest modus operandi. The whole process becomes a bit of an adventure if you have dodgy hips. I never approached an Alaturka loo exactly brimming with confidence. Practice didn't make perfect, but it was a help.

Before we set off in search of solids that evening in Sivas, we had a council of war to see if we could find a common geographical strategy to take us to Bombay. Differing views were forcibly expressed, senses of humour were stretched, Long John was gulped down – that evening the first bottle took us just over three-quarters of an hour, which remained the lap record for the journey. In the end, humour and good sense marinated by Long John won the day. As a result, Ady, Wooders and I ploughed on towards Bombay, with the Rover taking a more opportunistic approach to the route ahead.

In Europe, moving across the border from one country to the next had been a reasonably brief formality, but in Asia it became a much more complicated process. We were now driving along the road used by long-distance lorries taking their goods from Europe to the furthest stretches of the Far East. These huge vehicles choked the road and made Ady's job behind the wheel of the Rolls increasingly difficult, although the lorry drivers themselves took the 'Old Gal' to their hearts and did all they could to help us on our way. After two happily uneventful evenings in roadside hotels, we approached our first Asian frontier post with warnings from the lorry drivers that the people controlling these posts could come up with any excuse to hold you up for days before allowing you through. The main reason this was done was of course in the hope that quantities of baksheesh would be forthcoming.

The lorries had to join a long queue but it was much easier for cars. It still took us most of the morning to get through and it involved waiting in temporary huts in queues with other car drivers. We had to answer a lot of questions, first on the Turkish side and then later in Iran, but we were not seriously held up. The officials on the Turkish side were quicker and more amenable than their opposite numbers across the border. Even so, we were heading for Tabriz by mid-afternoon. It had been child's play compared to what we were told to expect when we entered Afghanistan a few days later.

Tabriz was uneventful and we set off in the 'Old Gal' at about half past six the following morning to drive to Tehran, where we were staying with Ady's prosperous legal friend who also had his own collection of old cars. His name was Fayed and he was not any old lawyer either, he was the Shah's lawyer, and in 1976 the Shah was still in charge, although the ayatollahs were already flexing their muscles behind the scenes. Fayed lived in a huge villa just outside the impressive high walls of the Shah's Saadabad Palace.

How Ady coped so well with the interminable traffic jams in downtown Tehran was remarkable, but after spending most of the afternoon negotiating the hold-ups in Pahlavi Avenue, Tehran's main artery, we somehow managed to find Fayed's magnificent house and, helped by his impressive head butler (there were three in all), we installed ourselves for what turned out to be almost a week. Fayed kept his collection of cars some distance away from the house and soon took Ady off to look at them. Jumping back into his smart dungarees, Ady began a two-day service of the 'Old Gal', something he had been greatly looking forward to. Even better was the fact that the spare tyres had arrived from London.

The week went quickly. Wooders and I got up very early one morning to go and watch a game of cricket between two sides from the British High Commission. It was a trial match to help them pick their best side for a short tour of India. The ground was on part of the land around Tehran Airport and every few minutes an enormous aeroplane flew over us so low one felt one could almost touch it – and at deafening full throttle in take-off mode. The pitch was appalling and within twenty minutes of our game ending at half past eleven, goalposts were being put up at both ends, which explained the pitch's condition.

Wooders and I both spoke at a dinner at the High Commission and the next day we all inspected the formidable Iranian Crown Jewels in the vaults of a bank in Pahlavi Avenue. One evening, from the roof terrace where we were staying we watched the sensational firework display on the other side of the palace wall to celebrate the birthday of the Shah's son. Earlier we had met our host dressed in a dinner jacket leaving for an unknown destination, obviously embarrassed that we were not going with him. When the fireworks began, we knew where he had gone.

Then it was off to Afghanistan by way of a night in Babolsar on the shore of the Caspian Sea, where the caviar was well up to standard. It then took us two days to drive on to the holy city of Mashhad. On the way we spent one night in Bojnurd, where we met some well-to-do locals who asked us to join the barbecue they were having just outside the city. We drove with them to a big roundabout a mile or so outside Bojnurd, where the barbecue was held – in the middle of the roundabout. There must have been about twenty people there and we ate lamb covered with succulent spices. During the evening one of the men told Michael that as we were going to Afghanistan it was important to take some cartons of matches because they were invaluable baksheesh. The next day Michael bought three large cartons and so we were prepared.

When we drove into the courtyard of the Hyatt Hotel the following day in Mashhad, the 'Old Gal' immediately became a major tourist attraction. Having been told by the reception desk that there were no rooms available, we bumped into the general manager, a German called Bruno, who had come out to see why the crowd had collected in his courtyard. He was greatly impressed by the Rolls, but even more so by Judy, who had never looked anything less than brilliant through the entire journey and was at her best. When we returned to the hotel lobby we were told that miraculously five rooms had just been discovered. Later still, Bruno discovered a cache of champagne in his office, which led to a party later that evening and hangovers in the morning. It was all a trifle incongruous, for there we were within a short distance of perhaps the most holy mosque of all.

The next morning the champagne also led directly to the launching of what I suppose has become my catchphrase of 'My Dear Old Thing'. By that stage of the journey we had established a satisfactory modus operandi. The 'Old Gal' never went much faster than 50 mph which, as it only had brakes on two wheels, was probably just as well. When we had a long drive ahead of us, the Rolls started off at about half past six in the morning. The Rover, capable of much greater speed, left at least a couple of hours later, overtook us late in the morning and would then find some café on the road where we could have lunch, and would wave us in when we got there. In the afternoon, they overtook us again and tried to find an hotel and again waved us in.

We were all bleary-eyed the morning after the champagne in Mashhad and before we left I had to leave a note for Michael about the little flasks of Long John whisky, which had been useful at the last frontier post and were likely to be come in handy on our way into Afghanistan. The flasks were all in the Rolls and we needed to pass some to the Rover at lunch. With my head aching, I wrote 'My Dear' and couldn't think of Michael's name, so I wrote 'My Dear Old Thing' at the top of the message and left it at reception. When we met up for lunch, Michael waved the note at me and said, 'I haven't been called "My Dear Old Thing" since my father died.' From then on that's what I called him. By the time we got to Bombay it tripped off the tongue pretty easily. I began to use it on other people and discovered that it could be a great help if I had forgotten someone's name. It still is.

While we had been planning the adventure, several people who had made the same journey told us that this border post was likely to be a problem. It was apparently supervised by a teenaged boy whose word had to be obeyed. We had had to get ourselves visas for Afghanistan and so we went to the Afghan Embassy in London to have them stamped into our passports. There was no problem with this, but while I was waiting at the embassy, they also told me about the boy and told me how important it was to do as he wanted. Not only that, but one of the officials there gave us a letter which we were told to give to him. As we now approached the border we made sure the appropriate documents were ready.

There was a huge queue of lorries and once again the cars joined another, much smaller queue. After a while we were told to park the car and go over to a large Nissen hut where there were a lot of people milling about, many of whom had been waiting for a long time and were not happy. The man who had told us to park came with us and, after waving his arms and shouting instructions, helped us force our way through to the door. The hut was hot and sticky beyond belief and smelt strongly of armpits. We told our friend that we had this letter from the embassy in London and we showed him the envelope. He was delighted and, smiling, told us to wait at the side of the hut until he returned, which he said would not be at once. He walked quickly to the door at the far end and disappeared.

We must have waited for getting on for an hour. I remember Michael and Ady both getting a bit restless and Wooders telling them they simply had to behave and sit this one out. There was much pushing and shoving as in their frustration people tried to gain an extra yard or two in this rather haphazard queue. Then suddenly a tall, youngish Pakistani came bustling towards us and he looked up at Michael's unmistakable large figure, with his drooping trousers and his half-moon horn-rimmed glasses perched on the tip of his nose. He immediately gave an extraordinary yelp of delight, almost jumped at Michael, put his arms round him and hugged him. There was no stopping the Pakistani, who spoke quite good excitable English. For a wonderful moment I thought he was going to kiss Michael, who had not seen the man approach him and was trying to back off because at this stage he was not sure whether he was a friend or an enemy.

It transpired that the Pakistani had been working for three years in London and was driving home to see his family. For quite a while he had worked for British Rail at Liverpool Street Station and for part of the time as a ticket inspector. Michael owned a holiday house on the Essex coast at Frinton. Most Friday afternoons when he had finished work in the City he would take the train from Liverpool Street to Frinton. As he went through the barrier he would show his ticket to the inspector, and for more than a year this Pakistani was that man who had been clipping Michael's ticket. Michael being the larger-than-life figure he was, there was no mistaking him, even in the crush at this border post on the road between Mashhad and Herat.

The general excitement caused by this remarkable encounter had not fully abated when our first friend returned with a serious-looking boy in tow. He had an air of authority about him and had to be the boy in charge. With hand outstretched, he asked for our papers and took us through to the far end of the Nissen hut into a sort of alcove. He sat down and read the letter we had been given by the embassy in London, and then told one of his minions to stamp our papers.

This done, he shook us all by the hand and our original friend, who was still with us, told us that this most impressive teenager, whose name I never heard, wanted to see the Rolls. We led him to it, and when we opened the doors he immediately saw the flasks of Long John. His eyes lit up and his face cracked into a smile for the only time.

'These are for me.' It was a statement of fact not a question, and before we could answer, two were in his hands.

'Oh yes,' Wooders now replied, 'we brought them from England especially for you.'

In the end, I think he took four of them, and when he disappeared he was as happy as Larry and still smiling.

And, unscathed, we were through an impossibly difficult border crossing in well under two hours.

7

A STREET CORNER
IN KANDAHAR

'From Curzon's embassy to Chicken Street'

WHEN we crossed into Afghanistan I didn't get the feeling that I was in a different country until we had passed through Herat, where we spent our first night. Perhaps the three of us in the Rolls were talking too much about all the recent excitements at the frontier post. When we arrived at our hotel we found that one of the other guests was the delightful Sikh we had already met a few times on the journey and whom we had nicknamed Pissy Singh. For the last ten days he had kept on turning up and had enlivened several evenings, although we had been unable to prevent him from considerably reducing our stock of Long John.

The next day the Rolls made an early start, for we intended to do the 282 miles to Kandahar that day. We found ourselves on a dead straight tarmac road which ran to the horizon and far beyond through a relentless desert which seemed to stretch away on both sides of the road to the edge of the world. There were a few cars along the way and some big lorries which, like us, had started their journey on the other side of the world and now looked like prehistoric mastodons in a movie as they chugged their way across the desert. There were some motorbikes too, the drivers backpacked to the hilt as they forged their way ahead. Most of those going east were probably returning to the Subcontinent after a spell working in Europe. This will have been their cheapest way home.

Every now and then there was a shack surrounded by fading advertising signs promising such universal thirst-quenchers as Coca-Cola, 7-Up and all the rest. Occasionally there were some ramshackle houses and a few desultory, dusty human beings shuffling along as fast as they dared in the broiling sun. Once or twice near a house there was an excited child on a makeshift scooter, usually being chased by its mother. It was gripping and beautiful but somehow a bit bleak and scary.

We had filled the petrol tank to the top, the cans on the running board were at bursting point and we had gallons of water for both ourselves and the 'Old Gal'. We had those cartons of matches too. The night before in our hotel-of-passage in Herat we had met a bearded professor in Eastern Arts and Languages and his lovely dark-haired young wife who were returning to their university in Spain. When we told him about our matches, his eyes lit up. He spoke with a strong accent, but his English was not bad. He had been making this journey for several years and explained that the local tribes lived in black-tented villages in the desert a long way back from the road. He told us that we would pass groups of children on the edge of the road who were from these tented villages, waving and shouting to the passing vehicles. They were hoping the occupants of the cars would throw goodies to them, and above all their greatest need was for matches.

During the summer months the tribes collected as much wood as they could find for the fires which would keep them warm in the freezing cold winter months. They needed matches to light their fires and they were hoping for boxes of matches to be thrown to them on the side of this extraordinary road, which was acting as a thin vein bringing the modern world briefly if not to their doorstep, at least within reach. The road had been built by the Russians and stretched from Herat to Kandahar, and then about the same distance on up to Kabul. The professor told us the best plan was to slow down as we approached the children and throw the matchboxes out of the windows as we passed. He assured us we would be astonished by their ecstatic reaction. Michael let us have a carton or two in the Rolls and we were looking forward to putting them to good use.

It was a while before anything happened. For miles, there were no children and not much traffic either – just dust and glare. In the front of the Rolls, Ady and I were beginning to wonder if we had been having our legs pulled, while Wooders, who was a believer, had piles of matchboxes at the ready and was looking like a benevolent potentate preparing to distribute largesse to his people. We then passed a small group of shacks and a couple of threadbare houses, outside of which were parked an elderly truck or two of the Steptoe & Son variety. The road surface was now more worn, with the odd pothole, and the road had become just a little narrower. The bigger lorries on their return journey from the still distant Far East sometimes seemed barely a couple of inches away as they came speeding past us. Long-distance lorry drivers are usually in a hurry and tend not to take prisoners. On this stretch, they were going at quite a determined pace and they kept Ady on his toes.

It must have been about ten minutes after we had passed those Steptoe & Sons that Wooders suddenly said, 'Look over there to the left.' Ady and I couldn't see anything but desert. 'No, no,' Wooders came back, 'in the far distance.' I looked again and, sure enough, some way off to our left we saw what at first looked like a collection of ungainly black mushrooms rising out of the desert. Wooders had his binoculars up and told us they were tents and he could see people walking about. Then, as if to order, we spotted a group of scantily clad children standing on the side of the road – waving and shouting at the passing traffic.

Wooders was ready for them and a couple of handfuls went out and in his excitement Wooders himself almost followed them out of the window. The children, who could not believe their luck, scrambled after the boxes, and one or two fights even broke out. Wooders then reloaded both hands and I grabbed a handful. We were ready for the next lot and in a moment or two we saw another group of madly waving children. Ady slowed down and Wooders and I pelted them with matches. The reaction was immediate and almost ferocious as the children fought for their winter fires. One furious rugger scrum developed and I saw a young girl snatch up a few small boxes and race off into the desert shouting to the heavens. She had become a matchbox millionaire, but not for long perhaps because the last we saw of her she was being chased hard by two small boys who were too young to be interested in anything else but the matches.

Michael and Judy must have started first that morning, for they were ahead of us and we could see Judy dispensing matches through the window with her usual vigour. Michael would all the time have been offering advice and giving instructions while keeping at least one hand on the wheel and his glasses on the end of his nose. When later we stopped for a break, they told similar stories of creating matchbox plutocrats.

We got through most of Michael's matches and the fun enlivened an otherwise relentless slog to Kandahar. In the evening the sun goes down fast and at one moment we thought we were going to drive into the city in sunshine, only to find that almost in the next we were winding our way through the narrow streets in an opaque dusk. This was no help to Ady, and although we had booked an hotel in Kandahar when we were in Herat, we had a difficult job finding it, not least because the 'Old Gal' was not exactly built to cope with narrow winding streets in eastern cities packed with free-range pedestrians all going in every direction at once.

Our arrival in Kandahar led to a wonderfully rich encounter between Michael and a bearded rogue on a dark street corner at a crossroads. Michael had jumped out of the Rover and he and Ady were in a muddle about whether we should go straight on,

Denis Compton batting against Eton College in 1956,
with the author keeping wicket.

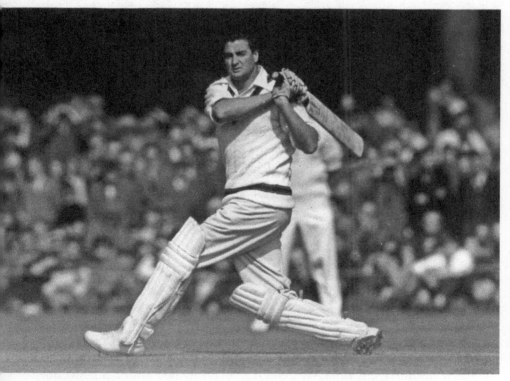

Cricket's number one matinee idol: that swashbuckling, inimitable
and charming Australian, Keith Miller.

The catch that never was. Bradman caught Ikin bowled Voce, Brisbane 1946. Given not out.

Australians touring the USA and Canada in 1932 included Don Bradman, left in middle row, on his honeymoon. Back row, left to right: P. A. Carney, E.K. Tolhurst, E.F. Rofe, W.F. Ives, L.O'B. Fleetwood-Smith, S.J. McCabe. Seated, left to right: D.G. Bradman, V.Y. Richardson, A.A. Mailey, A.F. Kippax. Front row, left to right: H. Carter, R.N. Nutt.

The Middlesex twins, Bill Edrich (left) and Denis Compton, in 1947, their *annus mirabilis*.

Great jubilation at The Oval in 1953! Compton and Edrich happily together when England won the Ashes for the first time since the Bodyline series in 1932–33.

An august commentary collection: John Arlott, Trevor Bailey, Bill Frindall, Neil Durden-Smith and Richie Benaud.

The Boy and the Boss: Fred Trueman and fellow Yorkshireman Len Hutton, his first England captain

BBC Television at full strength: Jim Swanton, Brian Johnston and Peter West.

Test Match Special getting in on the act: the author with
Brian Johnston and Christopher Martin-Jenkins.

More *TMS*: Tony Lewis, John Arlott, Johnners,
Blowers and CMJ at The Oval.

And again. Front row: CMJ, Fred Trueman, Johnners and Trevor Bailey. Back row: Peter Baxter, Bill Frindall, Farokh Engineer, Blowers, David Lloyd, Mike Selvey.

An unusually serene boss, our producer Peter Baxter.
All must have been going extremely well.

A 'script' of *Times* cricket correspondents: Mike Atherton, John Woodcock, Alan Lee and Christopher Martin-Jenkins outside Woodcock's house.

The Shah's palace in Tehran. On our epic drive to Bombay we stayed almost next door.

Blowers and Alastair Cook in the England dressing room. Not sure who's advising whom!

Blowers and Alison Mitchell discussing the finer points of commentary

A breathtaking view of Lord's from the present commentary box during a lunchtime discussion.

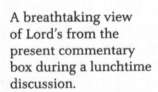

turn right or even left. Then we saw this cheerful vagabond standing on the corner smoking a cigarette. He gave Michael a cautious, watch-it-mate twitch of the mouth. Michael greeted him and showed him a piece of paper on which he had written in block capitals the name and address of our hotel. The vagabond began to speak through his heavy, almost W.G. Grace-like black beard, if a touch more unruly, as he dived into his flowing robes and came up with what in the loosest possible terms could be called a packet of cigarettes, which looked as if it had been partly opened. He held it up in front of Michael as if it was something the gods had sent, and Michael immediately dug into his own pocket and came up with a US ten-dollar note. Our vagabond grinned broadly and snatched the note, pocketing it at a speed which suggested he had been training with those children on the side of the road. Michael later said he had taken the packet in order to get the vagabond on our side, in the hope he would be able to tell us where our hotel was: 'At ten bucks, it's cheap at the price.'

There was a sublime moment when our friend turned to Ady, who was sitting in the Rolls peering out of the window, and began to speak in his direction rather than directly to him, whereupon Ady came back with a resounding 'I am sorry, I am afraid I have no Afghani.' Getting directions from our friend, who was now all over us, was still a problem. After trying to sell Michael another packet, he pointed with great conviction to the road straight ahead as though it might clinch the deal, but a few seconds later he was equally convinced we should go to the right. This crisis was averted by the arrival of another man, who looked a bit less evil if not exactly upmarket, but probably had even more exciting substances tucked away in his garments. After looking for a long time at Michael's piece of paper, he pointed with some certainty to the right. We were not brimming with confidence when we set off again after long and stirring farewells – our bearded friend wanted to kiss Michael, a feeling which was not reciprocated. As luck would have it, turning right and right again brought us to our hotel and, better still, they were expecting us.

Dinner that night consisted mainly of a spicy Afghan main course, which was delicious. We felt it was wiser not to enquire too closely about the origins of the meat. Afterwards we went back to Wooders's room for a nightcap and it was not long before Michael produced his unlikely-looking packet of cigarettes and suggested we light up. Which we did. There was a good deal of coughing and a strong taste and smell that certainly did not come from tobacco. We kept going for a bit and when I inhaled there was such a strange sensation in my chest I feared there was a good chance I might not live to tell the story. All I can tell you is that the next morning I had the most appalling headache which lasted for about three days. Wooders was not much better, and almost until the day he died, he and I, whenever we were together, touched on the saga of our life as junkies in Kandahar.

The drive to Kabul along another mercilessly straight road under the ever-searing sun took all day and it was late in the afternoon when, headaches and all, we reached our rather posh hotel with, thank heavens, sit-upon loos. This was Kabul before the bombs had begun to fall. Curzon's famous embassy still stood, impressive and unblemished, and although we only spent two nights there, it was lovely to have been able to look briefly at the old city before the explosives took over. We were kept busy during our day in Kabul too. We had duties to perform for Air India, the British Embassy kindly held a reception for us and we also had to pay the obligatory visit to the narrow, higgledy-piggledy Chicken Street, with its burning desire for American dollars, to buy a colourful Afghan coat. I tried to persuade Wooders to buy himself one too, but he was not sure how it would have gone down in Longparish. I think he felt that after the 'pot' in Kandahar, enough damage had been done to his reputation.

We were sad to leave Kabul so soon, but the blow was softened by the prospect of driving through the Khyber Pass on our way into Pakistan and on to Peshawar, where we were booked in for the night at the famous old Dean's Hotel, now sadly demolished. There was no spawning of black tents on our way to the Khyber and we drove through some highly fertile land, which was being busily farmed. It was a fascinating journey, with the mountainous frontier and the Khyber drawing ever closer.

The actual border between Afghanistan and Pakistan is near the bottom of the pass and on both sides we were quickly through the formalities. We suddenly found ourselves back in a world where English was spoken, and Ady was now thankfully back driving on the left-hand side of the road. While we were waiting in the passport queue we heard radio commentary on a Test between Pakistan and New Zealand. The match was being played in Lahore and while we were listening an off-spinner called Peter Petherick, who played only a handful of matches for New Zealand, took a hat-trick on his Test debut. I wonder how many other people remember where they were when Petherick had his moment in the sun.

The whole area of the Khyber Pass was bristling with aggression. It was in the middle of the tribal areas of Pakistan's North-West Frontier and it was a part of the world where anything went. Arms dealers thrived, contraband of every sort could be bought or at least ordered, and if you ventured into the forbidden areas I should think you were lucky if you ever came out the other side. Tribal warfare was pretty well continuous, and it was not a place to roam about without permission. The whole area was a haven for black-marketeers and smugglers, and it was also staggeringly beautiful in a stark and rugged way. It was alarming too, for it was hotching with police and soldiers, and there was an impressive variety of weaponry all over the place. An untimely spark might have produced an enormous explosion.

Driving up to the lovely old Dean's Hotel in Peshawar made us feel we were going back to the days of the British Raj. This was in

1976, almost fifty years ago, and as we pulled up that evening, an old bearer, seeing the Rolls – he would probably have been even older than the car – brought his hands together and bowed. When we got out, he told us how much it reminded him of the good (his word, not mine) old days of the Raj. The bearer will have perished by now and his hotel has given way to a brand-new shopping mall, which would not have made him happy. We had a drink in the old ballroom, which was being used as the Permit Room – a place where foreigners with the appropriate certificates were allowed to buy alcoholic refreshment. We had dinner in a huge dining room with a dank, musty feel to it, but even so it spoke of a vibrant and glorious past. It seemed appropriate that both Rudyard Kipling and Winston Churchill had stayed there. The 'Old Gal', parked outside in a position of honour, will have felt at home.

Dean's Hotel was somehow a fitting welcome to the Subcontinent. The tenor of the journey changed, partly because we were in an English-speaking part of the world, and partly because Wooders and I were in familiar territory, where we had friends and acquaintances. Of course, you never quite know what is round the next corner on the Subcontinent, but at least we could deal with problems in our own language. On that first night at Dean's, we sadly cut our last link with our recent past when, after a final evening hosted by Long John, we waved Pissy Singh farewell the next morning. He was incorrigibly cheerful and Wooders and I hoped we might meet up with him during the England cricket tour, but we never did.

The two cars now split up for about a week because Michael and Judy had decided they wanted to go and have a look at Kashmir. They drove straight from the Khyber to Delhi and flew up to Srinagar, where they stayed in a houseboat in one of those lovely lakes. From now on, for the three of us in the Rolls, even though Ady and the 'Old Gal' had never before encountered the hazardous driving conditions in Pakistan and India, the journey became a homecoming as well as an adventure. Although Wooders and I had been to India before, it is such an enormous country that on our previous visits we had only seen a tiny part of it. Nonetheless, we still felt we were back on familiar terrain. Our reception, principally because of the reaction to the 'Old Gal', was extraordinary. We were greeted for the most part as old friends returning rather than as foreigners in a machine which might have had a strange religious significance.

The reaction of the old bearer in Dean's Hotel was replicated many times as we drove down to Bombay, not so much by the young, who were mostly intrigued and curious, as by those old enough to remember the days when Rolls-Royces were a more common sight in India. When we drove slowly through villages and towns we were almost always followed as if we were a mechanical manifestation of the Pied Piper. When we needed assistance with directions or finding a petrol station, people were eager to help, and Ady was constantly being asked questions about the 'Old Gal', which he loved.

At this point I think all of us were relieved that we had actually reached India and were still in one piece. Ady had more reason than anyone to feel like this after driving the whole way himself and getting through against considerable odds, but he did so now without realising quite the task that still lay ahead, for he had to contend with the country roads in the remoter areas on the way down to Bombay. This was also the first time he had encountered the sacred cow, who can do as she pleases on the roads of India without fear of persecution or prosecution and takes pride of place even over a 1921 Rolls-Royce.

We had been on the Grand Trunk Road for a while before crossing into India, and now on the 300 miles from the border to New Delhi it took us in and out of plenty of potholes while also providing wonderful panoramic views of the north of the country. Many of the scenes of Indians going about their daily business seemed almost identical to those Kipling had described when writing *Kim*, which was published in 1901. In the more remote areas the hot sun, dust and wonderful colours combined with the natural elegance of the Indians, especially the ladies with their handsome, upright posture, to make a memorable picture. India never palls, for the unforgettable seems to be always just around the next corner. In these places the 'Old Gal', another supremely elegant and unforgettable old lady, sometimes received her own stirring round of applause.

Going through the frontier between Pakistan and India had made one immediately aware of the strength of the suspicion and distrust that exists between the two countries. There were many heavily armed soldiers on both sides of the border swaggering about. It felt like a tinderbox. There was no doubt that the 'Old Gal', in partnership with the remaining Long John flasks, helped to diffuse the tensions as, for a moment or two, she enabled the officials on both sides to find common cause, for they were all delighted to see her. Everyone was friendly and we were happy to pass through this important crossing point leaving cheerful faces behind us as we continued down the Grand Trunk Road to the city of Amritsar and its Golden Temple for our first night in India.

The British High Commission in Delhi pulled out all the stops to make us welcome. We had time in hand and had decided to spend three or four days there, mainly to see old friends. Wooders had alerted Ashwini Kumar, who had played hockey for India and now ran the sport there, as well as being the country's principal representative on the International Olympic Committee. Wooders, who was also the *Times* hockey correspondent for a time, had come to know him well. Ashwini, large and good-looking, was charming and no one could have been more determined to help us in any way he could. He had been a soldier all his adult life and was now head of India's Border Security Force (BSF), which was a huge job. When he discovered that our plan of action involved driving down through Rajasthan and Gujarat to Bombay, he insisted we spend time in Tekanpur, which was the headquarters of the BSF and not too far out of our way.

We were rejoined in Delhi by Michael and Judy, who had enjoyed their houseboat and their sojourn in Srinagar. After a final hilarious evening at the Maharajah of Baroda's house in the capital, we set off for Tekanpur. 'Jackie' Baroda had been one of the summarisers two years before at Old Trafford when I commentated on my first Test match for *TMS*. He was also a good friend of Wooders. On air in that series, we had called him the Prince, which was what Wooders and I continued to call him. The Indian princes had had their titles and privileges removed by Indira Gandhi in 1971, but they were still used most of the time in everyday life. The Prince knew about our journey and had promised he would put us up for the night in his palace when we reached Baroda. The only condition was that before dinner I should address the Baroda Cricket Association. He wanted me to speak for an hour, much to the dismay of my fellow travellers, for duty (to the Prince, not me) compelled them to attend. That evening in Delhi, he promised me that a three-line whip had gone out and there would be at least five hundred people in the Big Hall, which made it much more of a worry for me.

But first we had to visit Tekanpur. The town was not only the main base of the Border Security Force, it was also the group's equivalent of Sandhurst, where the potential officers were put through their paces before they passed out. Ashwini had promised us a display of tent-pegging – when riders at full speed spear the tent pegs so that the tent collapses on its occupants – but told us that pig-sticking was, unsurprisingly, no longer on the menu. There would also be military parades to watch, and some of the other disciplines it was necessary for BSF recruits to learn. We were given a wonderful send-off after breakfast when we left Tekanpur and I am sure that photographs, of the 'Old Gal' at any rate, will still be hanging on a wall somewhere there, such was the excitement and enthusiasm surrounding our visit. The centrepiece was a spectacular dinner the previous night when the silver in the mess seemed to be shining more brightly than ever.

The next day we were aiming for the magnificent Lake Palace Hotel in Udaipur, the seat of the Princes of Mewar. The lake itself is a shallow bowl with the city all around it, and the hotel stands on an island in the middle of the lake. We obviously had to leave the cars on the shore as a launch chugged us to our destination, where the plentiful supply of white marble gleamed enticingly in the late-afternoon sun. I remember it being hugely exciting as we arrived, but I felt slightly let down by my room, which was dark and dungeon-like, with the water lapping at the wall beneath the window. We had a jolly good Indian dinner, but I could not help feeling that a magnum of stirring champagne should have been produced with an appropriate feast to follow. Luckily, our supplies of Long John were still holding up and so we were able to make do and mend.

The next day our sights were on Jaipur, where we were put up in the Rambagh Palace Hotel with the help of Ayesha, the Rajmata (Queen Mother) of Jaipur, the widow of the late Maharajah, who for years was known as the most beautiful woman in the world. Even now in middle age she was amazing to look at, and what fun she was too. She had a lovely easy, slightly naughty laugh, a full smile and, as you would expect, wore the most beautiful clothes and was elegance personified. She lived in her own dower house, the Lily Pool, which she had had built after her husband had died. She was a keen but delightfully incompetent golfer and a wonderful hostess. Wooders and I returned to Jaipur during the England tour, when we stayed with Ayesha and played the only rounds of golf I have ever enjoyed in my entire life. The four was completed by Brigadier Himmet Singh, a serving soldier and friend of the Rajmata's. The golf was memorable for laughter rather than birdies.

*   *   *

We were now only four nights out of Bombay and our immediate goal was the palace at Baroda, which was about 450 miles from Jaipur, and we had another night on the road before reaching the palace. Our arrival got off to a poor start because a chap at the entrance to the grounds directed us to the Number Two Palace, which didn't do our morale any good. To add insult to injury, we drove past the magnificent Number One Palace on the way to our more modest quarters. We protested as politely as we could that this was not quite what was planned, and that we were sure 'His Highness' would sort things out, and rather begrudgingly they took us back to the main palace.

'His Highness', ever bonhomous and smiling, came bouncing down the steps. 'We're full up here. I am afraid you will have to stay over there,' he said, pointing in the direction we had just come from. And then to me, 'Henry, I have arranged for you to have a bat with some of my players. Vijay will look after you.' At that, a small man appeared with what seemed a slightly apprehensive smile. 'This is Vijay Hazare, who looks after my cricket for me.' Vijay was none other than the wonderful batsman who had captained India in the early fifties and led them to their first ever victory in Test cricket, against England in Madras in 1951–52.

We shuffled off back to the Number Two Palace. I changed into some cricket gear and didn't do very well against some keen young leg-spinners on the ground on which the state of Baroda play their first-class cricket. Then it was time to change again because the Baroda Cricket Association would soon be awaiting me. I climbed into a rather crumpled suit and the cleanest shirt I could find and was taken back to the Number One Palace for a glass of whisky in the VIP room, where there were about thirty people. It was there that I met three of the Prince's house guests who were staying in the main palace – Joanna Briffa, who hails from Malta, and Claude and Morag Brownlow, from Essex – all of whom have remained the greatest of friends. In the following years we had all sorts of fun at Test matches around England and in India when England played there.

But back to the Baroda Cricket Association. I was not at all confident. While having a drink, we were told the Big Hall was full, and when the signal was given we processed in behind the Prince, who loved this sort of occasion and was given a tremendous ovation. We sat in our appointed seats on a raised stage and the Prince then introduced me in Hindi. When he had finished, I stepped forward to the lectern and began. Every now and then I said something that seemed to go down pretty well, for suddenly there would be a loud burst of applause. Once or twice the audience clearly thought I had said something funny and they roared with laughter. I felt I was at the top of my form and it was all going pretty well. It was only the next day that I was told that the audience had taken their cue from the Prince, who was sitting behind me, and whenever he clapped or laughed they followed suit, and of course I lapped it up. When I had finished, the Prince thanked me in a mixture of English and Hindi, and I have never to this day received a standing ovation to match the one that followed. It went on for several minutes. I really thought it was my finest hour and was thrilled they had thought I was so good.

We all trooped back into the Prince's drawing room for much-needed drinks and then through into the dining room. There must have been about thirty of us. During the first course there was one of those moments when everyone stopped talking at the same time. It was just as Wooders leant across to our host, saying, 'Now, Prince, of all the six hundred people in the Big Hall tonight, how many do you think will have really understood what Blowers was talking about?'

Back came the answer: 'Practically no one.'

We spent the next night in the guest house of a cotton factory at Surat owned by the Prince himself and the following morning we drove into Bombay. About an hour later, we drove triumphantly into the short semicircular courtyard at the front of the Taj Mahal Hotel. It was a minute or two after half past one on 22 November. We had always said we would try and get there on the 22nd in time for lunch. We were disgracefully late. Before we left London we had booked a table for lunch at the Taj for one o'clock, but when we sat down, it was getting on for three o'clock.

8

OUR BRAVE NEW WORLD

'Banksy or Rembrandt?'

Now we come to the game's modern tumult. The way of life I have just walked, talked and driven you through flowed as easily as those rippling leg glances and delicate late cuts once found their way to the boundary. Not only are those elegant strokes heading towards extinction, but the way of life that seemed to go with them also belongs to the past. These days it has to be six or nothing on the cricket field and, off it, it is full speed ahead all day long regardless, while the past is viewed with deep suspicion, if it is not cancelled altogether. There is little time for reflection or persuasion as we plunge ahead, and to look over your shoulder in doubt will now be seen as a sign of weakness, or so it seems. In just a few years the world has moved on at a terrifying speed and cricket and all its appurtenances have been pulled along with it. Whether it is forwards or backwards is not always clear.

What we do now have in front of us looks pretty bleak. What can we do about it, or is it too late and therefore simply a matter of getting on with what we have left on a make-do-and-mend basis, rather than hoping to preserve something which has been intrinsically good for so long and deserves to be at any rate partially preserved? Are we gripped by an explosive evolutionary process, or are we lurching helplessly to a future dictated by multiple acts of self-destruction? Are the game's administrators, who are orchestrating what is happening by doing nothing to restore the balance of the game, being driven by a fear of being seen not to be 'with it' or by a feeling they should follow the latest social trends, or do they simply have no idea what to do? Or are they simply being taken over by events? Probably the latter.

Those who run the game seem finally to have lost control of it, for so much seems to be happening which they are unable to prevent. It is impossible for those of us who have loved and lived the game as I have not to throw our hands up in the air in horror too at some of the decisions the committee rooms around the world are failing to make to try and stem the tide that is turning cricket into a travelling T20 franchise circus. My fear is that it is too late to save the game I lived my life around in the first half of this book, but even so, all is not lost because at least we still have a game called cricket which is recognisable (just) as a direct descendant of our game.

Two recent occurrences point the way irrevocably to this different future. In May 2023 (before the start of the Ashes in England), Manoj Badale, lead owner of the Rajasthan Royals in the Indian Premier League, had a bit to say about the Test game and its place in the modern world alongside T20 and the IPL. He began by saying that Test cricket 'is still my preferred format', but that 'we're going to have to think creatively about Test cricket's future if we want it to work,' before suggesting it could be given a lift by making it 'more of an event'. He went on to say that Test cricket should be played in a condensed period 'at the same time every year … like Wimbledon'. Wimbledon only lasts a fortnight. It would be even harder to fit five Ashes matches into two weeks than it was to slot them into six. Mr Badale may love Test cricket, but he has done nothing to try and save it from being swallowed up in an undignified fashion by the T20 franchise world. The magnetic lure of money seems to be far more important than his professed love of Test cricket. One of the problems with the current situation is that the Ashes series is talked about for months beforehand in England and Australia and then, as in 2023, five Tests are crammed into six weeks as if the authorities cannot wait to get them out of the way. Of course, with The Hundred just round the corner straining at the leash. The reason for this is that although people love talking about and reflecting on Test matches in the periods between games, this fallow period is entirely unproductive in that it does not earn anyone a single penny.

Mr Badale also said, 'The number of times I hear arguments like "Ben Stokes wants to play Test cricket". That is important, but what is really important is what the fans of the future want to watch and where are they going to spend their hard-earned money.' It seems to me that Mr Badale is happily, if guardedly, waving goodbye to my old world of leisured intensity in which I learned and played the game. He is proclaiming, although he probably won't admit it, that his main interest in all of this is financial. T20 produces the goods, a five-match Test series does not. But hang on, what about that figure of at least two hundred and fifty million pounds a day grossed by the Ashes series? Few series will produce comparable numbers, but these impressive figures argue strongly in favour of the need to come to a compromise. That is not a story of financial incontinence, which is why I am going to discuss Bazball in the next chapter.

Although Mr Badale fell over backwards to be as accommodating as he could to Test cricket, it was, at best, cupboard love. He was, in my view, unable to disguise his speculatory intentions, hopes and expectations when he bought a large part of the Rajasthan Royals franchise and, by doing so, a strong position in the IPL. With all that is happening, an important franchise owner will stick like glue to the financial party line, however he may try to disguise it.

He seriously suggested that when the present reorganisation of the game is properly in place, all Test cricket will in the future be played in a restricted period each year when the T20 world gives permission. This can only mean that we can either learn to love

T20 franchise cricket with all its ramifications, or go and find something else, because you can only play so many Test matches in fourteen days, or however long he had in mind. It would be nice to think that having said all this, even he might have felt a trifle awkward, not to say embarrassed, after England and Australia played such a terrific Ashes series. Twenty-four exhilarating days' cricket were watched by twenty-four full-house crowds and the cricketing world was left spellbound and amazed. My guess is that with a condescending shrug, he would claim that this was one last hurrah and the exception which proves the rule. Wouldn't it be fun to prove him wrong, but my fear is that he is probably more right than wrong, especially in view of the apparent inability of the traditional game's administrators to fight back.

The other highly significant occurrence was the work of Cricket South Africa (CSA), who stated in January 2024 that none of their centrally contracted players would be picked for South Africa's tour of New Zealand the following month, which included two Test matches. They wanted to ensure their main players would be available for SA20, the new T20 franchise competition played in South Africa that clashed with the timing of the tour. In their defence, CSA made the important point that it was only this competition which enabled them to raise the money to be able to pay their leading players. This tournament is one of those under the aegis of the Indian Premier League. I expect the CSA, who seem to have signed a contract with SA20 which effectively gives the franchise competition greater importance than any Test or international series, will have received strong instructions from the Subcontinent.

The logical follow-through to this has horrendous consequences for the future of the traditional international game. To make it even worse, this series in New Zealand was part of the World Championship of Test cricket. Does the lack of these contracted players render the competition null and void? Already, we face the searching question: what is the point of a Test series if the best players are not allowed to take part? The answer is that there is no point. This decision of Cricket South Africa will be the first of many similar decisions around the cricketing world in the years to come.

There is an irony here too, because Kagiso Rabada, South Africa's most important player, has recently gone on record as a strong supporter of Test cricket. He said, 'It is concerning [that fewer Test matches are now played] because we want the game to continue growing. We want Test cricket to remain a priority in South Africa, especially when you have a young team.' He also said that the present South African side all love Test cricket and agree with everything Rabada has said. His words are unlikely to have brought much joy to the CSA. As we will see, he is not the only leading player to voice these sentiments.

Another, even more pertinent endorsement for Test cricket came from none other than the former Indian captain Virat Kohli, a hugely popular figure in India. While still captain, he said, 'Nothing comes close to playing an intense game in whites. What a blessing to be able to play Test cricket for India.' For the leading cricket icon in a country where Test cricket is being virtually relegated to second place, this is as remarkable as it is significant, for it shows that even there, this form of the game is far from dead. Kohli has millions of supporters who hang on his every word. We know Ben Stokes also loves Test cricket, and I am sure that many of the world's best cricketers would willingly back up everything these three great contemporary players have said. It goes without saying that no one understands the skills, the tension and the intrinsic value of Test cricket better than great players such as these three. Yet the administrators, lured of course by the cash tills, and who for some time have thought they are the ones who know what is what, are busily doing all they can to force the T20 game down the throats of the public all around the world, but the throats at the moment seem to be more than willing to be treated in this way. They are telling the public what they should like, and at the moment in most places they absolutely love it, but surely these administrators should be trying to protect the whole game. Attention spans have shrivelled and cricket is being shaped accordingly to meet new needs. The hope that the 'new' spectators will soon filter through to watch two-innings cricket has always seemed to me to be far-fetched. A crowd attracted by the showbiz razzmatazz of T20 and the way it is presented is, I think, most unlikely to settle for what can only seem to them to be a more sedate spectacle. This may be because of the absence of all the glittering showbiz extras. Before long, they will want to rush off in pursuit of the next sporting or cultural extravaganza, and I shall be surprised if Test cricket even gets a look-in when that happens. Test cricket still has a huge number of dormant followers whom they should be doing all they can to lure back to the game.

For the moment, T20 has been designed to grab the public imagination, but it is so crucially important that the classical style of cricket should be preserved. The time will come when fashions will shift and crowds will probably come back to the longer form of the game. Happily, the situation is not quite so dire in England, in spite of the administrators' best efforts to make it so. In the recent Ashes series, the public had their say. The twenty-four full houses at the 2023 Ashes prove the point. Test cricket is still a viable entity in England – the first three days of Test matches are sold out against all opponents – but even so it does not need to be further undermined from within by those running the game, who still seem hell-bent on playing catch-up with the rest of the cricket-playing world and its obsession with T20. But England need someone to play against, and shouldn't our administrators be spending at least some of their time and money trying to encourage other countries to continue to come here and play Bazball against us? It is interesting and relevant, and worth reiterating, that every day's Test cricket in 2023 will, when everything is taken into account, have grossed over £250 million. The ECB's current rate of expenditure needs an income stream of this sort. And yet Test cricket is being treated and spoken of as the poor relation with a crumpled shirt and baggy trousers.

This brings us to another important factor in the equation, which is the exorbitant price of tickets for spectators which puts a five-day Test match out of the reach of a great many people. A ticket for a day at a Test match at Lord's in 2023 costs at least £160. A one-day match is different, and T20 with all the artificial glitter is even more different, to say nothing of The Hundred. Of course this financial disparity is important and it is up to the ECB to get to grips with the problem and to try and find a way forward rather than just wring their hands and do precious little to nurture a hugely worthwhile tradition.

Another development which can only leave the traditional game of international cricket even more in tatters is the contracts which will almost certainly be offered by the franchise-owners to the game's leading players. For some years it has been the ambition of the world's best players to land a lucrative IPL contract. The time has come when these contracts will be more lucrative than ever. A player who signs for an IPL franchise is likely to be offered a twelve-month contract which will commit him to playing for all the other franchises his IPL franchise is tied to. This will leave him with precious little time to play for his country in any future Test series. In recent years, overseas tours have become increasingly compressed, which is something else which damages my charm factor. This, as we have seen, was perfectly illustrated by the 2023 Ashes series in England when all five Test matches were crammed into six weeks so that the cash tills could keep up the good work and leave elbow room for The Hundred which was to follow in August. The ECB were incredibly lucky that the matches were all so compelling that in the end no one was especially bothered about this.

In the old days, a tour to England would begin at the end of

April with a match against Worcestershire and not end until well into September. The five-Test series would start early in June, with the fifth Test being played at The Oval in late August. In between Tests, there were matches against the counties, which were not only huge local events but they gave out-of-form players the opportunity to sort themselves out. They also allowed the players who had not so far been selected for the Tests the chance to challenge those who had. Now, with tours pared down to the minimum possible time, the injured have almost no time to recover, but of course it enables more one-day series to be fitted in around the world and, above all, for the money to keep pouring in.

The first and most important aspect of all this is the shameful way in which the game's current crop of administrators have ignored Test cricket, for so long the bedrock and gold standard of the game. They have roared off headlong in pursuit of the wealth and popularity which they hope will come from the increasingly shorter and ever more frenetic modern slogathon interpretation of the game. One can only wonder if they have stopped for a moment to think about what they are doing to the game and what we all might be left with at the end of the day. Banksy is all very well, but surely Rembrandt will always reign supreme. Of course cricket has always needed more money and more sponsors who will buy into the game. I just hope that when push comes to shove, they will not find they have been sold a meretricious game at the expense of true cricket which we saw exhibited in unrivalled fashion for those twenty-four days in 2023. Is cricket not something more than four sixes an over all greeted at full blast by something from *Pick of the Pops*? All right, it is entertaining, but it is not cricket, and I am terrified that before too long it will drive the wonderful game which brought us this recent Ashes series near to extinction. One can only wonder how genuinely Mr Badale cares about Test cricket and the future of the game.

I have watched several of The Hundred games on television and the style of play makes a mockery of proper cricket. Take the surfeit of sixes: once, with good-sized boundaries, sixes were a joyful and much-loved rarity and were greeted as such. Now, with boundaries creeping ever closer, to make what commentators today insist on calling the 'maximum' even easier to score, an over without a six has become almost a surprise. All these sixes have their appeal, yet not only have they become an excess but they somehow unbalance the game, making it top-heavy and turning it into more of a rough-and-ready exhibition of slogging rather than a genuine and skillful contest. They make one long for a good old honest maiden over, but then it is a game which has effectively made the skills that go with an impeccable defence seem unimportant, and some of those lovely, delicate wristy strokes too. Bat and pad do not have to be close together in the way they once were, and deflections such as leg glances and late cuts are now a matter of optional last resort for a batter rather than a fully paid-up member of his armoury.

Bowlers have also had to make dramatic changes to hold their own in the T20 world. You will no longer see out-and-out fast bowlers who are bowling with perhaps four slips and a gully and a short leg or two. This is one of the truly gripping moments of Test cricket and why most of us try and arrive on the first day well before the first ball is bowled. But true fast bowlers, by their nature, have off days and these are not risked in T20. A field like this is the prerogative of fast bowlers at the start of an innings. It is not a moment to miss, any more than the moment the umpires in their gleaming white coats first appear at the top of the pavilion steps. In T20, umpires, like the players, wear anything but white, and so do not send the same shiver of excitement through the crowd when they first appear. If Test cricket is allowed to disappear – and remember that all two-innings cricket will disappear with it if it does go – this great moment of drama will never be seen again, nor will umpires in white coats or indeed players in white clothes; white sightscreens will go too. Fast-medium dobbers who aim at the batsman's toes will now be the order of the day for opening bowlers. Restriction is the name of the one-day game and bowlers must make it as difficult as possible for the batter to score runs. It is the job of spinners, by using flight, change of pace and length, with fielders strewn round the boundary, to buy wickets. The best way to win a Test match is to take 20 wickets; the best way to win a T20 game is to prevent your opponents from scoring runs: different objectives call for different methods.

Fielders have to be braver, faster and more agile than ever before. This is one aspect of the game which has been enormously improved by limited-over cricket. The modern game has greatly increased the mobility of cricketers, but it has also added to the strain they are under, and the physical demands have appreciably shortened the careers of some. The English season is the most demanding of all. It starts early in April and goes on almost seven days a week until the end of September. There are four competitions to be decided in addition to the seven Tests, the one-day internationals and the T20 games the two touring sides have to play. This will be the main reason that the old pros who I have mentioned earlier in the book and who played such an important part in the continuity and the development of English cricket are no longer there. It became too much for them and they did not fit into the modern cricketing scene.

The game has always been caught up in an evolutionary process. I only pray that my fears will be proved wrong and that the instincts of the game's modernists are not allowed to drive Test match cricket to extinction. Sadly, the mood for meaningful compromise was not glaringly obvious when the two sides of the argument met at Lord's in early July 2024.

9

IS BAZBALL THE SAVIOUR?

'The two Kiwis get together'

Can Bazball save Test cricket? Maybe this is the most important of all the imponderables which presently surround the future of cricket. As we bask in the vibrant and joyful aftermath of the 2023 Ashes, it is perhaps too easy to imagine Bazball as the saviour of Test cricket. If it was possible to guarantee that all Test series would follow a similar path, the answer to this question might well be yes. But to expect this to go on happening all round the world whenever a Test series is played is palpably ridiculous.

For a series such as this to happen again, even once, would require two sides with a decent sprinkling of individual genius, flair and bloody-mindedness. This would have to be coupled with an almost religious fervour of intent blindly to pursue an idea, all of which England managed to do in 2023 thanks to an inspirational captain and coach. All this, before you consider how much luck is needed to get the balance of the equation as right as it was then. There is a limit to what good organisation can do on its own. The odds against all this happening in just one series, let alone the whole lot, are too big to bother about. Mr Badale of the Rajasthan Royals may have been surprised by the Ashes, but it will not have cost him much sleep or caused him to have second thoughts about his and his bank manager's core beliefs.

Since its first manifestation, in 2022, Bazball has done wonders for the game in England, having had the luck to find exactly the right combination of players to make it so startlingly effective. That alone was an amazing piece of luck. England's coach Brendon McCullum, who had himself been a successful captain of New Zealand, was determined to change the way Test cricket is played. He had the good fortune to find the perfect apostle in Ben Stokes – who, coincidentally, was also born in New Zealand – to put his ideas into effect on the field of play.

It all began in 2022 when McCullum and Stokes joined forces as coach and captain of an England side which had been through a torrid time. In 2021–22, under the joint stewardship of Joe Root as captain and Paul Collingwood as the temporary coach, they had lost a series in the West Indies, which these days is sadly a most unlikely occurrence. McCullum and Stokes, brought together by Rob Key on his arrival as managing director of England's cricket, proceeded to drive the juggernaut that Bazball has become, a trifle recklessly at times, through the world of England's immediate opponents. They were lucky to find almost all the component parts they needed already occupying the England dressing room. It was the same squad of players that had come off second-best in the Caribbean. Metaphorically, these two shook them by the scruff of the neck and, almost overnight, their inspiration and enthusiasm generated a self-belief which turned them into a remarkable winning combination.

Now, what exactly is Bazball? The one thing that it is not is reckless slogging. McCullum, a wonderful attacking batsman in his day, a good wicketkeeper too, and the most positive of captains, felt with almost a religious fervour that Test cricket needed shaking up – and even more so after he had finished playing. Now he found himself in a position where he could begin to put his plans into action. He was well aware that a good deal of Test cricket, as it had been played, was boring and not the game to win back modern crowds with low attention spans. For spectators, cricket is mainly a batter's game and it was essential that runs should be scored a lot faster. If possible, the game should always be kept moving and there was no place for the draw. If this could be achieved, the product then would surely be more appealing to contemporary spectators.

He realised that one of the main obstacles to this was the understandable caution of batters who are not sure of their places in the side. Every time they go out to bat they want to make sure they are picked for the next game, and that is certain to be near the front of their minds. If they were now to follow the Bazball instructions and go for their strokes from the first ball, they needed an assurance that if they are caught driving at a wide-ish half-volley in the second over of the day, it will not count against them at the next selection meeting. Nerves must not be allowed to distort intentions and maybe ruin their batting lives. This was surely where Stokes's character and personality was so important. He was not only able to persuade his batters that they had to go for their strokes, but also that they would not be dropped if it went wrong and they got themselves out.

He and McCullum were also good at knowing who would best be able to deliver. Zak Crawley was a case in point. When McCullum took over, Crawley had been in the side for quite a while without scoring runs consistently enough to justify his retention. Although he had made 267 against Pakistan in 2020 and a hundred in the West Indies, there had been an awful lot of low scores in between, but the captain and coach saw something special in Crawley and knew he had it in him to do what they wanted. So it was to prove against Australia in 2023. He batted well throughout the series after cover-driving that first ball of the first Test at Edgbaston to the cover boundary in what was a colossal statement of intent. Anyone who still doubts Crawley was clearly not watching the fourth Test at Old Trafford, when he made 189 and played probably the innings of the series. He had been inspired by McCullum and Stokes's faith in him.

Ben Duckett, Crawley's opening partner, has a similar story to tell, even though he was one of the chief culprits when the second Test at Lord's was thrown away by batters who had not yet realised that to bring about the best results, Bazball sometimes needs to be disciplined and not just recklessly pursued. In that match, Duckett was out for 98 in the first innings and 83 in the second, both times to uncontrolled hooks played with reckless and almost suicidal intent, with the boundary littered with catchers. To miss a hundred against Australia at Lord's by 17 runs is careless, to miss one by two runs seems something much worse.

For me, the most surprising aspect at the start of Bazball was the way in which Root himself felt able to come to the party. It would have been so easy for the deposed captain, which he was, to have gone off in high dudgeon when he was suddenly told he had to play a completely new game. Then, when he saw how successful it was, a lesser man might have been jealous or peeved at the way it was panning out and been unwilling to join in. Yet Root not only took the dramatic change in his stride – perhaps the relief he felt at no longer being in charge was a help too – but with the bat he also willingly became a major contributor to the success of the new way forward. He deserves enormous credit for this. Then there was that other Yorkshireman, Jonny Bairstow, whose amazing form with the bat in 2022 and his glorious and crucially important partnerships with Root set the seal on an amazing summer.

New Zealand were taken by surprise and were well beaten in the first three Tests of 2022. They were unable to come up with an immediate and effective answer to Bazball. India were the next to perish, in a one-off match at Edgbaston, against an England side which at this stage of the summer was in overdrive. Then came South Africa, who located Bazball's Achilles' heel at Lord's and will have wondered, briefly, what all the fuss was about when they administered England's heaviest defeat for some years, by an innings and 12 runs, before succumbing in their remaining two matches.

No one relished the refreshing freedom of the Bazball approach more than Jonny Bairstow, who made 614 runs in the summer's first four Test matches with an enterprise and freedom of mind as well as a dashing array of strokes which he used with a merciless and joyful determination. He seemed himself to be the very essence of Bazball. But while the first part of the summer appeared to belong to Bairstow, with his red-headed bounce and ebullience, his fellow Yorkshireman Joe Root, with his more modest, fair-haired demeanour, his perfect but almost apologetic repertoire of classical strokes, together with his infectious schoolboy innocence, was almost as effective, scoring 569 runs in these same four matches. While the coaching books loved Root, it was Bairstow who made the crowds gasp. In three months, McCullum and Stokes had taken England's cricket to crazy new levels.

It was a visit to Pakistan next, in the winter of 2022–23, and their hosts were flummoxed, losing all three Tests. This was the first time England had ever won more than one match in a series in Pakistan and, of course, the first time Bazball had been taken overseas. It was then on to New Zealand, who showed they had thought long and hard about Bazball since their uncomfortable tour of England the previous year. They won the second of the two Test matches by one run at the end of a marvellous game of cricket, thanks to a brilliant hundred from Kane Williamson, a superb batsman who has never received quite the worldwide acclaim he should have done. It is interesting that individual New Zealanders should be having the impact they are on the contemporary scene. A match that ends like that last one in Wellington can only be a triumph for the game of cricket, but it is worth remembering that it was inspired by Bazball. The answer the

Kiwis had come up with to compete with this new approach was simply 'if you can't beat 'em, join 'em'.

The winter had gone well for an England side inspired more than ever by the mantra of Bazball. Yet they will all still, including McCullum and Stokes, have left New Zealand, whatever they may say, with an uneasy feeling in the pits of their stomachs. This England side and its newfound approach to the game was about to face its toughest test yet and the one on which its eventual authenticity would depend. A good Australian side was coming to England for an Ashes series, which has always been the ultimate challenge for England's cricket. The Australians professed to regard Bazball as nonsense – perhaps because it was not their idea. But for all their attempts to belittle Bazball and to pretend not to take it that seriously, an awful lot of thought and discussion will have gone into deciding how best to cope with it.

As usual, brave words were spoken before the series, and the England camp oozed confidence, but there was something slightly fragile about it. Pat Cummins's side contained some mighty good cricketers, such as Steve Smith, Marnus Labuschagne and off-spinner Nathan Lyon – in my view, the world's most underrated cricketer, as we were soon to see. It was difficult to imagine Bairstow, Root and the remarkable Harry Brook – the most significant newcomer since Stokes had taken over – scoring runs in their recent devil-may-care style. Also, would Jimmy Anderson, Stuart Broad and the other bowlers make quite the impact they had done against Pakistan and New Zealand, or in England the year before?

Something else that could have played on the minds of Stokes and McCullum was that as far as England supporters are concerned, against Australia victory is all-important. The method by which it is achieved is not so important. Dying bravely from Bazball was going to count for little if the Ashes remained in Australian hands.

As I have mentioned, one of the sadnesses of the modern game is that the build-up to a contemporary Test series is so quick that it is all happening almost before you have had time to read that the touring side has arrived in the country. This is yet another way in which old, familiar, leisured habits have recently been kicked into touch. I still remember the keen anticipation of the traditional opening match at Worcester preceded by the great worry that the spring floods that often submerge the New Road ground may not have abated in time. Don Bradman played four times at New Road, scoring double centuries on the three occasions before the war, and settling for a 107 on his final appearance in 1948. This game was usually played after the touring party had spent ten days or so getting themselves ready in the nets on the Nursery Ground at Lord's. After Worcester, the Australians then took on several of the counties, Oxford and Cambridge Universities and the MCC at Lord's. We were all involved for more than four months and it was part of the lovely leisured intensity I wrote about at the start of this book and which has now vanished.

Surprisingly, when the Australians came to England in 2023, the first match they had to play was a Test against India at The Oval on 7 June, a match which was the final of the World Test Championship, with both sides having arrived in the country somewhat breathlessly a day or two before the start. Australia won by 209 runs and they were then catapulted straight into the first of five Tests against England, which began at Edgbaston on 16 June, only five days after the finish of the match against India. The Ashes series was then completed in just six weeks.

Although the powers-that-be, both in Australia and at Lord's, will be reluctant to hold up their hands, this ridiculous pressure-cooker schedule was agreed simply to fit more lucrative tours and tournaments into an already hectic international programme. The ECB had a big part to play in this too, for they had decided they needed a free August so that The Hundred could be staged without any serious competition. The only other cricket then was the

Metro Bank One-Day Cup, not much more than a Second XI county competition paying a sort of lip service to the 50-over game. This format was once regarded as the potential saviour of the game in England, but it could soon disappear, even though, at the moment, the World Cup is still a 50-over competition. The players bought by the eight franchises for The Hundred were obviously not available for the One-Day Cup, but the tangled fixture list made this competition necessary, in 2023 at any rate. It provided about 70 per cent of contracted county players with their only chance of competitive cricket in August, England's prime holiday month of the year when the public enjoy their cricket and come along to watch. From this paragraph alone one gets a good idea of the state of confusion English cricket is in with such a muddled schedule of matches.

Nothing reflects the turmoil of the modern world of cricket more than the game's stately old bible, *Wisden*, or, to give it its full name, the *Wisden Cricketers' Almanack*. Published every spring in its magnificent traditional yellow jacket, it is the portly, reverential record of the previous year's top-level cricket from all around the world, although its main emphasis is on the English game. The statistics are accompanied by some excellent articles, not only describing the action behind the statistics, but also discussing in great detail the issues surrounding the contemporary game.

I think all of us who love cricket were brought up on *Wisden*, and I like to think I still know by heart some of the 1948 edition, the first to come my way, and which I devoured from cover to cover. It then had a nice, comfortable format and it was easy to find your way around. Seventy-odd years later the editor, Lawrence Booth, finds himself confronted by a problem which is well nigh impossible for him to solve. Each year, he has to try and make sense of today's cricketing confusion and to display it in a digestible and orderly manner. He does a noble job, but even if my eyes were good enough to spot a googly out of the bowler's hand, I would still need a literary satnav to find my way around his stately-looking volume as it is today – through no fault of his.

Maybe Groucho Marx, who will join us in a moment for the first two Ashes matches, would have enjoyed the contemporary scene better than the Test match against Pakistan he watched at Lord's in 1954. Cricket then was controlled without too much imagination by what would now be called the old-fuddy-duddy brigade, and the game plodded uneventfully along. At Lord's, Groucho was given a copy of that year's *Wisden*, which he accepted gratefully before giving it to the concierge at his hotel. It was not long before the start of the 2023 Ashes series that I watched a Marx Brothers film, *Animal Crackers*, a favourite of mine, and I thought it was time he resumed his cricket career, so I arranged for his spirit to come with me to Edgbaston for the first Test, to see what he made of Bazball. He was keen and made a joke about Marxball. At first he thought he could go back each night to the Savoy. In the end he agreed to slum it with me in the Midlands – and we had a lot of fun each day after the close of play.

10

GROUCHO LAPS UP BAZBALL

'The Ancient Mariner blows a gasket'

O N 16 June 2023, when Groucho's ghost saw Zak Crawley drive the first ball of the Ashes series, bowled by the Australian captain, Pat Cummins, like a shot out of a gun through the covers for four, he was able to guess from the crowd's reaction that the game had begun. And what a message of intent it will have sent to the Australians, and to Groucho too. He might also have stood up and waved a celebratory hat and cigar in the air, had Crawley not made him bite right through his first cigar of the game. He reckoned that opening blow of Crawley's would surely have warmed the hearts of many of his buddies in New York, where big cricket was hoping to make its first appearance in 2024.

When Groucho had settled in on the balcony of the committee room at Edgbaston, he enjoyed the return to red-ball cricket of that mischievous-looking off-spinner Moeen Ali. His neighbour, fortunately a former England captain, had to try and explain the difference between the red- and the white-ball game, another slight modern confusion, and not only for newcomers. Actually, this is probably only a confusion for us old-timers. Groucho listened carefully while his neighbour explained Australia's shrewd tactics at the start with a man back on the square-cover and square-leg boundaries to prevent a furious flow of early Bazball boundaries, which would have got England off to a riotous start.

He was confused by the field placings and kept patting his knee and muttering 'deep square leg' and 'silly mid off', and then chuckled. The old England captain was not sure what to make of it.

'I sure love this Bazball,' Groucho kept on saying.

He found so much to enjoy on that first day: Crawley's dashing strokes, Ben Duckett's little-boy-lost scampering between the wickets, and then there was the sublime Joe Root. He found himself nodding his head in appreciation at the class of Root as he went to his first hundred against Australia since 2015. Root clinched the deal with Groucho when he tried to play a remarkable reverse ramp to the first ball of the morning from Cummins. He missed and the ball went over the top of his off stump. 'Gee, any guy who tries to do that...' said Groucho. But when, in the next over, Root played the perfect ramp to Scott Boland and the ball soared over the wicketkeeper's head for six, Groucho loved it. They were sublime strokes and he shook his head in appreciation and then jumped up and shouted with delight, to the mild dismay of the old-fashioned lot around him on the Pavilion balcony. He had called the six a 'home run' and reckoned that Babe Ruth would have chuckled enviously at that one. Then he tapped Root on the knee and exclaimed, 'This Bazball's the goods!' The former England captain managed an uneasy smile.

Groucho not only sensed Root's instinctive skill as a batter, but also enjoyed the balletic elegance of his strokes, somehow underlined by his white clothes, which Groucho felt injected a certain Swan Lake beauty and romance into his batting. During Root's innings, he also found himself intrigued by the slow bowling of Nathan Lyon, even if his demeanour was much more West Side Story. Groucho thought Lyon looked awkward, almost unathletic, but vibrantly aggressive. His bowling troubled Root and he had to be pretty good to do that. It was a high-class game of cat-and-mouse as Root tried to attack him. His neighbour had told Groucho that Lyon bowled off-breaks, promising to explain more about that after lunch.

Groucho thoroughly approved of Stokes's declaration late on the first day to give his bowlers the chance of taking an Australian wicket or two before the close of play. It didn't work, but unlike most of those around him, Groucho was all for giving it a go. The next day, he thought seriously about taking up wicketkeeping, sure he could do the job better than Jonny Bairstow, who missed one chance after another. With a knowing nod, the former England captain told him what a difficult job wicketkeeping was. The game of cricket was beginning to come to Groucho. Later on, when Australia batted, he found it as difficult as the bowlers to get round Usman Khawaja, who was demonstrating the virtues of adhesiveness as he held the Australian innings together with admirable fortitude, reaching a worthy hundred.

In England's second innings, Root brought a frustrated groan from Groucho when, after making 46 runs, he set off down the pitch as if he had suddenly remembered that Bazball was the order of the day. He looked like a man who was late for his train. This was Root's only ugly moment of the match, and he was stumped for the first time in his career. Another thing which really tickled Groucho was the way the fielders appealed. Once or twice he could not resist joining in himself when the ball hit the batter's pads – to the laughing enjoyment of the committee-room balcony. He had to laugh when the fielders dropped catches – that didn't go down well either – and he even borrowed John McEnroe's 'You can't be serious' when Bairstow failed to stump Cameron Green. On the last day, right at the end, he leapt to his feet and dropped his cigar at the same time when Stokes dropped Pat Cummins and England's last chance had gone.

England were looking as if they were almost home when Cummins, Australia's gallant and splendid captain, took a step down the wicket to Root and drove him thrillingly back over his head for a 'homer', as Groucho's home run had become. And, just in case anyone had missed that first one, he did it again two balls later. Groucho loved his homers, which always produced a happy

laugh and more frowning chuckles on the balcony. In the circumstances, with Australia needing 40-odd runs to win, these two
strokes were as brave in concept and as magnificently executed as
they were decisive. It was those two blows that finally knocked
the stuffing out of England.

Groucho wanted to cheer, but when he saw the glum faces
around him, he had second thoughts. It had been inspiring topsy-
turvy cricket. At crucial moments, the Australian tactics had got
the better of Bazball, of which, being Australians, they had a
contemptuous opinion. This was eloquently voiced some months
later when Nathan Lyon, never a man to mince his words, told a
television interviewer in Australia that Bazball was 'a load of shit'.

Groucho enjoyed what he had seen at Edgbaston so much that
he lit another cigar, called the concierge at the Savoy and told him
to keep his suite for another week so that he would be able to see
the next match, at Lord's, his old stamping ground. He even asked
the concierge to buy him a copy of the latest edition of *Wisden*.
He promised Groucho it would be in his suite waiting for him.
And it was – and this time he would not be giving it back to the
concierge. Each day, he took it to Lord's with him.

After Australia had scored the winning runs at Edgbaston,
Groucho puffed contentedly away in the back seat as his driver
steered him to London and the Savoy. There was an elderly spring
in his step as he hopped out of the car and through the famous
doors, almost skipping into the hotel. Bazball and all that went
with it was his cup of tea, but, hang on, surely the object of it all
had been for England to beat Australia and not just to finish as
gallant losers. He couldn't work that one out, and until he remembered Bairstow's wicketkeeping in the first innings, but he was
still worried he was missing something.

The anticipation and excitement on the first morning at Lord's
was extraordinary as Groucho, *Wisden* tucked under his arm,
surveyed proceedings from the president's box in the Grandstand.

This was on the other side of the ground from where he had been stationed all those years before. Suddenly there was gentle applause and everyone turned to look at the grand old Pavilion and saw the two white-coated umpires coming down the steps. Soon the England side followed, and then two chunky batters in baggy dark green caps. He remembered that when he was last there he had thought of cricket as baseball on Valium, but now he was watching a different game. Bazball, well, it was almost baseball, wasn't it?

Groucho could not understood why England put Australia in to bat at Lord's and were then stupid enough to drop all those catches. Homers were in short supply too on this first morning. He was impressed by Steve Smith's classy century, but the batter he really went for was the left-handed Travis Head, with his flamboyant strokes and devil-may-care attitude, not to mention his cheeky moustache. Then, later, he didn't half scratch his head when England's batters began to pursue the dogma of Bazball to a point where it became sheer midsummer madness. The chap in the seat behind him, who had opened England's batting for many years, was apoplectic – Groucho rather enjoyed that too. He was already calling him the Ancient Mariner, and over the five days they became the greatest of friends. Groucho even offered to lend him his *Wisden*.

Australia were now bowling short and packing the leg-side boundary with fielders, and the Englishmen proceeded to give them catching practice. It was so unnecessary and so stupid, and even Groucho would have been able to spot that without the Ancient Mariner's assistance. Before that, England had reached 188–1 in reply to Australia's 416 and off-spinner Nathan Lyon – that former England captain at Edgbaston had given him a most confusing lecture about the art of off-spin – had damaged a calf muscle so badly when fielding that he had to be helped off the ground and out of the match and the series. Groucho couldn't understand why the substitute fielder who took Lyon's place was not allowed to bowl. When Groucho had first spotted Lyon at Edgbaston, he thought he looked the odd man out. He was not a natural athlete, but he soon realised that he was a determined and mighty clever bowler. He called him the 'stilted man', because when he bowled he looked as if he was walking on stilts.

The Ancient Mariner told him England's sights should have been on 600 and nothing less. The next thing he knew, Ben Duckett hooked wildly and departed looking like that woeful central character in an H.M. Bateman cartoon at whom all the world is laughing. 'Sheer madness,' the Ancient Mariner exclaimed furiously. 'Two runs short of a hundred against Australia at Lord's and a wild hook like that down long leg's throat.' Groucho puffed and nodded his head as if he agreed with every syllable.

It got even worse. Ollie Pope and Harry Brook seemed to think they were playing in a T20 jamboree, making Groucho feel he was right back on the West Side, while the Ancient Mariner looked as if he was contemplating suicide. Soon afterwards, Root didn't seem to be able to make up his mind whether he was on the West Side or in the West End as he nibbled naughtily to first slip and shuffled off in disgrace. Groucho took a long puff and groaned. England limped to 325 and Australia's lead of 91 was too big for comfort. Groucho invited the Ancient Mariner back with him to the Savoy for dinner that night, where he no doubt marked his card about baseball and dear old Babe Ruth.

England were left to score 371 to win after Lyon, batting on one leg, scored a stirringly defiant four runs from thirteen balls. Groucho loved each one of them and once shouted a throaty encouragement. Then it all began to happen, and in no time England had fallen to 45–4. Bazball had gone mad again and Groucho began to think he might just make it back to the Savoy Grill in time for a late lunch. Then, as Stokes came out to bat, the Ancient Mariner suggested a glass of wine and they watched him start his innings from the bar at the back of the box.

Believe it or not, Bazball's chief exponent now began to bat as if he had never even heard of his new creation. He went watch-fully to 50 in 99 balls and Groucho was able to concentrate on the Ancient Mariner's plentiful and rather pithy words of wisdom which, when it came to the England batting, were pretty spiteful, but at least Stokes did not get out. Groucho had just accepted what he thought would be his last glass when, hey presto, Stokes's memory, or maybe his anger, came surging back and, to Groucho's noisy delight, good old homers began to disappear to all parts of St John's Wood. But just as the crowd was beginning to be gripped by a feeling of distant hope, Duckett's suicidal tendencies suddenly came galloping back and another wild hook, every bit as crazy as his first-innings effort, ended up in wicketkeeper Alex Carey's gloves and Groucho and the ground groaned.

In came Bairstow, bustling with that cheeky-chappy energy – Groucho was grabbed by his jaunty walk. Here, surely, was the perfect partner for Stokes. Bairstow went easily to double figures before Dreamland, Disney World or the Chamber of Horrors took over. The Aussies knew Bairstow's habits at the end of an over: if he had let the last ball through to the wicketkeeper, he would just touch his bat or his foot down in the crease and then walk quickly up the pitch to do a spot of gardening – that appealed to Groucho – or to talk to his partner. He never waited for the umpire to call 'over', which would have signalled an official pause in hostilities. Now, the Australians were ready for him.

Cameron Green, tall and thin, whom Groucho would have been thinking of as an 'animated lamp post', bowled the preor-dained bouncer. Bairstow ducked, touched his back foot down in the crease and set off. Without waiting to look, Carey took the ball and instantly underarmed it at the stumps all in the same movement. He scored a bullseye and as the umpire, Ahsan Raza from Pakistan, had not yet called over, there was a massive Australian appeal. The square-leg umpire, Chris Gaffaney from New Zealand, hesitated for a moment and then made the signal that sends the question to the third umpire in the Pavilion, South Africa's Marais Erasmus, sitting in front of a TV screen in a box at the back of the top deck. After a while, with the whole ground holding its breath, he made the correct decision and Bairstow was given out stumped.

The Ancient Mariner, furious at Bairstow's stupidity, became visibly upset when the decision was greeted around the ground by much booing, obviously aimed at the Australians, and a highly indignant sense of shock/horror and shouts of 'cheats'. The Aussies were loudly condemned, while Groucho loved every moment of it. Of course he was not sure what had happened and his neighbours had the difficult job of trying to explain to the great man exactly what had occurred. Behind him, the Ancient Mariner, bright red in the face, was speechless at first and then kept muttering, 'Absolutely right, of course he's out, the stupid idiot.' Groucho thought back to that first visit to Lord's in 1954. Then, it had been sleepily peaceful, with lots of empty seats, no ice and warm drinks, and nobody talked above a whisper. Everyone was scrupulously polite and the personification of gentility – and 'oh so goddam boring'. This was fun, this was showbiz – it was all happening, right in front of him and now even the Limeys were getting all wound up.

Of course Bairstow was out and he only had himself to blame. The umpire had not called 'over', and this was a crucial moment in an Ashes series, in which, as the Ancient Mariner kept on telling Groucho, the pressure is as acute as it gets. Groucho was well aware that niceties do not apply on occasions like this, just like they don't always on a movie set. No one should have known that better than Bairstow, a tough competitor if ever there was one.

He was now walking slowly back to the Pavilion, trying to look both innocent and indignant at the same time. It was not long before irony stepped in. Television footage was found showing Bairstow and head coach McCullum, also a wicketkeeper, trying themselves to do exactly what Carey had just done to Bairstow. Oh dear. Before that disappointing discovery, McCullum had said, clumsily as it turned out, that he did not fancy having a drink with the Aussies after the match, while Stokes told the world he wouldn't want to win like that. Groucho, the straightest of guys, would not have cared for this hypocrisy, but these little titbits did not reach him until he read the papers the next day.

When the players came in to lunch soon afterwards, quite a few MCC members in the sacred Lord's Pavilion forgot themselves and seemed to think they were either watching the Globetrotters in Harlem or having a no-holds-barred session round the corner in the Bronx. The Australians were roundly abused and one or two members – yes, of the MCC – even appeared to clench their fists as David Warner and Usman Khawaja, the Aussie openers, went up the stairs to lunch. One member was eventually sacked from the club and two more had their memberships suspended for long periods. More than that, the prime minister of England, Rishi Sunak, and his Australian counterpart, Anthony Albanese, had their say, which made the whole thing even more absurd and ridiculous. This gave Groucho, who had loved every second of the drama, his biggest laugh of all. When he read about it at breakfast the next day he half-expected to see a meaningful quote from Donald Trump. Test cricket is a hard game, and Test matches for the Ashes harder still, and the indignant uproar in the ground and especially the Pavilion was as appalling as the hypocrisy of McCullum and Bairstow.

Groucho was beside himself with joy. He never expected to see the Brits behaving like this anywhere, let alone at Lord's Cricket Ground. This sort of thing might have been par for the course in downtown Harlem on a bad day, or even on a Broadway stage, but here at Lord's it was blissfully sacrilegious and too good to be true. He was tempted to join in the fun, before realising it was really none of his business.

But now at Lord's there was a game to be won. The tall figure of fast bowler Stuart Broad emerged from the Pavilion, ready as ever to take on the Australians with both bat and mouth. He had never been known to miss a chance of rubbing as much salt as possible into every Australian wound he had ever come across. He didn't half give it to them now, and when the Ancient Mariner explained what was going on, Groucho laughed his head off and managed to light two cigars at the same time. Broad made the staunchest of partners for Stokes too, who now moved effortlessly into overdrive and they put on 108 for the seventh wicket.

Stokes was amazing and Groucho was waving his arms for all he was worth as homers kept disappearing to all parts of Lord's. Even the Ancient Mariner was now smiling cautiously and even allowed himself a contented chuckle as Stokes really let the Australians have it. For a time they had continued to bowl short and, to Groucho's delight, Stokes took them apart. There was a rainbow of homers and three in a row took Stokes to his hundred. Groucho was on his feet and made himself hoarse from cheering.

The crack of the ball off Stokes's bat was magic and the crowd were really up for it. His second fifty came in just 43 balls and the crowd thought another Stokes miracle was on the cards. Groucho was enthralled and during the drinks interval the Ancient Mariner told him about his extraordinary innings at Headingley four years before. Stokes and the last man, spin bowler Jack Leach, had taken England to an incredible one-wicket victory over the Australians with their unbroken last-wicket stand of 76, with Leach scoring just a single.

Groucho looked at Stokes and thought of Joe DiMaggio. But Babe Ruth would have been in his mind when those three sixes soared into the crowd; Babe Ruth met Don Bradman in the Babe's private box at the Yankee Stadium in New York in 1932, but by all accounts, theirs had not been the most sparkling of conversations. Bradman, who was on his honeymoon, was on a private cricket tour of North America organised by that remarkable leg-spinning cartoonist, Arthur Mailey, who took 99 Test wickets for Australia in the twenties.

Back at Lord's, Broad, oozing determination, went on mouth-
ing away at the Aussies and defending his wicket. Standing there
in the middle with his arms outstretched to ward off Australian
blandishments, he looked as awkward and angular as the Angel of
the North on the Great North Road. Yes, Groucho was much
taken with Broad, the crash-helmeted batsman, just as he had
been with Broad, the bandana-ed bowler. He would have called
him 'The Mad Hatter'.

While Stokes and Broad were putting on 108, Groucho was
chewing his cigars, one at a time, as much as smoking them as
this new miracle drew ever closer, but it was too good to last. The
Aussies stopped bowling short and now aimed around the off
stump. Stokes went for yet another pull, got an edge and Carey,
the pantomime villain in the gloves, took the catch. Stokes, with
155 to his name, walked off furious with himself, while the
crowd saluted one of the greatest innings to have been played at
Lord's. Groucho applauded furiously, waved his fists and shouted
as Stokes, his disappointment obvious, stalked back to the
Pavilion. Groucho would have made him an honorary American
on the spot and given him the freedom of New York. It had been
that good, but now with only the bowlers left, it was all over.
Australia won by 43 runs and were now two matches up in the
series. Groucho couldn't help feeling this was just a little bit
unjust.

When the game had finished, the Ancient Mariner shepherded
Groucho round to the Pavilion to have a drink in the committee
room. He had made the same journey in 1954 to have a drink with
Gubby Allen, the stern but amiable ruler of all that he surveyed at
Lord's Cricket Ground. Back then, they had talked about the
Hollywood Cricket Club and the time Allen had played there on
his way back from the Bodyline tour of Australia in 1932–33. His
Hollywood captain that day had been the British actor Sir Aubrey
'Round-the-Corner' Smith, who had captained England in 1889
in their first Test in South Africa – which, curiously, was his only

Test match, although he took seven wickets and England won. He was called 'Round-the-Corner' because of the angle of his approach to the wicket as he came in to bowl. Allen's wicketkeeper that day had been none other than fellow actor Boris Karloff, who as William Henry Pratt had been educated at Uppingham School.

England v Australia
1st Test
Played at Edgbaston, Birmingham, on 16–20 June 2023

Umpires: Ahsan Raza & M Erasmus (TV: CB Gaffaney)
Referee: AJ Pycroft
Toss: England

England

Z Crawley c Carey b Boland	61	c Carey b Boland	7
BM Duckett c Carey b Hazlewood	12	c Green b Cummins	19
OJD Pope lbw b Lyon	31	b Cummins	14
JE Root not out	118	st Carey b Lyon	46
HC Brook b Lyon	32	c Labuschagne b Lyon	46
BA Stokes* c Carey b Hazlewood	1	lbw b Cummins	43
JM Bairstow† st Carey b Lyon	78	lbw b Lyon	20
MM Ali st Carey b Lyon	18	c Carey b Hazlewood	19
SCJ Broad b Green	16 (10)	not out	10
OE Robinson not out	17 (9)	c Green b Lyon	27
JM Anderson		c Carey b Cummins	12
Extras (lb 6, nb 3)	9	(lb 9, nb 1)	10
Total (for 8 wkts dec) (78 overs)	**393**	(66.2 overs)	**273**

Australia

DA Warner b Broad	9 (2)	c Bairstow b Robinson	36
U Khawaja b Robinson	141 (1)	b Stokes	65
M Labuschagne c Bairstow b Broad	0	c Bairstow b Broad	13
SPD Smith lbw b Stokes	16	c Bairstow b Broad	6
TM Head c Crawley b Ali	50 (6)	c Root b Ali	16
CD Green b Ali	38 (7)	b Robinson	28
AT Carey† b Anderson	66 (8)	c and b Root	20
PJ Cummins* c Stokes b Robinson	38 (9)	not out	44
NM Lyon c Duckett b Robinson	1 (10)	not out	16
SM Boland c Pope b Broad	0 (5)	c Bairstow b Broad	20
JR Hazlewood not out	1		
Extras (b 4, lb 6, w 1, nb 15)	26	(lb 10, nb 8)	18
Total (116.1 overs)	**386**	(for 8 wkts) (92.3 overs)	**282**

AUSTRALIA	O	M	R	W	O	M	R	W
Cummins	14	0	59	0	18.2	1	63	4
Hazlewood	15	1	61	2	10	1	48	1
Boland	14	0	86	1	(4) 12	2	61	1
Lyon	29	1	149	4	(3) 24	2	80	4
Green	6	0	32	1	2	0	12	0

ENGLAND	O	M	R	W	O	M	R	W
Broad	23	4	68	3	(2) 21	3	64	3
Robinson	22.1	5	55	3	(3) 18.3	7	43	2
Anderson	21	5	53	1	(1) 17	1	56	0
Brook	3	1	5	0				
Ali	33	4	147	2	(4) 14	2	57	1
Stokes	7	0	33	1	7	2	9	1
Root	7	3	15	0	(5) 15	2	43	1

Fall of wickets:

	Eng	Aus	Eng	Aus
1st	22	29	27	61
2nd	92	29	27	78
3rd	124	67	77	89
4th	175	148	129	121
5th	176	220	150	143
6th	297	338	196	192
7th	323	372	210	209
8th	350	377	229	227
9th	–	378	256	–
10th	–	386	273	–

Close of play:
Day 1: Aus (1) 14–0 (Warner 8*, Khawaja 4*, 4 overs)
Day 2: Aus (1) 311–5 (Khawaja 126*, Carey 52*, 94 overs)
Day 3: Eng (2) 28–2 (Pope 0*, Root 0*, 10.3 overs)
Day 4: Aus (2) 107–3 (Khawaja 34*, Boland 13*, 30 overs)

Man of the match: U Khawaja
Result: **Australia won by 2 wickets**

England v Australia
2nd Test
Played at Lord's Cricket Ground, London, on 28 June–2 July 2023
Umpires: Ahsan Raza & CB Gaffaney (TV: M Erasmus)
Referee: AJ Pycroft
Toss: England

Australia

DA Warner b Tongue	66	(2)	lbw b Tongue	25
U Khawaja b Tongue	17	(1)	c sub (MJ Potts) b Broad	77
M Labuschagne c Bairstow b Robinson	47		c Brook b Anderson	30
SPD Smith c Duckett b Tongue	110		c Crawley b Tongue	34
TM Head st Bairstow b Root	77		c Root b Broad	7
CD Green c Anderson b Root	0		c Duckett b Robinson	18
AT Carey† lbw b Broad	22		c Root b Robinson	21
MA Starc c Bairstow b Anderson	6		not out	15
PJ Cummins* not out	22		c Duckett b Broad	11
NM Lyon c Tongue b Robinson	7	(11)	c Stokes b Broad	4
JR Hazlewood c Root b Robinson	4	(10)	c Root b Stokes	1
Extras (b 12, lb 14, nb 12)	38		(b 14, lb 9, w 7, nb 6)	36
Total (100.4 overs)	**416**		(101.5 overs)	**279**

England

Z Crawley st Carey b Lyon	48	c Carey b Starc	3
BM Duckett c Warner b Hazlewood	98	c Carey b Hazlewood	83
OJD Pope c Smith b Green	42	b Starc	3
JE Root c Smith b Starc	10	c Warner b Cummins	18
HC Brook c Cummins b Starc	50	b Cummins	4
BA Stokes* c Green b Starc	17	c Carey b Hazlewood	155
JM Bairstow† c Cummins b Hazlewood	16	st Carey b Green	10
SCJ Broad lbw b Head	12	c Green b Hazlewood	11
OE Robinson c Carey b Head	9	c Smith b Cummins	1
JC Tongue c sub (MT Renshaw) b Cummins	1	b Starc	19
JM Anderson not out	0	not out	3
Extras (b 9, lb 4, w 2, nb 7)	22	(lb 3, w 10, nb 4)	17
Total (76.2 overs)	**325**	(81.3 overs)	**327**

ENGLAND	O	M	R	W	O	M	R	W	Fall of wickets:				
										Aus	Eng	Aus	Eng
Anderson	20	5	53	1	19	4	64	1					
Broad	23	4	99	1	24.5	8	65	4	1st	73	91	63	9
Robinson	24.4	3	100	3	(4) 26	11	48	2	2nd	96	188	123	13
Tongue	22	3	98	3	(3) 20	4	53	2	3rd	198	208	187	41
Stokes	3	1	21	0	12	1	26	1	4th	316	222	190	45
Root	8	1	19	2					5th	316	279	197	177
									6th	351	293	239	193
AUSTRALIA	O	M	R	W	O	M	R	W	7th	358	311	242	301
Starc	17	0	88	3	21.3	2	79	3	8th	393	324	261	302
Cummins	16.2	2	46	1	25	2	69	3	9th	408	325	264	302
Hazlewood	13	1	71	2	18	0	80	3	10th	416	325	279	327
Lyon	13	1	35	1									
Green	9	0	54	1	13	3	73	1					
Head	7	1	17	2	(4) 4	0	23	0					
Smith	1	0	1	0									

Close of play:
Day 1: Aus (1) 339–5 (Smith 85*, Carey 11*, 83 overs)
Day 2: Eng (1) 278–4 (Brook 45*, Stokes 17*, 61 overs)
Day 3: Aus (2) 130–2 (Khawaja 58*, Smith 6*, 45.4 overs)
Day 4: Eng (2) 114–4 (Duckett 50*, Stokes 29*, 31 overs)

Man of the match: SPD Smith
Result: **Australia won by 43 runs**

11

A MIRACLE DENIED

'Wood and Woakes to the rescue'

Now that Groucho's ghost and I had gone our separate ways, I settled down at Hoveton for the next four weeks to listen to the rest of the 2023 Ashes series on *Test Match Special*. Just occasionally my loyalty wavered and I would have a quick look at the replays on my mildly recalcitrant television set, which is elderly and fitful. This was, I suppose, one advantage of packing the Ashes into six weeks, for it meant I did not have too many blank days between the last three Tests.

Hoveton is a village in Norfolk about eight miles north of Norwich and on the River Bure and is where my family has lived for a long time. I was born there just after the war had begun in 1939, and I returned to live in a tiny but splendidly ancient cottage in time for my eightieth birthday. I have found since that there is something wonderfully reassuring about being able to retrace your old footsteps, working out who used to live where, remembering when a tractor almost ran you over – and then there was that corner where the wheel of my bike suddenly came off. What a joy it is too to commune with so many ghosts of the past, for I am afraid they all are now ghosts. The butcher and the fishmonger have gone, the post office and the chemist have moved, but remarkably the station, having survived Dr Beeching, is not only still there, but, with a change in Norwich, it gets you to London in a touch under three hours. Then, there was an amazing village cricket ground . . . but I think that's enough to be going on with.

The Australians had worked out Bazball pretty well and were now in the almost impregnable position of being two matches up in the series with three still to go. Ironically, Australia are the only side ever to have pulled themselves back from this precipice and win a series. It happened in Australia in 1936–37 against Gubby Allen's England team, who had won the first two matches. We met Gubby, a fast bowler, briefly with Groucho at the end of the last chapter. It was now England's turn to do some serious thinking to see if they could manage something similar.

Two defeats like this, especially when in both matches they had thrown away brilliant positions, can be seriously debilitating. The energy, exuberance and enthusiasm that new faces would bring to the dressing room were badly needed for the third Test at Headingley. This was particularly important, for with the matches coming up so thick and fast, there was almost no time to recover, regroup and take a deep breath. With any luck, the impetus the new faces would bring with them would invigorate the main group of players, who would obviously remain the same.

At every press conference, Stokes himself was wonderfully upbeat, but behind the scenes he and McCullum will have had plenty to talk about, although I am sure neither will have considered changing their essential views about Bazball. But they had to be more flexible and tell their players that at times caution would have to be an important ingredient in the Bazball vocabulary. They also had little time to decide on the players they wanted to bring in to help kick-start the side back into winning ways.

Headingley itself will have let out an enormous sigh of relief that this Test match was being played there at all. The Yorkshire County Cricket Club had been roundly accused by one of their own former players, Azeem Rafiq, who was born in Pakistan, of being institutionally racist. The immediate and dramatic response of the ECB – now under Tom Harrison's stewardship, had not before appeared unduly concerned by worrying reports of this nature coming out of Yorkshire – was, among other things, to tell Yorkshire they could no longer play Test cricket at Headingley. This was a damaging blow, for the Tests made an important contribution to the income of the club. The ban did not stay in place for long, because the club was soon considered to have made a good start to the job of sorting itself out, and so this ban had been withdrawn.

In view of the ECB's original reluctance to intervene in Yorkshire's affairs, could it have been that this decision was helped maybe by the thought that if the club which had played such a big part in the success of England's cricket was now deprived of this income for a long period, it would go bankrupt and perhaps out of business? The aftermath of Rafiq's accusations had cost Yorkshire a great deal of money, more than £3 million in all, as employees at whom he had pointed a finger were dismissed and compensated. Rafiq himself was paid around £200,000, an amount authorised by the new chair Lord Patel, who had been parachuted in as a temporary replacement for the previous chair, Roger Hutton, who had resigned. They also unsurprisingly lost a number of important sponsors because of Rafiq's claims. There will have been considerable relief that such an important source of income would again be available to them. There had to be a reason why a county with such a considerable number of Asian immigrants had seen so few come through to the top level of cricket. From Azeem Rafiq's evidence it looked to be that this was the result of a most disgraceful and unspeakable culture within the county club which no one in a position of power at Headingley had thought to question. Perhaps their stewardship of those in charge was somewhat lax and they did not realise what had been going on, or maybe they looked at it with a blind eye. One can only wonder what the fate of a less significant county might have been if it had been thought to have gone down a similar path to Yorkshire. Essex is another county which has faced serious accusations of racism and there still some way to go before that is sorted out.

This was the unhappy background to the third Test. The selectors made three significant changes to the England side which had lost the first two matches. Chris Woakes, a bowling all-rounder, who had not played Test cricket since the ill-fated tour to the West Indies, took the place of the injured Ollie Pope, while Mark Wood, who would have played in the first two matches if his right elbow had fully recovered, now came in for the unlucky Josh Tongue because of his extra pace. Spin was needed at Headingley, and even though Moeen Ali's hand, badly blistered after bowling so many overs in the first Test, would not yet have fully recovered, he was brought back and effectively replaced Jimmy Anderson, who was rested, with his home Test at Old Trafford coming up.

While Moeen's enthusiasm plays a useful role in any dressing room he occupies, it was those two great friends, Woakes and Wood, who now made the difference and enabled England to win this third match. Woakes, a more dangerous cricketer in England than he is abroad, swung the ball both ways and bowled with excellent control at a lively fast-medium. It was then his batting which made sure of victory for England on the last day, while Wood also made important and defiant runs in both innings and was batting with Woakes at the end. Wood was terrific with the ball, as he underlined the huge difference between bowling at, say, 85 and 92 mph. In every stride you could see his joy at being back and also his single-minded determination. He found an extraordinary rhythm in taking five wickets in Australia's first innings and two in the second. Moeen, as game as ever, may only have taken two wickets, but what wickets they were. Late on the second day he sent back Labuschagne and Smith in quick succession and more than earned his keep.

It is a sign of the times that Mark Wood was thinking hard about turning his back on two-innings or red-ball cricket and going solely for the rich takings that come from the franchise T20 game. In the end, later in 2023 he signed a three-year central contract to play for England, after his mind had been made up by both the length of the contract and its much increased value. His marked lack of success in the World Cup in India when England, the holders, were eliminated in the group stage may have been another relevant factor as he was almost thirty-four, which is fast approaching old age for a fast bowler. The irony was that David Willey, who, bowling fast left arm over the wicket, had taken 145 wickets in 113 white-ball games for England since 2015, was not one of the twenty-nine players offered a new central contract. He was not pleased and decided to turn his back on England's white-ball game, complaining loudly that he was at the peak of his career and would now only be available for the highest bidder in franchise T20 competitions. The difference between Wood and Willey is that Willey, unlike his father, Peter, had never played Test cricket for England. We catch up later with the full drama from the World Cup.

Meanwhile, back to the Ashes. I got up early and made my preparations to listen to the first day at Headingley: a comfortable chair, radio – the age of mine suggests it still deserves to be called a wireless – coffee, newspapers and pencil at the ready. And a corkscrew too. I think I was almost as excited as I ever was when I was going to the commentary box itself. When I was working as a commentator, I invariably felt the pressure on the first morning of every Test match. Right to the very end, I was on my toes – not exactly nervous, but anxious to get it right. Now, funnily enough, I had exactly the same sort of feeling of tingling excitement, and then suddenly there was the lovely old familiar voice of dear old Aggers starting the day off, which almost made me feel I was back in the box with him. Then came the day's first moment of suspense: the toss. Cummins called wrong and, never one to do the obvious, Stokes made the first positive move of a match England had to win when he metaphorically shook a challenging fist at Australia and put them in to bat: typical Stokes, typical Bazball.

Broad and Robinson started things off on this first morning and in no time Broad had dismissed his favourite bunny, David Warner, gobbled up at second slip by Crawley, who doesn't miss much there. I only got the tail end of the replay then, but saw it later on, in one of the many repeats. There is something happily comforting about a replay when you know it is going to produce the right answer. When, after half an hour, Stokes gave the ball to Wood, I found myself moving my chair an inch or two closer to the wireless. The first question – was his elbow fully healed? – was soon answered: yes, it was. Wood was like a racehorse which had been shut up in its stable for too long and had been kicking at the door. Nose flared, arms going, legs pounding, he raced in for four overs.

Every ball was over 90 mph. His rhythm – that great will-o'-the-wisp, there one moment, gone the next – has surely never been better. He made it look so relaxed and easy, and yet he was extremely fast. Suddenly, the batters looked as if they were trying to balance themselves on a tightrope in a high wind. They were all over the place. With the last ball of his first spell he knocked Usman Khawaja's leg stump flat – wouldn't Groucho have loved that – and what a moment that was: first on the wireless, and then this time I got the full replay. There's nothing like flying timber. I had the luck to be commentating when Bob Willis took the last wicket at Headingley in that incredible match in 1981. Australia needed 19 to win and he knocked out Ray Bright's middle stump and England had won by 18 runs. What a moment it was.

The Australian innings at Headingley now stuttered along to 85–4, when Mitchell Marsh, who had last played for Australia in England in 2019 and was now a late replacement for the injured Cameron Green, joined Travis Head. Soon, they were both dropped. It was that dreadful Bairstow again. He put down a straightforward one down the leg side standing back when Head was nine. Groucho and I would have swallowed it. When he was starting out, they used to call Rod Marsh 'iron gloves', and poor old Bairstow was fast becoming a worthy successor to the title: Edgbaston and now this. I am ashamed to say I felt angry. And then Joe Root, of all people – what happens to his concentration? – put down a sitter when Marsh (no relation to the late Rod) was 12. If it was to go on like this, I was going to need something stronger than coffee and I eyed my corkscrew. I caught the replay of both misses too, and then I began to put it to good use.

These two then put on 155, with Marsh making the fastest hundred by an Australian in England since the immortal Victor Trumper who had done it from 85 balls before lunch on the first day at Old Trafford in 1902. One of the joys of cricket is that an innings like this can take us back to an innings played 121 years before, and to one of the greatest batsmen of all time, who did much to develop the art of batsmanship in those early days. Of course the game was different then, but I am sure that in its way the Ashes were just as challenging and competitive as they are now, and that victory was just as important. Test cricket produces such fascinating and romantic comparisons of a kind the one-day game can never do – it is just not that sort of cricket, and for most of the time one remembers results but not individual performances. The excellent commentary on *TMS* was making the most of a great story. It is a little bit different to what it was in my day, but everything moves on and it was none the worse for that. The team had a good narrative to put across and one that got better and better as the match went on. It was a good listen.

Marsh batted magnificently for 118, in spite of having had no recent batting practice except in the nets, and his strokeplay was spectacular. Every time the guilty pair, Root and Bairstow, were mentioned on *TMS*, I wondered what was going through their minds, although I suppose if you play at this level you learn not to dwell on these things. Earlier, I had found myself daydreaming that Aggers might hand over to me, but at 240–4 I was happy he didn't. But then the splendid Woakes, bowling magnificently and swinging the ball late, dismissed both Marsh and Head. Just before tea, Marsh got an inside edge onto his pad and it looped to Crawley in the slips. After the interval, Root also dropped Carey, but managed to hang on to Head the very next ball.

It was gripping listening and I was surprised how involved I became with it all. The commentary nowadays is a part of an ongoing conversation between the commentator and the summariser. When I was there, I always felt I had the over to myself and was able to indulge myself in all sorts of descriptions of all that was going on around me while waiting for the summariser's words of wisdom at the end of the over. As I listened now, I hardly dared blow my nose in case I missed something. I couldn't help wondering if, when I was commentating, I tore at listeners' nerves in the same way that these tales of dropped catches were tearing at mine. But then it was back to Wood who, with that wonderful combination of rhythm and pace which come one from the other, devoured the Australian tail in a blistering blur of speed. I have to admit my loyalty wavered and I watched Wood run in for a couple of overs on tele. It was worth it and Australia collapsed to 263 all out. It was only then that I realised that in my preparations for the day I had forgotten the wine glass which should have accompanied the corkscrew. Only a minor setback.

Stokes had won his first challenge but found his next was upon him much too soon. England's early batting was even more threadbare than Australia's. The first five wickets fell for 87, and I was hugely disappointed and I thought we were heading for another defeat. I even considered turning the radio off, but that would show what a bad loser I am, and so I stuck it out. When, early on the second day, the score had reached 68–4, Stokes came bustling out with that no-nonsense stride of his even though he was now suffering from a muscle problem in his behind, all this in addition to the damaged knee that was preventing him from bowling. Maybe Stokes has taken a leaf from the book of that great West Indian batter Gordon Greenidge, in that he often seems to be at his very best when he is suffering from an injury, for he now proceeded to bat as he had done at Lord's.

He was cautious at first, just as he had been in St John's Wood, until he was set in motion by another extraordinary display by the incorrigible Wood. The Australians were bowling short and after lunch Wood faced Starc. He swung the first ball for six and the next two went for four and another six . . . and it was at that moment that the postman rang the doorbell, which was irritating, but as he is a cheerful Italian with no obvious love of cricket I had to forgive him. When I got back, I found myself continually turning from radio to TV replay and back. By then, Wood had dispatched Cummins into the crowd for a third six before top-edging him to midwicket, having made 24 in just eight balls.

Stokes wasn't going to let his fastest bowler steal his thunder and was quick to change gear and carry on in the same thrilling vein. In Starc's next over he hit him for three fours and then turned his attention to off-spinner Todd Murphy, whom he proceeded to hit for a total of five sixes. It was terrific to listen to and no one was enjoying himself more than Tuffers, who was in boisterous form on air.

In the end, Stokes gave Murphy his first Ashes wicket when he holed out at long on, but by then Australia's first-innings lead of 26 was nothing like as important as at one time had seemed likely. While this was happening, it had been hard to work out the best moment to go to the bathroom. It was all about Bazball. The non-stop strokeplay and the speed and excitement of the commentary which faithfully and entertainingly reflected Bazball was terrific. It was not often that the tempo was like this when I was doing it, unless Viv Richards or Ian Botham were at the crease. I kept smiling as I wondered again how John Arlott would have coped with Bazball. He was such a great pro that he would never have been left behind. As it is, his original cricketing world and the present one were now a long way apart on the field of play, but he would have relished them both, and anything in between.

In Australia's second innings the wickets were shared around by England's four main bowlers and Usman Khawaja's anti-Bazball 43 was the highest score. I was able to listen without too much anxiety, although Head and Marsh were again a bit of a worry and caused me to eye my corkscrew for a moment or two. They added 41 before Marsh was caught behind off Woakes. I think I reacted to the appeal just before the commentator, who had been engaged in a conversation with a summariser. It was one of those deafening jobs which often seem to produce the right answer for the bowler.

England were left to score 251 to win and it was now that Moeen Ali made a brave and important decision for England by offering to bat at number three. The obvious candidate for that all-important position has for a long time been Joe Root, England's best player, but he has several times declined the invitation, preferring to stay at number four. Is this merely a personal preference or a weakness? Harry Brook may in time be the man, but he is not yet ready for it, and so Moeen gallantly stepped forward, but as this was his last Test series he was only going to relieve the situation for the time being.

Crawley and Duckett put together a reasonable start of 42, but I have to confess that as I listened to them batting during this series I often had the awful feeling that either of them could be out at any moment – except of course for Crawley later on at Old Trafford. Maybe that was because I was not then as confident of Bazball as they were. As the series went on, I became a great supporter of them both, even after Duckett's suicidal exploits at Lord's, and there is no one who communicates the joy and the aim of Bazball better than Crawley. Moeen survived for only 15 balls, but by coming in third he may have eased tensions within the dressing room. Brook, in front of his home crowd, was the only batsman to prosper, and when the Australians bowled short at him, he did his best to discipline a compulsive urge to hook. By the time the urge did get the better of him, his exciting strokeplay had taken him to 75 from 93 balls and England to the brink of victory. Even so, it still required the cool nerve of Woakes, with flamboyant assistance from Wood, to make sure of England's three-wicket victory.

The final square drive for four by Woakes off Starc was a wonderful moment. It was a glorious stroke which kept the Ashes alive and did English cricket a power of good. It had something in common with that glorious cover drive with which Crawley began the series. This third Test at Headingley was an absorbing match which Groucho would have found as compelling listening in Los Angeles as I had done in the middle of the Norfolk Broads, and at the end of it the Ashes were still up for grabs. Groucho would have been listening, because an English friend of his would have told him how to twiddle the knobs on his wireless so he could pick up the commentary on *Test Match Special*.

Then it was on to Old Trafford, with its reputation for rain, for the fourth Test match. It was surprising that the main players on both sides in this daunting series had kept going as well as they had after three such demanding matches in quick succession, and that muscle fatigue had been held at bay. Anderson, who in the first two matches had sadly looked a bit past his sell-by date, was now reinstated for what was his last Test at Old Trafford, where one end of the ground had already been named after him. He and Broad, who had bowled his heart out, had always been the most unlikely to survive the ridiculous planning of this series, but Broad miraculously gave no sign of creaking muscles or exhaustion, and was still bowling as well as ever. I think all of us listening and watching at home, to say nothing of the actual spectators, were just about as knackered as the players.

For all that, England will have been buoyant when they came to

Old Trafford – until they heard the weather forecast. Mark Wood and Chris Woakes had made all the difference at Headingley and had given the side the lift they badly needed if they were to have a chance of bringing back the Ashes. The one big problem now was out of their control: Manchester's appalling weather forecast, which promised unrelenting rain for most of the last two days.

Once again, I repelled all visitors at Hoveton and established myself in front of my wireless with the tele just round the corner. The match was given an interesting start when for the second Test running Stokes decided to put Australia in to bat, in spite of knowing – I can't imagine he didn't – that no side had ever put their opponents in at Old Trafford and gone on to win the Test match. Being Stokes, who loves bucking trends, maybe it was this that helped him to make the decision.

England bowled well, but not devastatingly so, and Wood was not quite the force he had been at Headingley. Australia were bowled out for 317, with seven of their batsmen reaching 20 without any of them going on to make more than Labuschagne and Marsh, who both reached 51. Stokes would probably have settled for this when he put them in. He owed most to Woakes, who, bowling superbly, took five wickets in an innings for the first time against Australia as he continued to stamp his mark on the series.

England's batters were shown the way by the magnificent Crawley, who made a prodigious 189 from only 182 balls. This was an unthinkable rate for an opening batter in a crucial Test match in an Ashes series and it took one back to Bob Barber's 185 at the Sydney Cricket Ground in 1965–66. Crawley now took England to 592, their highest score against Australia in England since 1985.

Crawley had been growing in confidence throughout the series and now he was fulfilling all the hopes that had persuaded McCullum and Stokes to keep him in the side. His innings was a joy to listen to and the commentators brilliantly described his splendid array of strokes and, yes, I would very much have liked to be back in the commentary box while Crawley was playing this innings. There was something marvellously compelling about his approach to batting, especially when taken together with his enthusiasm and his obvious enjoyment of what he was doing, although he had the luck to be dropped twice. In fact, this was a series which saw a surprising number of dropped catches by both sides, which was one of the reasons that the quality of the cricket did not quite match that in the thrilling series in 2005 when Michael Vaughan's England side won the Ashes for the first time for nearly twenty years.

Crawley almost knocked another old-timer off his perch, for in 1897–98 in Sydney the Australian opener Joe Darling reached his third hundred of that series in 91 minutes off 85 balls. I find these old scorecards quite irresistible, and what fun it was to look at this one. Darling was the first left-hander to score a hundred in a Test match, and in this innings he made 160 out of 252 before he was out. Records like this are such an important part of the game's heritage, but I fear that today, when there are so many different forms of the game, they may not seem as important as they once did. I do hope I am wrong.

In the later stages of Crawley's innings he was scoring so freely that the fielders were constantly changing positions as Cummins did his best to staunch the flow of runs. In the commentary box it is at moments like these that identification of fielders, which always gave me more of a problem than anyone, becomes even harder. This is when I often used the fielding positions rather than the name of the actual fielder as a way out. As I listened now I occasionally heard mentions of 'deep mid off' or 'deep extra cover' or perhaps 'short fine leg', and I couldn't help smiling at the memory of having been there and done that myself. This works well enough until, say, third slip takes a catch and then the name of the catcher is imperative. I probably won the prize for getting things wrong, and I was relieved to hear that perhaps it still happens, even if nothing like so much now that I have been put out to grass.

One thing which has recently crept in and I don't care for is the use of 'leg gully' instead of 'backward short leg'. I think there is rather more romance about 'backward short leg' than 'leg gully', a bureaucratic-sounding position in the field if ever there was one. It seems to be used much more nowadays than it was and I always wonder who started it, although I suppose there is a clear logic behind it. They have their own cricketing language in Australia, but I don't think we can even blame them for this. For all that, I would love to know why 'extras' are called 'sundries' in Australia, although 'sundries' has a nice ring to it, and for what reason do they insist on giving the score the wrong way round? For example, 200 for 3 becomes 3 for 200. Maybe it has something to do with being on the other side of the Equator.

We must get back to Crawley. Although he took centre stage on the second day at Old Trafford, the impish Moeen, still going in at number three, Root, Brook and Stokes made classy fifties, while Bairstow was helped in a last-wicket stand of 66 by Anderson, who was then out, leaving Bairstow marooned on 99 for the second time in a Test match at Old Trafford. It was hereabouts that my elderly wireless developed a severe case of snap, crackle and pop, which used to happen all the time when I first listened, probably under the bedclothes at school, to Test match commentary, when Freddie Brown's England side was in Australia in 1950–51. Then, it was like listening to something from outer space, and I still think it was just about the most exciting thing I have done in my life. Now, I missed the dismissal of Anderson, which was irritating, and I was sad we didn't get to 600, which always has a nice ring to it.

When Australia went in again, 275 runs behind, Wood suddenly found his rhythm and took three wickets, reducing them to 108–4, before Marsh joined the ever-adhesive Labuschagne. With storm clouds gathering, they had put on 103 and Labuschagne reached a patient, fighting hundred before he was caught close to the wicket off Root. After that, only three more runs were scored before the heavens opened when only 30 overs had been bowled on this fourth day. No play at all was possible on the fifth, and so the Ashes were damply retained by Australia. Manchester cannot claim that it does not deserve its reputation for rain, for this was the thirty-second day of Test cricket at Old Trafford to have been completely rained off. This became the first of the seventeen Test matches since Stokes had taken over the England captaincy to end in a draw. The blame for that lies squarely with the miserable Manchester weather.

It was now that the top echelon of the cricketing world went completely bonkers. There were a number of extraordinary suggestions that in the future the regulations for a series should, in the event of this situation happening again, allow an extra day to be added to the match, or that play on each day should be allowed to finish later. These serious suggestions all came, of course, from people sitting on the English side of the fence, so that England should in any similar situation be allowed to win, for that is what it amounts to. Joe Root suggested that each day's play should continue until the allotted number of overs for the day had been completed. Maybe this should happen anyway.

Remarkably, the chair of the ECB, Richard Thompson, then went much further the following morning on the BBC's *Today* programme. He said he was going to talk to the chair of the ICC to make sure that schedules can be made more flexible to accommodate this type of strange eventuality. Thompson's arrival at Lord's as chair of the ECB is one of the best things to have happened for a long time for the game in England. His shrewd common sense and refusal to panic has done much to sort out the confusion in those offices. But he must surely have got out of the wrong side of his bed on the morning he made those remarks on *Today*. You cannot change the rules just because they don't suit you, for this was what he was trying to do. The feeling of deep disappointment the morning after that blank day at Old Trafford led to many strange and improper thoughts. I have no doubt that none of them came from the Australian camp. We now live in a climate where inappropriate suggestions like this can be made without fear of ridicule or condemnation. If such a thing had been suggested sixty years ago, Gubby Allen would have suffered immediate heart failure in the committee room at Lord's.

Let us go back sixty years to another extraordinary rain-affected Test match, against the West Indies at Lord's in 1963. I watched the last day sitting in the row of seats immediately below the windows of the broadcasting boxes in the Warner Stand. (Sir Pelham 'Plum' Warner, an immense figure in English cricket, had been born in Trinidad. It was later in 2023 that the new chair of the MCC, Bruce Carnegie-Brown, suggested that the name of the Warner Stand might have to be changed because of Plum's family's earlier connections with the slave trade, which had been abolished many years before Plum was born. Carnegie-Brown did not stand for a second term of office.)

With one ball of the final over of that 1963 Test remaining, all four results were possible. England, at 228–9, needed six to win and the West Indies to take one wicket. The day before, when England had begun their second innings, Colin Cowdrey, who had come in when the third wicket had fallen for 31, had fractured his arm trying to play a short ball from Wes Hall, who was bowling in dreadful light from the Pavilion End, where there was no sightscreen. On the last day, rain delayed the start until well into the afternoon, which heightened the drama still further. Now, when the last over began, Hall, who bowled throughout the 200 minutes' play on this last day, was bowling at off-spinner David Allen. Derek Shackleton, who was thirty-eight and playing his first Test for eleven years, had been run out off the last ball of the penultimate over as he went for an impossible single in order that Allen should be facing the last over.

England were now nine wickets down and Cowdrey, left arm in plaster, walked slowly out of the Pavilion to the non-striker's end for this final over. Somehow, Allen saw it through in appalling light and the match was drawn. We did not then hear a word from the captain, Ted Dexter, or indeed from Gubby Allen, who in those days ran English cricket with an extremely firm hand, about the need for longer hours each day, or extra time on the last day, or a possible sixth day just in case. Their West Indian counterparts, from whom any such demand might have been more likely, also remained silent. The thoughts of 2023 would never have crossed anyone's mind in 1963. The rules and regulations were the rules and regulations and were respected as such. Sixty years later, little appears to be sacred.

Back to the 2023 Ashes. There is nothing more difficult than listening to a rained-off day like this on the radio. The commentators did their best, but it is not easy to massage this sort of irritated frustration. As a listener, you have to make lots of tricky decisions. If you leave the room for any length of time, there is the fear you may miss a significant announcement. It is as well to stay within earshot for these periodic situation reports, and also when the guys in the box get into an interesting conversation it becomes difficult to drag yourself away. But this was one of those days with a ghastly inevitability submerging it. Fate was cruelly robbing us of the ultimate cricketing nirvana, with England and Australia coming to The Oval with the visitors leading 2–1. Even worse, this deluge meant that the Ashes still belonged to Australia. I have to admit that I went to bed that night thinking more nasty thoughts about poor old Bairstow's wicketkeeping at Edgbaston.

Nonetheless, England, probably the better side, if woefully undisciplined at crucial moments in the first two matches, could still save the series, even if the Ashes were out of their reach. Also, they had to try and prevent Australia winning their first series in England since Steve Waugh's side in 2001. There was plenty to play for, even though the main prize had gone.

England v Australia
3rd Test
Played at Headingley, Leeds, on 6–9 July 2023
Umpires: HDPK Dharmasena & NN Menon (TV: JS Wilson)
Referee: RS Madugalle
Toss: England

Australia

DA Warner c Crawley b Broad	4	(2)	c Crawley b Broad	1
U Khawaja b Wood	13	(1)	c Bairstow b Woakes	43
M Labuschagne c Root b Woakes	21		c Brook b Ali	33
SPD Smith c Bairstow b Broad	22		c Duckett b Ali	2
TM Head c Root b Woakes	39		c Duckett b Broad	77
MR Marsh c Crawley b Woakes	118		c Bairstow b Woakes	28
AT Carey† c Woakes b Wood	8		b Woakes	5
MA Starc b Wood	2		c Brook b Wood	16
PJ Cummins* lbw b Wood	0		c Bairstow b Wood	1
TR Murphy b Wood	13		lbw b Broad	11
SM Boland not out	0		not out	0
Extras (b 10, lb 10, nb 3)	23		(b 5, lb 2)	7
Total (60.4 overs)	**263**		(67.1 overs)	**224**

England

Z Crawley c Warner b Marsh	33		c Carey b Marsh	44
BM Duckett c Carey b Cummins	2		lbw b Starc	23
HC Brook c Smith b Cummins	3	(5)	c Cummins b Starc	75
JE Root c Warner b Cummins	19		c Carey b Cummins	21
JM Bairstow† c Smith b Starc	12	(7)	b Starc	5
BA Stokes* c Smith b Murphy	80		c Carey b Starc	13
MM Ali c Smith b Cummins	21	(3)	b Starc	5
CR Woakes c Carey b Starc	10		not out	32
MA Wood c Marsh b Cummins	24		not out	16
SCJ Broad c Smith b Cummins	7			
OE Robinson not out	5			
Extras (b 4, lb 3, w 5, nb 9)	21		(b 7, lb 7, w 1, nb 5)	20
Total (52.3 overs)	**237**		(for 7 wkts) (50 overs)	**254**

ENGLAND	O	M	R	W	O	M	R	W
Broad	11.4	0	58	2	14.1	3	45	3
Robinson	11.2	2	38	0				
Wood	11.4	4	34	5	17	2	66	2
Woakes	17	1	73	3	(2) 18	0	68	3
Ali	9	1	40	0	17	3	34	2
Root					(4) 1	0	4	0

AUSTRALIA	O	M	R	W	O	M	R	W
Starc	14	3	59	2	(2) 16	0	78	5
Cummins	18	1	91	6	(1) 15	0	77	1
Boland	10	0	35	0	11	1	49	0
Marsh	3	1	9	1	6	0	23	1
Murphy	7.3	0	36	1	2	0	13	0

Fall of wickets:

	Aus	Eng	Aus	Eng
1st	4	18	11	42
2nd	42	22	68	60
3rd	61	65	72	93
4th	85	68	90	131
5th	240	87	131	161
6th	245	131	139	171
7th	249	142	168	230
8th	249	167	170	–
9th	254	199	211	–
10th	263	237	224	–

Close of play: Day 1:   Eng (1) 68–3 (Root 19*, Bairstow 1*, 19 overs)
Day 2:   Aus (2) 116–4 (Head 18*, Marsh 17*, 47 overs)
Day 3:   Eng (2) 27–0 (Crawley 9*, Duckett 18*, 5 overs)

Man of the match: MA Wood
Result: **England won by 3 wickets**

Dressed to kill: Manoj
Badale, owner of the
Rajasthan Royals,
a hugely important
contemporary figure.

Groucho Marx showed up at a Test
at Lord's in 1958 and was bored
stiff. Sixty-five years later, his
re-energised spirit found Bazball
and the modern game irresistible.

Kagiso Rabada at full stretch with
the safest pair of hands: South
Africa's brilliant all-rounder.

The man of the moment: Ben Stokes, England's extraordinary
captain, the chief engineer of Bazball.

Australia's Nathan Lyon is a wonderfully competitive cricketer and a brilliant off-spinner.

Pat Cummins, Australia's outstanding captain and opening bowler, clubs Joe Root straight for six at Edgbaston.

Zak Crawley and Ben Duckett, England's exciting Bazball openers.

Back to the box. Blowers in full flow alongside that
supreme scorer, Andrew Samson.

India's superstar captain, Virat Kohli, a passionate supporter of
Test cricket, modestly acknowledging the applause.

Bazball's architect and chief apostle: Brendon McCullum,
England's coach (right), and Ben Stokes, the captain.

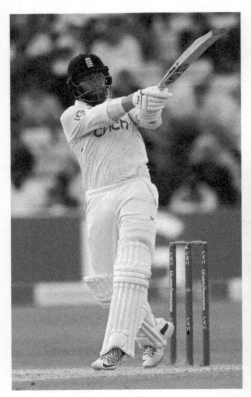

A typically exuberant Jonny Bairstow, who launched Bazball with a series of brilliant innings in 2022.

Another Yorkshireman who has come to stay. Harry Brook has made a wonderful start for England.

Ramp or reverse sweep: Joe Root plays them all with equal brilliance – and elegance too.

Stuart Broad about to dismiss Alex Carey with his last ball in Test cricket.

What an end! Stuart Broad swings the last ball he faces in Test cricket for six.

A huge thank you to all you listeners and the unending supply of cakes. This was the best!

My last day's commentary, at Lord's in 2017. It was a sadly wonderful and unforgettable occasion.

Sharing my love of cricket with Graeme Smith, and a smiling Jonathan Agnew in the background.

England v Australia
4th Test
Played at Old Trafford, Manchester, on 19–23 July 2023
Umpires: NN Menon & JS Wilson (TV: HDPK Dharmasena)
Referee: RS Madugalle
Toss: England

Australia

DA Warner c Bairstow b Woakes	32	(2) b Woakes	28
U Khawaja lbw b Broad	3	(1) c Bairstow b Wood	18
M Labuschagne lbw b Ali	51	c Bairstow b Root	111
SPD Smith lbw b Wood	41	c Bairstow b Wood	17
TM Head c Root b Broad	48	c Duckett b Wood	1
MR Marsh c Bairstow b Woakes	51	not out	31
CD Green lbw b Woakes	16	not out	3
AT Carey† c Bairstow b Woakes	20		
MA Starc not out	36		
PJ Cummins* c Stokes b Anderson	1		
JR Hazlewood c Duckett b Woakes	4		
Extras (b 8, lb 3, nb 3)	14	(b 1, lb 2, w 1, nb 1)	5
Total (90.2 overs)	**317**	(for 5 wkts) (71 overs)	**214**

England

Z Crawley b Green	189
BM Duckett c Carey b Starc	1
MM Ali c Khawaja b Starc	54
JE Root b Hazlewood	84
HC Brook c Starc b Hazlewood	61
BA Stokes* b Cummins	51
JM Bairstow† not out	99
CR Woakes c Carey b Hazlewood	0
MA Wood b Hazlewood	6
SCJ Broad c and b Hazlewood	7
JM Anderson lbw b Green	5
Extras (b 15, lb 9, nb 11)	35
Total (107.4 overs)	**592**

ENGLAND	O	M	R	W		O	M	R	W	Fall of wickets:		
											Aus	Eng	Aus
Broad	14	0	68	2	(2) 12	2	47	0				
Anderson	20	4	51	1	(1) 17	5	30	0	1st	15	9	32
Woakes	22.2	4	62	5	(5) 12	5	31	1	2nd	61	130	54
Wood	17	5	60	1	11	0	27	3	3rd	120	336	97
Ali	17	1	65	1	(3) 13	2	44	0	4th	183	351	108
Root					6	1	32	1	5th	189	437	211
										6th	254	474	–
AUSTRALIA	O	M	R	W						7th	255	486	–
Starc	25	0	137	2						8th	294	506	–
Hazlewood	27	2	126	5						9th	299	526	–
Cummins	23	0	129	1						10th	317	592	–
Green	15.4	1	64	2									
Head	7	0	52	0									
Marsh	9	0	57	0									
Labuschagne	1	0	3	0									

Close of play:	Day 1:	Aus (1) 299–8 (Starc 23*, Cummins 1*, 83 overs)
	Day 2:	Eng (1) 384–4 (Brook 14*, Stokes 24*, 72 overs)
	Day 3:	Aus (2) 113–4 (Labuschagne 44*, Marsh 1*, 41 overs)
	Day 4:	Aus (2) 214–5 (Marsh 31*, Green 3*, 71 overs)

Man of the match: Z Crawley
Result: **Drawn**

12

PAINTED WITH A BROAD BRUSH

'The perfect ending, broadly speaking'

I MADE rather a business of listening to the last Test mostly on *Test Match Special*, while again backsliding to my television set for the replays. I did my best, too, to catch up on all the other cricket which had been going on. The Women's Ashes was also a really close-run and exciting series, but inevitably and sadly suffered by being played simultaneously with such a dramatic men's Ashes, which will have claimed more attention, but the big advance in women's cricket had sparked a wonderful new interest at all levels of their game. Then, in the men's world, there was the County Championship, the T20 competition and all the bits and pieces about who was signing for who in the next round of all the franchise tournaments around the world. There were also bits to read about the forthcoming World Cup in India and, of course, the fast-approaching men's and women's Hundred, which of course had the month of August pretty well all to itself. Phew! What a world, and I am sure I have left a few things out.

The pile of newspapers I had stacked up in the corner for future reading grew bigger and bigger, for The Oval was now all I could think about. I made sure there were enough spare batteries for my old wireless, which would have been able to remember cricket when it was only played in white clothes and 229–3, or 3–229, was a good score on the first day of a Test match. It may also just have remembered Denis Compton and Len Hutton, although news as far back as that was more likely to have come by way of a plug in the wall.

On the first morning at The Oval, Cummins won the toss for the first time in the series and decided to put England in to bat. This was the third match in succession where the winner of the toss had put the other side in – whatever had happened to the old dictum: 'If you win the toss, think about putting the opposition in before you decide to bat'? This leads me to another complaint. Scorecards in papers and magazines do not these days always say who has won the toss. In the good old days of leisured intensity, I like to think the toss always got a mention at the top of the score-card, at the ground or in the paper.

England wasted another useful start from Crawley and Duckett. Then, it was a typically carefree innings of 85 from Brook – one day he will learn to convert these little gems into meaningful hundreds – and useful runs once again from Woakes and Wood that took England to 283. By now, Bazball was becoming irresistible, but it still badly needed to be tempered by discipline if it was to achieve the victories it promised. If it does not, I fear it will ultimately go down as a passing phase rather than a new religious movement. If McCullum is to become the high priest rather than the leader of the insurgents, he must stand on a chair in the dressing room and preach meaningfully with a long-term emphasis on the occasional need for caution.

England were bowled out in 54.4 overs with two hours of the first day left. It was gloriously entertaining and yet infuriatingly wasteful to see another chance to rub Australian noses in it thrown away. What on earth was as good a batter as Joe Root doing dragging Hazlewood into his stumps trying to play a stroke that may again have fulfilled the demands of Bazball, like that time he was stumped at Edgbaston, but certainly not those of common sense?

I feared both the pace and the content of this first day would be too much for my venerable wireless, but it bravely lasted the course. It had me jumping up and down a bit too. The commentary was a frenzy of thoughts, opinions, explanations, conversations and expectations, some of which were excellent and others as wide of the mark as Root's choice of stroke. But then commentary has always naturally adjusted itself to the approach and tempo of the game that has to be described. Not even Sir Geoffrey Boycott was able to be right all the time.

This frenetic tempo is never more evident than when listening to a T20 game. I have to admit that I was only allowed to commentate on one T20 game, when England played Australia at what was then called the Rose Bowl in 2005. That game was memorable because at one point Australia were 31–7 and even a game of beach cricket is memorable if Australia are 31–7. I must have made an awful mess of it, for I was never asked to do another. It was the only time I have ever commentated from an hotel bedroom too, for *TMS* took over a couple of bedrooms in the Hilton Hotel at the Rose Bowl as their commentary point.

The *TMS* output from The Oval during this fifth Test was all a bit different from when England played Australia there in 1953. I shall never forget listening to almost every ball of the fifth Test then, from a more staid commentary box – it was not called *Test Match Special* until 1957 – and there was no television then, at least not at Hoveton. England won the match and with it the Ashes for the first time since the Bodyline series in 1932–33. I so well remember running flat out to relay the news of falling Australian wickets to my mother and father, who were sitting in the peace of a commentary-free summerhouse, where sadly they showed only a head-nodding interest in events at The Oval.

For the last two hours on that first evening at The Oval in 2023, Australia's openers played old-fashioned cricket. Khawaja would have been quite incapable of buying into Bazball. He would almost certainly have photographs of Geoffrey Boycott and himself on his bedroom wall and a framed snapshot of Ken 'Slasher' Mackay's forward defensive stroke on his desk; Garry Sobers or Viv Richards would not have got a look-in. On the other hand, I think a younger David Warner might easily have bought into this new craze, but in his old age he was learning discretion, probably because, being about to retire, he wanted to make sure of keeping his place in the side so he could wave good-bye in Sydney in the New Year of 2024. In the first 25 overs, Australia crawled to 61–1 and by the end I was almost blaming my wireless for not taking another wicket.

The second day went England's way after that supreme batter Steve Smith had tried to play Chris Woakes away on the leg side and skied a gentle catch to Bairstow, but even so, right at the end, we had to stomach some splendid warrior-like strokes from Nathan Lyon's stand-in off-spinner, Todd Murphy, which brought him three of Groucho's homers and took Australia to a lead of just 12. The contrast between the helter-skelter of Bazball and the old-fashioned ways of the Australians was perfectly illustrated when after 54.4 overs, the length of England's complete innings of 283, Australia had reached 130–4. Marnus Labuschagne had set the tone at the start of the day with an innings of prodigious and record-breaking boredom as he took 82 balls to amass nine runs – and on a good wicket too.

On the third day, the Oval Test was taken over by Stuart Broad's decision to make this not only his final Test match but also his final game of first-class cricket. Now a veteran of 167 Tests, and with a tally of wickets poised to pass 600, he had decided that the time had come. Ashes battles were the joy of his cricketing life; he was now thirty-seven and the next Ashes was two years away. His decision gave this fifth Test another wonderful storyline. Broad, just like his father Chris, who once scored three hundreds in an

Ashes series in Australia in 1986–87, has always been the most wholehearted and fearless of cricketers. When I heard the news, like many people, I suspect, my thoughts turned to Trent Bridge in 2015, when he took 8–15 bowling Australia out for 60 before lunch on the first day. I was lucky enough to be the first commentator that day, and when I handed over to Ed Smith Australia were 15–4.

At The Oval now, Crawley and Duckett again showed they are the ideal Bazball opening partnership, even though Duckett found a wasteful way of again getting out when they had put on 79. Thereafter, Root batted beautifully for 91 and should have gone on to a big hundred, while Stokes and Bairstow both played extremely well, but even so, England's second-innings total of 395 was not quite enough to shut Australia out of the game, and this same undisciplined Bazball carelessness was the reason. The fourth day began with England at 389–9 and the two not-out batters, Broad and Anderson, were met by an Australian guard of honour as they left the pavilion. Broad then faced Starc and pulled what turned out to be the last ball he faced in a Test match for six. After that, the script went haywire for a while. The weather allowed only 40 overs to be bowled in the rest of that day and Warner and Khawaja, going carefully about their business, put on their first century partnership of the series. Australia finished the day at 135 for no wicket, needing 249 runs to win leaving England with the feeling that it might all go horribly wrong.

They had had one great piece of luck, although they were not to know it until play began on this last day. The previous evening, Khawaja had been hit on the helmet by Wood and the umpires had decided to change a ball which had allowed the bowlers hardly any movement, in the air or off the seam. Now, on the fifth morning, in similar overhead conditions, there was much more movement from the replacement ball. Australia complained that due care and attention had not been shown when choosing that replacement ball. There was, too, maybe as a result, more urgency about the England bowling as Woakes and Wood, that duo again, took the wickets of Warner, Khawaja and Labuschagne.

Smith and Head now built a good partnership and then, just before lunch, Stokes held a good one-handed catch at leg slip as Smith played forward to Moeen, but his hand then banged against his leg and the ball popped out. After a two-hour break for rain, which heightened the tension still further, Moeen now cleverly flighted one to Head, who went for it and was caught by Root at slip, and then, ten runs later, Smith followed a beauty from Woakes ·and was caught at slip. Australia were 274–5. Before another run was scored a brilliant reflex catch by Bairstow accounted for Marsh off Moeen. Starc and Cummins were soon gone and with two left-handers at the crease, Carey and Murphy, and another, Hazlewood, to come, Stokes threw the ball to Broad, who had always made life a misery for left-handers. This was the start of the final act.

It took Broad 40 balls. First the exuberant Murphy, who again showed he knows how to hit the ball, put on 35 with Carey. Then Broad decided it was time for his favourite party trick. In the first innings, when Labuschagne had established squatter's rights, Broad had switched over the bails at the non-striker's end and Wood's next ball had Labuschagne caught in the slips. Now, Broad did the same at the bowler's end before bowling to Murphy. The next ball, from round the wicket, was up to the bat and moved just enough in the air and off the seam to find the edge, and Bairstow took the catch. Then, soon afterwards, Broad bowled to Carey, also round the wicket. It was an identical delivery, again finding the edge, and the ball thumped into Bairstow's gloves.

Broad had taken a wicket with his last ball in Test cricket and England had won by 49 runs, preserving their unbeaten record at home against Australia since 2001. It was the perfect ending, but of course the major prize was Australia's, for they still held the

Ashes. It will be a long time before we see another series like this one. It has put Test match cricket back on the map with some emphasis, but for how long? Broad may have done it for the last time, but we are left with the big imponderable: can Bazball do it again?

England v Australia
5th Test
Played at The Oval, Kennington, on 27–31 July 2023

Umpires: HDPK Dharmasena & JS Wilson (TV: NN Menon)
Referee: RS Madugalle
Toss: Australia

England

Z Crawley c Smith b Cummins	22		c Smith b Cummins ...73
BM Duckett c Carey b Marsh	41		c Carey b Starc...42
MM Ali b Murphy	34	(7)	c Hazlewood b Starc...29
JE Root b Hazlewood	5		b Murphy...91
HC Brook c Smith b Starc	85		c Carey b Hazlewood...7
BA Stokes* b Starc	3	(3)	c Cummins b Murphy...42
JM Bairstow† b Hazlewood	4	(6)	c Carey b Starc...78
CR Woakes c Head b Starc	36		c Khawaja b Starc...1
MA Wood b Murphy	28		c Marsh b Murphy...9
SCJ Broad c Head b Starc	7		not out...8
JM Anderson not out	0		lbw b Murphy...8
Extras (b 9, lb 7, nb 2)	18		(lb 4, nb 3)...7
Total (54.4 overs)	**283**		(81.5 overs)...**395**

Australia

U Khawaja lbw b Broad	47	(2)	lbw b Woakes...72
DA Warner c Crawley b Woakes	24	(1)	c Bairstow b Woakes...60
M Labuschagne c Root b Wood	9		c Crawley b Wood...13
SPD Smith c Bairstow b Woakes	71		c Crawley b Woakes...54
TM Head c Bairstow b Broad	4		c Root b Ali...43
MR Marsh b Anderson	16		c Bairstow b Ali...6
AT Carey† c Stokes b Root	10		c Bairstow b Broad...28
MA Starc c Duckett b Wood	7		c Crawley b Woakes...0
PJ Cummins* c Stokes b Root	36		c Stokes b Ali...9
TR Murphy lbw b Woakes	34		c Bairstow b Broad...18
JR Hazlewood not out	6		not out...4
Extras (b 17, lb 12, w 1, nb 1)	31		(b 10, lb 10, w 5, nb 2)...27
Total (103.1 overs)	**295**		(94.4 overs)...**334**

AUSTRALIA	O	M	R	W	O	M	R	W	Fall of wickets:				
										Eng	Aus	Eng	Aus
Starc	14.4	1	82	4	20	2	100	4	1st	62	49	79	40
Hazlewood	13	0	54	2	15	0	67	1	2nd	66	91	140	141
Cummins	13	2	66	1	16	0	79	1	3rd	73	115	213	169
Marsh	8	0	43	1	8	0	35	0	4th	184	127	222	264
Murphy	6	0	22	2	22.5	0	110	4	5th	193	151	332	274
									6th	208	170	360	274
ENGLAND	O	M	R	W	O	M	R	W	7th	212	185	364	275
Broad	20	5	49	2	20.4	4	62	2	8th	261	239	375	294
Anderson	26	9	67	1	14	4	53	0	9th	270	288	379	329
Wood	22	4	62	2	(6) 9	0	34	1	10th	283	295	395	334
Woakes	25	8	61	3	(3) 19	4	50	4					
Root	7.1	1	20	2	9	0	39	0					
Brook	3	1	7	0									
Ali					(4) 23	2	76	3					

Close of play: Day 1: Aus (1) 61–1 (Khawaja 26*, Labuschagne 2*, 25 overs)
Day 2: Aus (1) 295
Day 3: Eng (2) 389–9 (Broad 2*, Anderson 8*, 80 overs)
Day 4: Aus (2) 135–0 (Warner 58*, Khawaja 69*, 38 overs)

Man of the match: CR Woakes
Result: **England won by 49 runs**

13

THE HUNDRED
AND BEYOND

'The two Richards must show the way'

THE summer of 2023 had, so far, been too good to be true. In the previous three chapters we have seen the reasons why the country, and much of the cricketing world, was gripped by one of the most exciting Ashes series ever. Bazball had taken over and considerably quickened up the traditional Test match game, but without making it in any way unrecognisable from the one we have always watched. The series was crammed into six weeks, but it was so exciting that in the end that will not have harmed anyone's enjoyment.

When the series was over, the players hardly had time to unbuckle their pads before cricket's new Punch & Judy show was thrust upon them. The logistics of the summer had been planned by the ECB under its old leadership of chair Colin Graves and CEO Tom Harrison, who were determined to get the Ashes out of the way by the end of July. This was done so that they could release from its cage a far from toothless tiger which they seem to have regarded as the major event of the season: The Hundred. They had cleared the decks as much as they could, leaving the 50-over county competition, the Metro Bank One-Day Cup, as the only other domestic competition to be played in August. It was hardly an existential threat to The Hundred, which had already deprived the Metro Bank Cup of its best players. Once The Hundred was out of the way, these same players would then be returning to their county sides to play out the second half of the County Championship amid the autumn mists and with the football season in full swing – just as the previous one had been when the first half of the Championship had been played in the spring. Those running the ECB had shown what they thought of Test cricket by pushing the only two-innings competition, the training ground for Test cricketers, to the extreme ends of the season, almost as if it was an irrelevance. Once the County Championship had finished, the relevant players would almost immediately be climbing into an aeroplane and heading for India and the World Cup.

As we can now see, The Hundred, in 2023, was a most disruptive competition. It was never properly thought through before being thrown into the mix of an already hectic English season. As a result, it was allowed to elbow everything else out of its way. Another problem was that the T20 Blast has an uncomfortably similar format. But it has to be said that not all is bad, for The Hundred has proved to be a really good day out for the whole family.

The young spectators have loved the funfair-like added extras and will have woken up the next morning with exciting thoughts about the fireworks, the balloons, the music, the DJs, the stuffed animals and the hamburgers. The actual cricket, although exciting, is unlikely to have been that high on their list, but it was good fun and they will be keen to go again. The day will also have been greatly enjoyed by the ladies, particularly the first part of it when the two women's Hundred teams will have been in action. The recent improvement in the standard of women's cricket and its fast-growing appeal will have made the ladies feel much more a part of the overall scene. The women's matches in The Hundred have provided great entertainment. The Hundred has done a huge amount for their game and the idea of playing both the women's and the men's games on the same day has been an important factor in making the competition so popular. It has also become a splendid evening out for the family and parents will have been happy their kids were having a really good time of it.

Some of the men may have begun the day with mildly cynical views about the women's game, but those will surely have disappeared during the first half a dozen overs. The women's game is now watched as an entertainment on its own without endless and boring comparisons being made with the men's game. A by-product of all this is that some men *will* have been delighted that they no longer have to find an excuse to go off on their own for a day or an evening at the cricket, even if they were not allowed to escape to the bar as often as they would have liked. All of this could hardly be further from the era of cricket I have tried to bring to life in the first part of this book. In those days, let's be honest, women's cricket on this scale would have been unthinkable.

A day of The Hundred at Lord's may seem an oil-and-water contradiction, rather like turning a side chapel in Canterbury Cathedral into a nightclub, but I had the greatest of fun when I went to a match at Lord's. The hamburgers were delicious, although some of the other delicacies on offer looked as if they might struggle to survive a stewards' inquiry. Strictly speaking, though, the occasion had little to do with real cricket and will have given Father Time, next to the Mound Stand and above the scorers, a serious bout of hiccups, but hang on, I am sure I spotted a twinkle in his eye and when it was time to go home, he looked positively sprightly and slightly roguish. He and I both realised it was sensible to move on with the times – to an extent.

I have no doubt that the original concept of The Hundred was dreamed up in good faith, but with a large helping of saving-face thrown in and a determination not to let India and the IPL have it all their own way. After all, it was the ECB that had first put the T20 game together. The problems came later when the bare bones were given flesh and a certain amount of blood by an ECB led by a chair, Colin Graves, who had had a brilliant career running the Costcutter supermarket chain, and had taken over from Giles Clarke who had been nothing if not a controversial figure. Graves inherited a chief executive, Tom Harrison, who had been appointed by Clarke in order to negotiate the all-important television contract with Sky. Harrison then found he had to deal with issues for which he was not really qualified and found he was to a great extent out of his depth through no fault of his own.

As I hope I have shown, the competition itself has not been by any means a failure, but then nor has it been an unqualified success either. It has brought in good crowds and has attracted maybe an important new audience to cricket, which was one of its main stated purposes. It is a moot point whether any of these newcomers will make the journey to the longer-drawn-out forms of the game. I can see some going on to test the waters of the Blast, when the evening is only 40 balls longer, but is there a realistic chance of them being more ambitious than that and moving up to the ODI level, with a hundred overs or 600 balls in the match, let alone to a Test match, the length of which is measured in days and not balls, even though draws are almost an extinct species? How interesting it would be to discover what the actual follow-through has been. Sky Television, who have bought the rights of The Hundred until the end of the 2028 season, seem to have been delighted with the product. It is this contract, more than anything else, which will keep the competition going, at least until 2028, even though plans for the future beyond that date are being drawn up. The ECB have now opened the doors to private investment, and with the franchise world interested in buying their way in, The Hundred may prove to be the vehicle that brings IPL-like prosperity to English cricket. Mr Badale will be doing handstands, but what will this do to the game itself?

What, therefore, are the problems? The starkest at the moment these words are being written is England's lamentable performance in the 2023 World Cup in India. The only practice England's players were allowed with the 50-over game came deep into September, when well before the close of play the shadows were lengthening across the ground. The tournament started in October, and England's batters behaved as if they were still engaged in The Hundred. They were roundly beaten by New Zealand in the opening match, and then by Afghanistan, Pakistan, India, South Africa and Australia and were on their way home before the knockout stages of the competition.

What we saw in the recent Ashes series makes me feel that the ECB were playing catch-up and not concentrating on the whole picture when they hurled The Hundred at us. The full-house crowds in the Ashes series showed that Test cricket in England is clearly a long way from being thought of as old-fashioned nonsense and an obsolete form of the game hanging on to the rafters for dear life. It is not only the Ashes that is such a draw either, for Test cricket in England remains as popular as it has ever been, if not more so, whoever the opponents may be.

Has The Hundred therefore been an unnecessary show of bravado by the English authorities trying to make up for their failure to take advantage of their own invention? Did they see The Hundred as a form of virtue-signalling, to prove they had not lost their way in this brave new world and that the ECB were cool and trendy after all? They wanted to make it even more over-the-top than T20, to say to the rest of the world and particularly India, 'Anything you can do, we can do better.' But the IPL franchise juggernaut is pretty well unstoppable. The Ashes in 2023 showed not only that Test cricket is still the gold standard of the game, but also that the ECB had got it wrong. They were only trying to nurture and sell the lower end of the game. They were putting the cart before the horse.

Now let's look at the mindset of those who ran the game in England when The Hundred was on the drawing board. It was apparently their intention to invent a new form of the game which had been reduced to its basic fundamentals even more than it was in the rest of the world and did not require any great intellect to be able to understand what was going on. Also, The Hundred would never be involved in international or franchise tournaments, as it would only be played in England. This isolation gives it a sterility, and I wonder if it occurred to them that this might be a problem, especially with the franchise world likely to outbid them in their attempt to buy the services of the world's best players. Why did they not make an effort to encourage people to come to *all* forms of the game, instead of only to the most basic? All they had was a hope that by a sort of natural progression those who came to watch The Hundred would automatically want to climb the ladder which leads to the longer forms of the game. Nothing was done to entice them up that ladder.

The least-spoken-about competition in the cricket calendar is the County Championship, the only domestic two-innings competition, whose job it has always been to produce Test cricketers. The Championship was pushed to the side, partly so that The Hundred could have August almost to itself and maybe partly because they felt that Test cricket was also a diminishing asset. Over the years, a variety of efforts have been made to make county cricket more attractive for spectators. One of the first moves was the introduction of overseas players. The playing conditions have often been altered to try and quicken up the game and to lessen the number of draws. Matches were extended from three days to four and other little tweaks were always being considered in an attempt to attract more than the sadly small numbers of members that most county clubs have these days, a sprinkling of whom will always turn up for County Championship cricket.

The Championship is an important and relevant part of the English summer. It will never again attract the big crowds that came to watch in the immediate post-war years, when entertainment opportunities were much more limited. However, the Championship is the pathway to the Test side, and this will guarantee it a hard core of support. The members of county clubs love nothing more than watching young players develop and go on to play for England, and this is the main purpose of the Championship, and, quite properly, it will remain as a prior charge on the profits that come from the international game. The two-innings game teaches the basic disciplines of cricket, and those who have gone on to make a success of the limited-over game would not have found it so easy to do so without this basic grounding in the syntax of the game which they will have had in their early cricketing years. The importance of the County Championship therefore reaches further than some may realise.

The County Championship is a competition, too, which I hope will also benefit from Bazball. Aspiring young Test cricketers will know by now that the best way of attracting the attention of McCullum and Stokes is to show that they buy into their approach to the game. These two New Zealand-born Bazballers have all but eliminated draws in Test cricket, which is a remarkable achievement in itself. It would be wonderful if Bazball was now to have a similar effect on county cricket, even if it will never be able to take command of the English weather. The influence of Bazball should make County Championship games more attractive, although in today's hectic world maybe only those who have retired will be able to take advantage of this. If Bazball can influence the pathway to Test cricket by enlivening the county game, it really might be the catalyst to increase the Championship's popularity in England and help bring back a better balance between red- and white-ball games.

The arrival of Richard Thompson and Richard Gould in the ECB offices at Lord's is an excellent stabilising influence on the game just when it is most needed. In earlier days, when they were steering Surrey's cricket, they had both been outspoken in their criticism of The Hundred and its effect on all the competitions around it. Now, they are in charge of the ECB offices that have spent so much time and money setting up The Hundred. When they settled down at their desks in their new home in February 2023 they will presumably have found all around them much support for this competition, which may have made them see it from a different perspective. As a result, they appear to have changed their minds, but it may be that these new opinions are only for public consumption. With the Sky contract in place, The Hundred will run at least until 2028 and it would have been clumsy, to say the least, for these two, as soon as they took office, to criticise a competition with six years still to run. Gould has said that the competition has been a terrific success, especially for women's cricket, and he is sure that it will run for many years beyond 2028. Thompson has sounded equally enthusiastic, and in the circumstances they could hardly have said anything different.

With the men's and the women's competitions being played the same day, it has meant that the women have also been playing in front of full-house crowds and getting much more exposure. It has been a wonderful PR exercise for them and they would not want this arrangement to stop, although Gould has said that he is sure that after the recent rise in popularity, the women on their own would pull in big crowds. This is potentially a tricky situation, for neither the men nor the women would want to harm the other's game, but the way of the world just now might make it harder for the men to go it alone if this is considered the best way forward. The ECB will surely no longer allow The Hundred to have August to itself for much longer, and it could be that the men's Hundred will one day join forces with the T20 Blast, although this would leave the women on their own, which would not be popular.

If this were to happen, The Hundred would then become part of a new T20 competition, with private money invested in it. The ECB has already refused one offer from a commercial organisation eager to buy its way into The Hundred. In turning it down, they said, quite reasonably, that it is too early in the life of the competition to be able to have an accurate guess at its value in the years ahead. The time is bound to come when private investment can no longer be refused, and in May 2024 it was announced that plans to encourage private investment in The Hundred are well advanced and at this early stage all eighteen counties are agreed on how the money should be split between them. An American bank is already rolling up its sleeves to lure investors from India, Australia, the United States and elsewhere to invest in The Hundred. The T20 franchise world may have made a slow start in England, but it is now doing its best to catch up. When that moment arrives and outside finance comes in, the ECB will have to be careful not to lose control of part of the English season. If some of the competition is in private hands, there could easily be the problem of who owns what. At this early stage, Thompson and Gould have made all the right noises about this enigmatic competition, and a lot of other things which cannot now be foreseen may have happened to change the landscape still further before 2028.

The profit-and-loss account of The Hundred in its present form is also a major worry. The ECB, pre-Thompson and Gould, doing everything it could to make sure its new infant was seen in the best possible light, announced that in its second year the competition made a decent profit of several million pounds, but this was not easy to believe and depended on what costs were included. The Hundred was given extraordinary publicity, even though nearly all the world's best players refused to be lured by the competition. So far, in its first years precious few household names have been involved, but even so, the wage bill has not been small. After its first two years, the counties were extremely worried about the obfuscating ways of the ECB when it came to its finances. It was either unwilling or unable to provide clear-cut details when it came to the amount of money spent on the competition. It is surprising that those in charge should have been either so incompetent or simply unwilling to face up to what had actually happened.

As a result, the counties got together and asked Fanos Hira, the chair of Worcestershire and a highly qualified chartered accountant, to head an inquiry to get to the bottom of this. Hira was shown the full figures, which did not make happy reading. They showed that The Hundred had been extremely expensive to set up and run and had cost at least £110m in its first two years; it was also losing money and likely to lose more as it continued. The profligacy of the ECB had been painful, and this increased expenditure stretched much further than The Hundred itself, for the staff numbers of the ECB had increased by a colossal 83 per cent during Tom Harrison's time as CEO, which meant that the wage bill had shown a correspondingly enormous leap.

The founders of The Hundred have a lot to answer for, even though a great many people who have been to watch The Hundred thought it was wonderful experience and great entertainment – and, as we have seen, I am one of those. We will all surely be back for the next few years. But the competition will take some sorting out and it would be lovely to think the best bits can somehow be kept, but it will not be easy, any more than it is easy to guess what will happen after 2028.

In 2023, in order to try and get round the effects of giving August to The Hundred, the ECB had cobbled together an extraordinary September, having extended the season almost into October. In the old days, cricket bags were on their way up to the attic by then. New Zealand arrived to play four T20 matches against England, and then four 50-over ODIs. The last one was on 15 September at Lord's, and five days later, at Headingley, England began a series of three ODIs against Ireland which ended on 26 September.

This allowed the players just about enough time to go home, pack and then get to the airport in order to catch the flight to Ahmedabad, where England were playing New Zealand again in the opening match of the World Cup nine days later, on 5 October. If I had had any serious thoughts of making my way to India after the England season had ended in anything other than an aeroplane, and most certainly not in a 1921 Rolls-Royce, for this match, the gentlemen in the white coats would have been hastily summoned. This crazily packed schedule caused the players, through the Professional Cricketers' Association (PCA), to protest soon after the start of the 2024 season. Over two-thirds said too much cricket was being played, but if the amount of cricket was reduced so would the contents of their pay packets which would go down as well. The players said they needed three blank days between the four-day County Championship matches, and at times they had not been arriving home until one o'clock in the morning after away matches and were expected to play again the next day. This situation was the product of unthinking administrators driven by the lure of money.

The England setup were happy to believe that all they, the holders, needed to do was to turn up in India and everything would fall into place and they would again win the competition. The match against New Zealand was an event the citizens of Ahmedabad found distinctly underwhelming. The television cameras seemed to have a tough job locating a big enough group of spectators on the vast new ground to suggest to viewers that there was a decent crowd. It was not an exciting game either, for England were annihilated by the huge margin of nine wickets. The Indian administrators had got the script badly wrong, for they surely should have had India playing in this opening game, and then there would not have been a single empty seat in a stadium which holds close to 150,000. This would have been the best possible PR exercise for the competition. Now, in spite of their activities in September, England's batters were still in Hundred mode, while the bowlers all looked as if they wished they were somewhere else. England's progress in the tournament continued to be an humiliating disaster. They were well beaten by Afghanistan, and so it continued, with them losing six of their first seven matches. This meant that far from reaching the knockout stages, they were in the ignominious position of having their work cut out to finish as one of the top eight teams, in order to qualify for the next Champions Trophy in 2025.

One exciting aspect of the World Cup was the excellent form shown by some of the seemingly less fashionable sides. Afghanistan, a country where there is great cricketing talent, is now ruled by the Taliban and cricket is not high on their list of priorities, which does not help the development and spread of the game. Yet they now beat England and Pakistan with some ease, which shows that their game is fast improving in spite of the country's unhelpful political leadership. Afghanistan's form in India was repeated soon afterwards, in 2024, when they reached the semi-final of the T20 World Cup in the West Indies and the United States – which would have made Groucho sit up. Afghanistan's progress is the best possible news for the game as a whole, which has just become an official Olympic sport for the Los Angeles games in 2028, although at the moment of writing we cannot be sure what form of the game will be played there.

The Netherlands, where cricket has been played for many years, were also successful in India, beating both Bangladesh and South Africa. Their showing is also good news for the game, for it means that it is likely that yet another country will soon be thought good enough to join an increasingly important second tier of emerging Test and T20 match-playing countries. This helps to give the game a stronger base across the world, even if it does look as if these new members will find themselves playing a lot of limited-over cricket and few Test matches. Traditionally, full membership of the ICC brings with it the right to play Test cricket, but from the way the cricket world is going, this may soon have to be changed.

The problems caused by the competing demands of the franchise world and the international game were once again highlighted during the World Cup. With atrocious timing, forced upon them by circumstances beyond their control, the ECB released during the competition the details of the new central contracts which were being offered to twenty-nine England players across all three formats of the game. It would have been better if this had not happened until after the World Cup. England's disastrous performance must have meant that the value of some of the players had fallen while some may no longer have had a future in the ODI game and others, like Joe Root, would now be used only for Test cricket. As it was, the ECB had to act when they did because the players' existing contracts ended while the World Cup was still being played, which would have meant they were out of contract. The ECB would therefore have temporarily lost control of them and the franchise owners may well have swooped down with irresistible offers.

With so much money about, the players find themselves in a stronger position than ever. Ben Stokes, for example, was offered a new three-year contract which he turned down in favour of a one-year agreement. He took the view that the contract he will be offered in a year's time will be for a significantly larger amount of money than the one that was now on offer. This looks like a shrewd business move, no doubt inspired by his agent, which again illustrates the extraordinary difference between then and now. It would hardly have been surprising if worries about the contracts had not taken some of the players' minds off the job in hand.

While this was going on, Rob Key, the man in charge of English cricket, flew out to India with twenty-nine contracts in his briefcase. Once they had all been signed, he took them back to London, locked them in his office safe, left his dirty laundry at home and then came back to Kolkata for England's last match, against Pakistan. Unless he was badly short of air-miles, it struck me as a masterpiece of faulty planning and reminded me of what Ernest Hemingway once said to Marlene Dietrich: 'Kraut, never confuse movement with action.' As it was, Key's presence in Kolkata may have been the inspiration England needed for victory.

One of the joys of cricket for me is the game's ability to keep coming up with the controversial, the comical and the completely unexpected. One day, the news burst upon us from Delhi that Angelo Mathews of Sri Lanka, who had come in at the fall of their fourth wicket in their match against Bangladesh, had become the first batter in 146 years of international cricket to be timed out.

The World Cup was approaching the final knockout stage when Bangladesh and Sri Lanka met in the qualifying round. This was a relatively meaningless game except that it would also help to decide which of the countries playing in the World Cup would qualify for the Champions Trophy in 2025. This was very much on the mind of Shakib Al Hasan, the Bangladesh captain. He had won the toss and put Sri Lanka in to bat, and Mathews had come in during the 25th over, when they had reached 135–4.

The playing conditions for the competition stated that an incoming batsman must be ready at the wicket within two minutes of a wicket falling – in first-class cricket it is three minutes. Mathews arrived with five seconds to spare. It was then that he tried to tighten the strap on his helmet and it broke. He signalled to the dressing room that he needed a new helmet and walked off to meet it. It was while this was going on that Shakib, who was also the bowler, appealed to the umpire, Marais Erasmus, who then told Mathews, who had not yet put on his new helmet, that he was out. At first, Mathews thought it was a joke, but when he realised Erasmus was being serious and the decision had been ratified, not surprisingly he became extremely angry with both the umpires and Shakib. In his fury, he threw the replacement helmet down on the ground as he stalked off.

Shakib later said that one of his players had told him that if he appealed, Mathews would be given out. 'The umpire asked me if I was serious [when the appeal was made]. And I said, "It's in the Laws."' Then Shakib went on, 'I felt like I was at war. Whatever I had to do, I did it.' Mathews made it abundantly clear how he saw it: 'It was obviously disgraceful from Shakib and Bangladesh. If they want to take wickets like that and stoop down to that level, there's something wrong, drastically ... within two minutes I was at the crease.'

Shakib is unlikely to be awarded the freedom of Colombo anytime soon, just as Alex Carey had not been in danger of being made an honorary member of MCC after his long-range stumping of Bairstow. Anyone who thinks that Shakib's behaviour would never have occurred in the old days should remember that England's captain, Douglas Jardine, took Bodyline to Australia in 1932–33 in order to stifle the genius of Don Bradman and arrogantly defended the tactic when batters, but not the Don, were injured by the torrent of bouncers bowled deliberately at their bodies. Bradman was curtailed rather than neutralised and still managed to average just over fifty runs per innings. Jardine certainly would not have been squeamish about timing out a batter if the opportunity had arisen.

My view is that while Bairstow was dozy and had deserved his fate at Lord's, Mathews, with a suddenly-broken helmet in his hand, was a victim of faulty legislation and did not deserve to be given out. He had arrived at the crease in time and it was simply fate that the helmet strap had broken when it did. If he had had any idea that he would be given out for taking the time to collect a new helmet, he would have faced one ball with his broken strap. Then he would have signalled for a new helmet and all would have been well. That regulation needs to be amended.

In the days before the Decision Review System (DRS), an experienced umpire, seeing a batter's helmet had broken like this, would almost certainly have felt able to use his common sense and not given him out. But with DRS coming into play, the letter of the law has to apply and there is sadly no longer any room for common sense to come to the rescue. Mathews was scurrilously treated.

The turmoil and tumult of the modern cricket world does not only affect the best sides, and another story which was both comical (unless you were involved) and disturbing at the same time came to my notice during the World Cup, if from a much more minor level of the game. There are about two thousand licensed cricketers in France, where the women's game is developing well too. The governing body, France Cricket, report annually to the ICC and receive financial help for the development of the game. This amounts to an annual grant of over €100,000, but the integrity of those who run the governing body in Paris is being questioned.

France Cricket, who demand an annual subscription from every registered player, have told the ICC that they are using this grant to encourage the development of both the women's game and youth cricket. The ICC are particularly keen to support this and France Cricket keeps them posted about how rapidly both are growing. But the cricketing community are accusing France Cricket of boosting their figures in order to impress the ICC, so that they continue to receive this not insignificant financial handout, although those who run France Cricket are refusing to say how it is being spent.

According to their critics, the organisation advertises forthcoming women's matches which do not appear to have been played. Apparently, France Cricket later publishes scorecards for matches which critics say have not been played and these are sent to the ICC. They also allege that France Cricket is not being transparent about the way the ICC grant is being spent and how very little of it goes on the development of the game. The cricket community in France are claiming that the behaviour of the governing body is seriously holding back the development of the game in France. It seems to me that the ICC would be well advised to put a call through to Inspector Maigret as quickly as they can.

The World Cup ended in Ahmedabad with Australia beating India in the final by the comfortable margin of six wickets, leaving a billion and more Indian fans in the depths of despair. Australia were brilliantly led by Pat Cummins, who put India in on a sudden whim and then helped bowl them out with a wonderfully disciplined display of controlled hostility for 240. Australia then lost three important wickets before Travis Head, who had opened the batting, played the innings of his life, making 137 not out, while at the other end Marnus Labuschagne showed that his adhesive qualities had not melted under the hot Indian sun and also had their uses in the one-day game.

The India of 2023 had moved on a long way from the India that we had found at the end of our drive in that lovely old Rolls-Royce nearly fifty years before, not least because Tony Greig's England side went on to win that series in 1976–77. Just before the end of the World Cup now, there was one piece of cheerful news for England, which was that Freddie Flintoff was ready to be involved once again with cricket. He had made a remarkable recovery after an horrendous car crash while making an episode of *Top Gear* for BBC television.

England's cricketers badly needed Flintoff's inspiring example, not only as a player, but also as a human being – no one will forget that wonderful moment when he put a consoling arm around a devastated Brett Lee at the non-striker's end a moment after England had beaten Australia by two runs at Edgbaston in 2005.

It was incredible that he had made so good a recovery after suffering such a dreadful accident and the resulting injuries to his face. Through it all, Flintoff had remained amazingly strong both physically and mentally, and yet humble and modest at the same time. After this World Cup fiasco in India and then their uncertain form in the T20 World Cup in the West Indies, it looked as if his inspiring example needs to find its way back into the England white-ball dressing room as fast as possible.

14

NEW KIDS ON THE BLOCK

'The United States and Saudi Arabia join in the fun'

THERE has been a trail of cricket in the United States in these pages ever since Groucho Marx's unlikely appearance at Lord's was allowed to creep into the Introduction. This was followed by the posthumous antics of his ghost at Edgbaston and then back at Lord's in 2023. First-class cricket was played in America until the First World War, at which point the game bowed its head to baseball, a not-so-distant blood relation. It is mildly ironical now that cricket owes its at any rate temporary re-emergence in America largely to India and the IPL: former colonial cousins making common cause, perhaps.

The main inspiration behind the foundation in the United States of the Major League Cricket (MLC) T20 franchise – whose first season was played in July 2023 – will have come from the IPL, four of whose franchises have a financial interest in four of the first six franchises in America. The other two were partly financed by Australian money coming from Cricket New South Wales and Cricket Victoria. (Indian influence had reached Australia through its own T20 franchise, the Big Bash, which although financed by Kentucky Fried Chicken will have been inspired and underpinned by the example of the IPL.) In addition to the Indian financial interest in MLC, there was a sprinkling of Subcontinental players in the six American teams and, in the early stages, successful Indian businessmen in the States were eagerly flexing their financial muscles in support.

Major League Cricket was several years in the planning, and one reason was that those involved wanted to make sure this new competition had the full approval of the ICC, which would instantly guarantee cricketing respectability, and this took time. But it is a mystery why it took quite so long, considering the strength of India's influence within the ICC.

Australia has had a long, if somewhat tentative interest in cricket in the United States and, over the years, a number of private tours have gone there from Australia. That wonderfully idiosyncratic leg-spinner Arthur Mailey, one of the most delightful and engaging of characters ever to have played the game, took 99 wickets for Australia in the early twenties with his extravagant leg-breaks and googlies. In 1932, six years after his retirement, he took a party of twelve players including Don Bradman, whose presence the sponsors insisted upon, on a tour of North America. The tour was financed mainly by the Canadian Pacific Railway and the team played 51 one-day games in 60 days: quite a schedule, although the opposition was not greatly testing.

Mailey was a frequent visitor to England, and when I was a child, I was lucky enough to meet him several times, for he often stayed in Norfolk with friends of my parents who organised splendid boys' cricket matches in the early fifties. He was an old man then but enormously friendly, with an outrageous twinkle in his eye. He had a great sense of humour, a necessary attribute for any wrist spinner, and he tried to show us how to bowl leg-breaks and googlies. He occasionally spoke about this tour to America, and especially on the occasion when he brought Don Bradman along to Norfolk with him. Mailey was a great admirer of the American fast bowler Barton King, who played in Philadelphia from 1890 for more than twenty years. King was probably the best cricketer America has ever produced, and he took a great many wickets when sides from Philadelphia toured England soon after the turn of the century, playing matches against some of the first-class counties. Mailey, who met King some years after he had finished playing, liked to include him in his side whenever he was asked to pick a World XI. He loved talking about King and told us that he was the bowler who invented swing, which 'he was able to explain better than any expert on ballistics'.

I met Mailey again when I was a few years older and he once told a wonderful story about King which may have needed a touch of poetic licence, but I hope not. King was playing for Belmont, his club in Philadelphia, against another club, Trenton, whose captain arrived very late that day, but just in time to be ready to bat when his side's ninth wicket fell. On his way out to bat, he was heard to say that this batting collapse would never have happened if he had been able to get there in time. King, who was bowling, overheard this assertion. He immediately sent all his fielders off the ground except for one, whom he stationed with care at fine leg, just over the boundary. The non-striker asked King what the fielder was doing there, but he didn't answer the question and walked back to his mark. He now bowled to the Trenton captain; the late inswinger hit the outside of his leg stump and the ball went straight to the man over the fine-leg boundary. King turned to the non-striker and said, 'Now you know why I left him there.'

Cricket has always been the poor relation among the world's major sports and one reason is that the game has not prospered at any significant level in America after it had ceased to be a lingering adjunct of colonialism. When the IPL and T20 franchise cricket began, however, it suddenly became a game with a huge money-making potential, and it was then only a matter of time before the owners of the IPL turned their attention to the huge migrant population from the Subcontinent living in the USA. They at once embraced their fellow countrymen who had climbed to the top of the business world there, and they were only too happy to come up with the $120m needed to get the idea of an American T20 franchise tournament off the ground.

Although they had been planning it for a long time, it was in the end a mad rush to get everything ready for the start in 2023. Two grounds were prepared – they would have liked two or three more, but any others that might have been available were nowhere near the standard required. The two they came up with were good enough, at least for this exploratory first year. When it was over, they saw that the expatriate Indian community had responded just as they had hoped. Buying into it the way they did was the start the organisers needed and it was the beginning of the massive PR exercise necessary to try and attract the rest of the country.

In Texas, an old baseball ground which held only 7,200 spectators, had been hastily converted from the former baseball home of the now defunct Texas AirHogs into the Grand Prairie Stadium. The other ground, Church Street Park in Morrisville, North Carolina, was already a cricket ground. It was the smaller of the two, but good enough to help get the competition off the ground if not much more. The comparisons between cricket and baseball would always be there to be made, but for the Indians living in the States the difference would have been huge, and they would surely come running to seize hold of something that had always been such an important part of their heritage. Or that was the thinking, and as far as it went, it proved to be right. They revelled in the ambience of the game and the increased sense of self-identity it will have given them in a foreign land. It made them feel that home was not quite so far away, even if the Grand Prairie Stadium was only the most distant of relations when it came to, say, Eden Gardens in Kolkata, where the official full-house crowd numbers around 100,000, to say nothing of the new Narendra Modi Stadium in Ahmedabad, which fits in nearly 150,000.

Cricket in the United States is being given a double boost because in June 2024 the T20 World Cup was being hosted jointly by the West Indies and the United States. Let's hope those living in America who grew up with cricket do all they can to sell the game to their disbelieving neighbours so that they come along to see what the fuss is about. They will have to be ready to explain the game to their American friends, which, as anyone who has tried knows only too well, is far from easy – as those sitting around Groucho Marx found out all those years ago at Lord's.

By Indian standards, Major League Cricket made a modest start in 2023, with six teams, two small grounds and fifteen games. The smattering of imported talent was joined by players from within the USA, where vibrant league cricket is played by teams of expatriates, most of them of Subcontinental or West Indian origin. With the MLC teams coming from as far away as San Francisco and Los Angeles, Seattle and New York, the two grounds, in Texas and North Carolina, did not have visiting supporters queuing up for seats. Considering this, they did well to sell 80 per cent of the available seating for the whole tournament, taking over $2m in receipts from 70,000 spectators. These may not be big numbers, but the people who went along were those at whom this initial tournament was aimed and their feedback would be extremely important to the future of the competition.

This first sortie – which saw Mumbai Indians New York defeat the Seattle Orcas in the final – was considered to be a success and prompted much excited planning for the future. The organisers were originally hoping that for the second year's competition they would have four grounds ready, with one of the new ones a 34,000-seat pop-up venue in New York City at Van Cortlandt Park in the Bronx. This proved wishful thinking and New York's ground was situated in the Eisenhower Park in the County of Nassau in Long Island with a 34,000 capacity. The other two venues were at Lauderhill in Florida and Grand Prairie in Texas. The World Cup is a joint venture between the ICC and MLC. After the opening

MLC tournament in 2023, we were promised a big new stadium in Los Angeles and within a year or two the hope was that they would have grounds seating between 10,000 and 20,000 in all their key marketplaces. But for 2024 the competition will be back to the original six franchises and these matches will be played on the two grounds used in 2023, Grand Prairie in Texas and Church Street Park in North Carolina. America has been discovering that it takes longer than they will have hoped to build cricket grounds and, as a result, while MLC is growing it is not doing so at the the dizzy pace it was at first envisaged.

A number of good international players, some of them at the stage of their careers where they were edging towards retirement and were unlikely to turn their noses up at a decent pay cheque, were bought by the six franchises. These included Kieron Pollard, Sunil Narine and Andre Russell from the West Indies, Trent Boult from New Zealand and Faf du Plessis and Quinton de Kock from South Africa. Liam Plunkett, already playing regularly in America, and Jason Roy, who gave up his white-ball contract with England to join MLC, were the two imports from England. Then there were the Australians Aaron Finch and Marcus Stoinis, the latter a player who should have a good white-ball future ahead of him, and Rashid Khan from Afghanistan. They will all have had their own reasons for joining up and will have been delighted to take part in such a fascinating adventure. As a result, there were enough decent players around to ensure a reasonable standard, which was important for this exploratory exercise. The expatriate Indian community they were primarily aiming at would not have settled for rubbish cricket. Most of these players will return for a second year when Pat Cummins, Steve Smith, Glenn Maxwell and Travis Head will be leading another Australian sortie to America and the 2024 MLC.

Now, we come to the problems – at least as far as English cricket is concerned. MLC will be played in the middle of the English summer, at around the same time as The Hundred and the T20 Blast. This is also likely to be the time of year that the proposed T20 franchise jamboree in Saudi Arabia will take to the field. It is almost inevitable that the MLC and Saudi Arabian franchises, with their strong Indian support and ownership, will be able to outbid the English franchise-owners when it comes to buying up the best players. This is bound to affect the content, quality and impact of The Hundred and the Blast.

At the same time, the world game is seething with so many other problems arising from the ongoing battle between Test and T20 franchise cricket. As I mentioned earlier in the book, South Africa sent a seriously weakened side to New Zealand to play two Test matches in order to protect their own IPL-inspired T20 franchise. South Africa's contracted players were forbidden by Cricket South Africa from going to New Zealand for matches which were a part of the official ICC World Test Championship. This makes the ICC's subsequent silence on this matter even more astonishing. Only seven of the fourteen of those selected for this tour had played Test cricket and they did not include the captain, Neil Brand.

This decision by CSA was roundly condemned, and former Australian captain Steve Waugh declared it to be a 'defining moment in the death of Test cricket', calling on the ICC and the boards of the 'big three' cricketing countries, England, Australia and India, to intervene in order to 'protect the purest form of the game'. Cricket New Zealand, an uncontentious body if ever there was one, fell over backwards to help. First they tried to move the dates of the tour so that South Africa's best players would be available, but this did not work. They then suggested that the matches should be moved to Darwin in Australia's Northern Territory to make it easier for the South Africans to travel there, but that also was not acceptable.

There is a more than plausible explanation for Cricket South Africa's extraordinary decision. The financial situation for cricket there is dire and the game is almost insolvent. They had no option but to agree to the T20 home series, which is heavily backed by the IPL, being played at the time of the tour to New Zealand because it gave them their only chance of raising the money to pay their leading players enough to keep them in South Africa. Their presence was therefore essential. Cricket in South Africa is low down on the government's list of priorities when it comes to giving financial assistance.

One reason New Zealand were content to play this makeshift side was that they had never before defeated South Africa in a Test series. New Zealand won both matches by big margins, but it was nothing if not a Pyrrhic victory. Yet this first ever series win over South Africa, together with Kane Williamson's batting – he made three hundreds in the two games – will surely have appealed to the New Zealand public and provided some consolation for New Zealand's sponsors. One can only wonder how they and the broadcasters and the public will look at things if this state of affairs continues.

Two other examples of Test cricket playing second fiddle to the limited-over game cropped up as 2023 turned into 2024. First, the West Indies picked a weak side for another series, of only two Test matches, against Australia in January, with their best players unavailable, as usual, because of their T20 franchise commitments. The West Indies board is always short of money and their players are not well paid. This makes it understandable that they snap up any franchise contracts, which means the West Indies selectors are almost never able to pick their best side. Although the Australians had much the better of things, the West Indies won a remarkable victory by eight runs in the second Test at the Gabba in Brisbane. This was their first victory in a Test match in Australia for twenty-seven years. The Australians enjoy seeing England beaten 5–0 in the Ashes, but the present West Indies side does not have the same pull, and on that last exciting day at the Gabba there were only a handful of spectators in the ground.

In the second example, Pakistan played three Tests in Australia over Christmas and New Year in 2023–24. For the final match, the New Year Test in Sydney, the Pakistan selectors decided to rest their best fast bowler, Shaheen Afridi, so that he would be in good shape for the five T20 games they were about to play in New Zealand. This decision, which seems likely to have been made in accordance with Shaheen's own wishes, brought withering criticism from those two great Pakistan fast bowlers Wasim Akram and Waqar Younis, who both emphasised strongly that Test cricket was the best and most important form of the game. Waqar said that he would never have missed a Test match and that Shaheen's workload in the first two Tests had been far from excessive. It somehow seemed like a dose of rough justice that in the third match of the T20 series, which New Zealand won 4–1, their opening batsman, Finn Allen, hit 16 sixes in his innings of 137, which dear old Groucho would have loved. Allen will also be playing in the second year of the MLC.

These decisions are a great threat to Test cricket as we know it, and this is why I had hoped that meeting at Lord's in early July would turn out to be a peace conference, but, alas, the franchise lot did not at this stage seem willing to give much ground. If the present situation continues, it would reduce Test cricket to a most unsatisfactory sort of second-XI competition which would quickly become both boring and irrelevant. Above all, Test cricket as we know it is a demonstration of excellence as the world's best players challenge each other, but, as we have seen, increasingly this is no longer what is happening.

It is, at the time of writing, impossible to gauge the long-term effect reborn cricket in the USA will have on the rest of the game, let alone on America. The IPL will naturally do all it can to protect its investment and make sure the MLC builds on its satisfactory beginning. There is one danger: if it becomes a real hit, the Americans will want to make the most of it and who knows what that will lead to?

One can only wonder about the additional streamlining that might be proposed if it is felt that the present mix is not quite strong enough for the American market. Will they try and bring the overs down to ten? Will boundaries be shortened even further, so that the flow of homers becomes too much even for Groucho? And what will happen if Mumbai, Kolkata and Chennai, the engine rooms of the IPL, are not prepared go along with it? But if American enthusiasm does prevail, what will we be left with? There are already T10 competitions, in Abu Dhabi and the West Indies, and there are plans for something similar in Sri Lanka and Zimbabwe. There will hardly be time to settle comfortably in your seat, and I could see Groucho and the Ancient Mariner having a lively chat about all this. The T10 game lasts for ninety minutes and is known as The Sixty (balls per innings) and its supporters include the former England one-day captain Eoin Morgan, who also thinks T10 is the right format for the Olympic Games. Virender Sehwag and Shahid Afridi are two more influential supporters of this minuscule affair. So, watch this space.

The white-ball world is made almost daily more confusing by the far-reaching tentacles of the IPL. The pursuit of wealth is man's inalienable right, but there comes a time when one begins to feel that when that pursuit becomes as relentless as it has, we are moving closer than ever to the point of no return when the game is ruled only by the urge to make money. The people who are in charge of the T20 franchise game in India now seem to be hell-bent on creating as much wealth for themselves as they can regardless of anything, especially the history and tradition of the game. They revel in the power and influence that comes with their success. When I began this book I feared I would soon be looking down the barrels of a weapon that might destroy even the modern version of Test cricket; in the time I have taken to get to this point, relevant people have been talking and things may have just begun to happen. There is room for hope. I begin to feel there are influential forces about who realise the danger of putting all the

NEW KIDS ON THE BLOCK   191

game's eggs in the T20 franchise basket and are anxious to prevent this from happening.

Let me now go back to the original purpose of this chapter, which, before I sidetracked myself, was to look at the newcomers to the T20 franchise world. The two principal ones are Major League Cricket and the budding league in Saudi Arabia, a country which is throwing enormous sums at sport. The Saudis have promised no less than $5 billion to launch their T20 franchise competition. As we have seen, both these newcomers are potential threats to the game in England as it is presently structured. If the IPL does buy its way into English cricket, and I shall be surprised if this does not happen, its right hand might soon be fighting against the left, which is another intriguing prospect. Saudi Arabia and the MLC are both children of the IPL, to whom they owe their existence, and will do their bidding.

The IPL and Saudi Arabia have been in discussions for a while. The Saudis want to make their competition the richest and most glamorous of all, and the IPL has already made one important concession to help them on their way. The Indian board, the BCCI, do not allow their cricketers to play in any other franchise competitions, but they have indicated that they will be allowed to play in Saudi Arabia, which is presumably why none have signed for the MLC. The BCCI may even have done this to ensure that the Saudis do not one day attempt to go it alone. The Saudis are planning a tournament which lasts for two months, while the IPL is said to be thinking about turning theirs into a three-month event. It is unlikely the two competitions will be played simulta-neously now that the Indians are allowed to play in both. We could therefore have five consecutive months of T20 franchise cricket in India and Saudi Arabia. MLC will be played in the same period, and one can only wonder about the composition of any side that comes to England to play Test cricket during these summer months. The hope is that the BCCI will be able to persuade the all-embracing franchise-owners to release their players for Test cricket. There is so much at stake.

There is one unhappy cloud hanging over all the money that Saudi Arabia is paying to enhance its place in the world of sport. It is being said that this T20 tournament is intended to be another big step along the path towards gaining international respectability and taking the world's attention away from Saudi Arabia's shocking record over human rights. The rulers are being accused of being involved in a process of sportswashing. What will the eventual reaction be to this?

The Hundred is not under the IPL umbrella, yet, although it was obviously spawned by the IPL's influence and example. Because it is deliberately different, 100 balls as opposed to the almost universal 20 overs or 120 balls, there is an element of rebellion in its make-up which will not have been lost on India. Another factor which almost certainly and understandably plays a part in all this is that for many years Indian cricket had to obey the firm instructions issued from Lord's, where the ICC was based and from where, with considerable local influence being brought to bear, the game was ruled. All that has now gone, with the ICC headquarters having moved to Dubai. India, who produce 80 per cent of the game's worldwide income, are very much in control of cricket's immediate destiny. They will be understandably happy that everyone, especially England, should now respect this.

Then there are the other recent newcomers to the franchise world. The International League T20 (ILT20) in the United Arab Emirates (UAE) is comprised of six franchises playing in Dubai, Abu Dhabi and Sharjah and had its first season in 2023. The Abu Dhabi Knight Riders is owned by the Knight Rider Group, which began life as the owner of the Kolkata Knight Riders. In its first years, the statistics of the ILT20 matches were not included in players' career records because the UAE is not a Full Member of the ICC. The ILT has now been granted official List-A status and is the first of the Associate Member T20 franchises to be elevated like this. The league's close attachment to the IPL and therefore the BCCI will obviously have helped this process and lends more weight to the argument that the ICC bends increasingly to the will of the BCCI and therefore of the IPL, for the former effectively owns the latter.

Now we come to the Pakistan Super League (PSL), vying with the IPL for first place on the Subcontinent and fighting a losing battle. When the PSL played its first season, in 2016, with five franchises, the games were played in the UAE. It was not until 2021 that security was considered good enough for the fixtures to be moved to Pakistan. The competition prospers, as does, and perhaps more surprisingly, the franchise league which was set up in 2022 in Nepal. By the end of 2023, a total of ten T20 franchise leagues had been set up around the world, and no doubt there are still more on the drawing board, to say nothing of what is happening in the world of T10.

Those of us who love and want to preserve Test cricket will by now realise that it will need a miracle to reverse a seemingly inexorable process which looks as if it will lead first to the trivialisation and then to the gradual disappearance of Test cricket. But, and we must be thankful for small mercies, the game of cricket, albeit an amazingly different game to the one those of my generation learned to love, will still be flourishing. India beat England 4–1 in the 2023–24 Test series in India having lost the first Test, which must have heightened local interest. This final result will have caused great jubilation in India and the hope is that it may have underlined the ongoing importance of Test cricket in a country which is being led unblinkingly down the path of T20 franchise cricket. There have been rumours, too, that the BCCI is aware of this and wants to make sure the importance of Test cricket is understood by the IPL, who might as a result begin to think differently. If this is so, it is an extremely important shaft of light to brighten what has increasingly seemed to be a bleak future. It is also worth pointing out that Bazball, on spinning Indian pitches against surely the best Test side in the world, was not seen at anything like its best. In fact, events in that recent series will have given McCullum and Stokes plenty to think about, as well as a series of blinding headaches. But, at least, there were no draws. McCullum and Stokes must be beginning to understand that Bazball is not a one-size-fits-all solution for Test cricket. Would Bazball ever work in Indian conditions against their high-class spin bowling? Probably not.

15

FRIENDLY BANTER

'What has cricket come to?'

ONE of the reasons those of us who love cricket find the game irresistible is that it represents everything that is decent in life. The immortal phrase 'it is not cricket' plays an important part in the standing of the game. It stretches far beyond the parameters of cricket itself and is used to describe anything in life that is underhand and does not measure up to accepted standards. In the English language, at any rate, the game is portrayed as a talisman of morality and honesty. Imagine the shock, therefore, when this elegant and stately idea of English cricket was blown to pieces the day before the start of the second Ashes Test match, at Lord's, in June 2023. The Independent Commission for Equity in Cricket (ICEC) handed in its massive, far-reaching and explosive report just as the finishing touches were being applied to the famous ground. It was doubly ironic, for not only is Lord's nothing if not the high temple of the game, but also this Test match, like all the others in the series, was to see cricket at its best and most compelling.

The ICEC had been set up by Ian Watmore, who was chair of the ECB for just thirteen months, and his chief executive, Tom Harrison, whom he inherited, and was inspired by the murder of George Floyd by a white policeman in Florida in May 2020. Watmore's choice as chair of the commission was Ms Cindy Butts, who had long experience in dealing with issues connected with equity, diversity and inclusion (EDI). Now, their extensive report filled 317 pages and was produced after more than 4,000 people had been interviewed. The conclusions were shattering: 'Institutional racism, class-based discrimination, elitism and sexism are widespread and deep-rooted in English cricket.' In other words, the game was morally rotten from top to bottom.

By then, the report had been given even greater significance by the devastating accusations by the Pakistan-born Azeem Rafiq, about the racist behaviour he and other cricketers with an Asian background had encountered while they were involved with Yorkshire cricket. Rafiq went so far as to say that what happened to him at Yorkshire took him to the brink of taking his own life. These accusations led to violent upheavals within the administration of what was for years England's best-known and most successful cricketing county. After the Yorkshire chair, Roger Hutton, stood down, a retired political figure, Lord Patel, was shoehorned in to take his place and immediately authorised a payment of around £200,000 to be made by Yorkshire to Rafiq. A number of celebrated players – including Michael Vaughan, the former captain of England, and three other former England players, Matthew Hoggard, Tim Bresnan and Gary Ballance – were accused of making offensive racial remarks to the Asian players in the county side which, in their defence, they considered to be nothing more than 'friendly banter'. In the end, the Cricket Discipline Commission (CDC) found some of the case against Hoggard and Bresnan proved, and Vaughan was cleared. Most of the coaching staff were dismissed, and the chief executive, Mark Arthur, was eventually forced to resign. The leading figures on both sides of the argument, including Rafiq himself, came to Westminster to be interviewed by a parliamentary committee. It was all greeted by a mixture of shock, dismay, injured disbelief and, it has to be said, a touch of self-righteous bravado, but the unanswered question was inescapable: had it really been as bad as this, and if so, how had it been allowed to sink to these levels?

The ICEC was set up to examine discrimination in English cricket and came back with an horrific answer which stretched far beyond the game and into society as a whole. All of the problems the ICEC has identified are appalling and it is alarming to think that attitudes like this are still prevalent even to a limited extent in modern Britain. This is not being written in any way to let cricket off the hook, but views like this do not belong to just one small segment of society, which is what cricket is.

This goes as much for the approach of some people to mass immigration as maybe it does to the behaviour in the Yorkshire dressing room when faced with what are considered to be outsiders. Of course it should never happen and I am in no way trying to excuse behaviour that is completely indefensible and intolerable, but simply trying to find a reason for it. But what this cannot explain and is utterly beyond comprehension is another of the commission's discoveries. They found that in club and more minor cricket some players from overseas were held down, presumably by their fellow players, and urinated upon. Some were even forced to drink urine. There is something seriously wrong if the perpetrators of this cannot, even now, be made to pay for what they have done.

When it comes to the perceived lack of respect for both women's cricket and its players, this is, as much as anything, a matter of old bad habits dying hard. Women's cricket has come a long way in the last few years, but inevitably there are still people who remember their game when it produced nothing like the entertainment or the skills it does today although of course respect should not depend on quality. I remember early in my commentary career watching a men's Test match at Headingley which finished in three days. I went back to London when the match ended on the Saturday evening and Peter Baxter, the producer of *Test Match Special*, asked me to go to The Oval the next day to commentate on the women's Test match against Australia. I remember Rachael Heyhoe Flint, England's captain from 1966 to 1977, who did so much for the women's game, making a big hundred against some accurate spin bowling. It was a long afternoon with very few runs and lots of maiden overs, which did not make for much excitement, and it was hard work in the commentary box and for a sparse crowd. It was all so different from the women's game today, even though some people have been slow to appreciate the remarkable improvement, but happily this seems to be changing fast.

We now come to elitism and class-based discrimination. I played a lot of cricket when I was at school at Eton College before going on to Cambridge University. Both these places will probably be regarded as institutions which harboured if not taught class-based discrimination. I suppose there was a certain nose-in-the-air snobbery, but only because at Eton when I was there, we were all of a sort and knew our way round accordingly – although we too formed our own protective squares, which again would have been a sort of instinctive defence mechanism against intrusion. At Cambridge the first captain I played under, in 1958, was the redoubtable future England captain Ted Dexter, who was roundly known as 'Lord Ted'. I could not live up to that and, indeed, was not selected by him for that year's match against Oxford.

At the risk of being thought mildly flippant in an extremely serious context, the first player from India I came across was the fourteen-year-old Nawab of Pataudi, who revealed an extraordinary ability with the bat playing for Winchester College in 1956. He went on, like his father, to captain India, even after losing an eye in a car crash. I could be in retrospective trouble here because we threw Pataudi into the swimming pool on the first evening of a two-day game, but this did not in any way dampen his batting skills or his charm the next morning. The Cambridge side at the end of the fifties was quite a cosmopolitan affair and I was fascinated and delighted by my overseas team-mates. They lent a touch of excitement to almost everything, not only with their form on the field of play, but also with their lifestyle off it, neither of which could be matched by their Anglo-Saxon colleagues. I remember especially the joy of Santosh Reddy's twinkling foot-work and wristy strokeplay, which was matched only by the exuberant form he showed behind the wheel of his sports car during the week I spent in his home city of Calcutta during a Test match in early 1964.

On a more serious note, it was felt by some, including the ICEC and the committee of the MCC, that continuing to hold the annual match between Eton College and Harrow School at Lord's was an elitist mistake. This fixture was first played in 1805 on the first of the three grounds set up by Thomas Lord. This made it the oldest fixture at Lord's and it is the only remaining link between the present ground and the first. The high-handed way in which the MCC committee tried to remove the game without consulting the members caused a furore. After a lengthy squabble, when the members looked like winning the vote on the future of this game and the University Match between Oxford and Cambridge, it was agreed to continue both games because of their historic importance – the University Match was first played in 1827 – for at least another five years, when the issue will again be debated. Of course, the continuation of these games at Lord's will be seen by some as both elitist and class-based discrimination by the MCC. The club is also planning competitions for schools and universities with the finals being played at Lord's. The MCC is the guardian of cricket history and must surely not wantonly jettison its historical links without careful thought.

With the huge number of Asians living in the country, it is appalling that so few from this background have come through to the top echelons of the game. Their talent is indisputable and if they had been given a fair opportunity to develop their game, we would surely have seen many more come through. As it is, they will undoubtedly have come up against attitudes and obstacles which will have made it harder for them to get through to the next stage. This pathway which leads ultimately to county cricket and beyond must be made easier for players from all backgrounds to access, and cheaper too, for the expense will have made it impossible for many to start this journey. This must be done quickly so that the immigrant community can see not only that the opportunity is there for them, but also that they are encouraged to make use of it. Perhaps a new Saqlain Mushtaq or Sachin Tendulkar will then one day be playing for England.

West Indians living in England have suffered similarly. Forty years ago there were a good number of all-West Indian club sides across the country showing off their own infectious style of play and they were happily accepted, their exhilarating influence doing much for the game in the UK. Brilliant West Indians like Devon Malcolm, Gordon Greenidge and Phil De Freitas learned their game here, and what wonderful ambassadors for the sport they have been. Greenidge plied his trade with great brilliance on behalf of Barbados and the West Indies and Hampshire, and who will forget his amazing 214 not out which won a Test match against David Gower's England side at Lord's in 1984? Malcolm bowled at frightening speed for England, and his 9–57 against South Africa at The Oval in 1994 will be never be forgotten and is unlikely ever to be improved upon. DeFreitas was an important member of Mike Gatting's Ashes-winning side in Australia in 1986–87 and a considerable all-rounder. And there have been plenty of others.

I have to admit that I was once accused of being racist in my writing, and it is ironical after what I have just written that it was by the West Indians. In the eighties and nineties, when I was in Australia I wrote for *The Australian*, the only national newspaper in the country, owned by Rupert Murdoch. The West Indies were touring Australia and one day I wrote a piece which touched upon the West Indies tour to New Zealand in 1979–80, a three-match series won by New Zealand which was probably the most ill-tempered Test series ever to have been played. The New Zealand umpire Fred Goodall was probably the principal reason for this. He was an umpire who loved not only to make his somewhat bristly and self-important presence felt, but he also thrived on controversy. When New Zealand won the first Test in Dunedin by one wicket, he had upset the West Indians with some of his decisions in a match which saw twelve players given out to lbw decisions, a record at the time. In the second Test in Christchurch, the West Indians considered his umpiring to be heavily biased against them. When, on the fourth morning, there was a huge appeal for a catch behind against Richard Hadlee and Goodall gave him not out, Colin Croft, the bowler, ran in to bowl the next ball and in his final approach to the crease he shoulder-charged Goodall from behind. Earlier, Michael Holding, in an exaggerated follow-through, had kicked out the middle stump when John Parker had survived a similar appeal. The West Indies team locked themselves in their dressing room after the tea interval that day and refused to continue the match for twelve minutes afterwards. Much diplomacy was needed that evening to persuade them to continue not only the game the next day, but also the rest of the tour.

In my piece for *The Australian* I pointed an accusing finger at some of this unbecoming behaviour, and an even bigger finger at the dubious umpiring. Their team now in Australia was being managed by Clyde Walcott, one of the famous three Ws who dominated West Indies cricket after the war. Walcott read my piece and rang up a firm of lawyers. I was simply repeating what had happened in New Zealand as a result of the atrocious umpiring. I was accused of libelling the West Indian team, and in the end Murdoch's News International paid the West Indies barely enough money to take the players in Australia out for a good dinner. One amusing sequel was that during the Test in Sydney which was being played while all this was going on, I was having an early schooner of beer in the bar under the Noble Stand when an attractive girl came up to me waving a big piece of paper. Thinking she wanted my autograph, I began to sign my name on it. 'No, no,' she cried, 'I am serving you with a writ for libel,' to the huge amusement of those around me.

There would be no argument with surely everyone's total disgust and horror at the revelation that an overseas player was urinated on. This, on its own, defies belief and I say again that the perpetrators deserve to be retrospectively punished for this unforgivable bullying behaviour. But even this charge pales before the next, which is that another was forced to drink urine. There are no words to describe the horror of this and it is unbelievable that such despicable behaviour should take place in the twenty-first century let alone between players in a cricket pavilion. Everyone who reads this will see it for what it is, and I only hope it hangs heavy on the consciences of those who did it – in the unlikely event of any of them having one in the first place.

The ECB has already, through its new CEO, Richard Gould, made a sensible and reasoned initial reply to this report. They have promised that certain things will be done at once, while all the issues raised will be thoroughly examined to make sure that appropriate actions are taken to ensure cricket becomes truly a game with a level playing field for everyone. These things are not going to be put right overnight, and the ECB have sensibly avoided knee-jerk reactions, which can sometimes turn out to be counter-productive. They have already said that as far as match fees are concerned, women will now be paid as much as men for playing for their country, which is a modest move in the right direction. Their central contracts will not yet be brought into line with the men because at the moment there is not the money to go round and the women's game does not earn as much as the men's.

So far, the response to the ICEC report has brought the immediate reaction Cindy Butts will have been counting on.

The ICEC was set up by the ECB in March 2021 and eight months later, in November, Azeem Rafiq, who was born in Pakistan and later became a Yorkshire player, made his shocking accusations of institutional racism against the county club. This obviously resonated strongly with Cindy Butts and her colleagues and indeed gave even more point to their final report. She will have been almost as surprised as Azeem Rafiq when, during the winter months of 2023–24, Colin Graves was given back control of Yorkshire Cricket. Graves had been chair of the club from 2012 to 2015, the period for which, after Rafiq's accusations, the club was sanctioned for failing to deal with the 'systemic use of discriminatory and racist language'. Graves himself went on to become the chair of the ECB in 2015, effectively running English cricket for five years.

After Rafiq's accusations had come out, Graves apologised 'personally and unreservedly to anyone who experienced any form of racism at Yorkshire'. Rafiq's complaints cost Yorkshire a great deal of money, as we have seen, but in addition to what I have mentioned earlier, the ECB fined the club £400,000 and took away their right to hold Test matches at Headingley, which was soon restored. Their head of cricket, Martyn Moxon, was sacked and they took Darren Gough away from his broadcasting career to replace Moxon. After two apparently highly paid years, at the end of which the county club was still marooned in the second division of the Championship, he left Headingley and returned to the airwaves.

It was a turbulent time for Yorkshire, and it was not long before they faced bankruptcy. The county already owed the Graves Family Trust over £14m, a further large injection of cash was urgently needed. At that point, in the autumn of 2023, three potential saviours were flexing their muscles. Mike Ashley, the businessman who owns Sports Direct and is always putting his name forward when this sort of rescue operation is needed, had yet again thrown his hat into the ring. One of the franchise owners in the Indian Premier League showed what was only a brief interest in buying into Yorkshire cricket although rumour has it that the IPL franchises are keen to build a financial interest in domestic cricket in England. Then there was Graves and his family trust, which was considered to be the most reliable option. In February 2024 his offer was approved by the Yorkshire membership and this decision was accepted by the ECB. Graves had promised an immediate million pounds in cash coupled with the promise to raise a further four million. He was again installed as chair and Yorkshire were saved – for the time being at any rate.

Graves's return to his old job shocked a number of people. Rafiq immediately accused the ECB of being 'not fit to govern' and again urged Yorkshire's sponsors not to accept the deal and to walk away from the club. He also said that Graves's return 'exposes a failing game'. Cindy Butts was more measured and said 'a lot of concerns' had been raised after Graves's controversial return was approved. And Dame Caroline Dinenage MP, who chaired the Parliamentary Select Committee for Culture, Media and Sport, said, 'The return of Colin Graves to Yorkshire and English cricket risks undermining what progress has been made so far.'

The last few years have also not been entirely happy for the ECB offices at Lord's. Ian Watmore lasted for only thirteen months in the chair. It was on Watmore's watch that the tours to Pakistan by England's men and women in 2021 were cancelled. This was a shameful decision, for Pakistan had toured England during the Covid pandemic in 2020 and the Pakistan board had done everything within its power to ensure the safety of the England players. Touring sides had not visited Pakistan since 2009, when terrorists attacked the Sri Lankan tourists.

Tom Harrison, whom Watmore inherited as chief executive, also had an eventful time in his seven years in office. After negotiating the television deal for Giles Clarke, he presided over a massive increase in staff at the ECB offices, with a corresponding increase in the wage bill, and he helped Colin Graves set up The Hundred, which for all its good points was not the best-thought-out of competitions and, as I have suggested earlier, had been over-promoted. Harrison also supported Watmore in the setting up of the ICEC, although he had apparently ignored the earlier reports of racist behaviour which had previously been coming down from Yorkshire. Harrison had previously worked for the International Management Group, which was the brainchild of Mark McCormack and a business which knew a thing or two about writing good contracts for sportspeople. When Harrison resigned from the ECB, his final severance payout amounted to no less than £1.31m. All credit to him for negotiating such a splendid deal for himself, but since his departure, the ECB have rearranged a few things so that no one in the future will receive such a handsome payout.

There is one ambiguous phrase which keeps recurring in these arguments around Azeem Rafiq and his fellow Asian cricketers which I am sure will have made Cindy Butts prick up her ears. The accused players speak of the remarks which Rafiq and the others found highly offensive – such as the infamous P-word – as being nothing more than 'friendly banter'. When deciding they were not going to take disciplinary action against any of its employees, the Yorkshire club itself used this same phrase as if to justify or at least take the sting out of what had been said. Of course, this was what the people who ran the club were told by their players, and it appears that they chose to look no further. These executives will have had no idea how the words in this 'friendly banter' were used or the tone of voice in which they were uttered, let alone what the essential relationship between the players concerned really was.

It is imperative that we all give the ICEC and its comprehensive final report our full respect and support, and indeed our thanks. These five commissioners have done what the game should have done for itself some time ago. The commission has done its best to make sure that cricket returns to the secure and blameless path we all, in our blindness, imagined the game had been travelling down all along. Don't let's pussyfoot around: there is more than enough evidence to suggest that quite a number of people are never going to be held to account for what has been totally unacceptable behaviour. Let's hope that what has now happened will finally put a stop to it all in the world of cricket. The game is a precious part of our heritage, and we must all do our best to make sure that a Cindy Butts is never again needed to pull us back from these sickening depths.

16

THE MIXTURE
IS RICH

'And what a mess it has left us in'

THE mixture is rich and all over the place. England has just seen one of the best Ashes series ever, T20 franchise tournaments are popping up everywhere, and serious cricket (of the T20 variety) has returned to the United States and is about to blossom in Saudi Arabia. Meanwhile, The Hundred, that illegitimate baby, both loved and yet not trusted, hovers like an awkward misfit over England's summer. Elsewhere, in the first few months of 2024, both South Africa and the West Indies have sent out weakened Test teams because of the contractual demands of T20 franchise competitions, while Pakistan's leading fast bowler was rested from a Test in Australia to be ready for a T20 series in New Zealand.

The dangerous precedents being set are all ganging up against Test cricket and in time may be a threat to its very existence and therefore that of all two-innings cricket if action is not taken. Perhaps the most surprising aspect of this story has been the reluctance of the game's governing body, the ICC, to make even a comment about the changing face of the traditional game. The reason for the ICC's existence is to oversee and protect the game, and yet it appears to be happy to stand aside, act as a bank for the countries involved in international cricket and allow Test cricket to be threatened like this. Cricket South Africa claims it was forced because of financial problems to make the decision not to take its leading players to New Zealand. The hands of the IPL weigh heavily on all these things. Five of the twelve Full Member countries of the ICC – India, Pakistan, Sri Lanka, Bangladesh and Afghanistan – are part of or joined to the Subcontinent, and will not vote against their neighbour's wishes. South Africa and Zimbabwe are supporters of India too, which gives them an automatic majority within the ICC. This means that India is in control of the worldwide game.

On a more positive note, just before finishing this book, I heard that the BCCI are now prepared to speak to the IPL about the importance of not suffocating Test cricket. It may seem curious that India, the epicentre of the T20 franchise world, is still interested in playing Test cricket, but it is brilliant news, for Test cricket's best guarantee of survival would come with the BCCI's support. Unless it is prepared to do this, Test cricket's journey to the margins of the game will continue. Test cricket is such an important stabilising influence and without it, the standards of a game without the necessary balance between bat and ball, will fall alarmingly. For how long will the craze for sixes and thirteen runs an over, hold the world's attention?

Another piece of good news is that Test cricket itself is doing its best to fight back on its own. This depleted West Indies side may have been predictably beaten by ten wickets in Adelaide in the first of the two Tests in Australia, but the West Indies then won a remarkable victory by eight runs in the second, which produced a memorable fairy story to go with it. The hero for the West Indies, an unknown fast bowler, Shamar Joseph, who was only twenty-four and comes from a remote part of Guyana, took 7–68 in Australia's second innings, bowling 12 successive overs on the last day with a nasty injury to his foot.

The previous day when batting, Joseph had been hit on the toe by a yorker from Mitchell Starc and had to retire. He did not at first expect to be able to go to the Gabba the next day, but after a painkilling injection he took the field and proceeded to take seven wickets with a truly great spell of fast bowling which won the match for the West Indies. Sadly, this last day was only watched by just over 3,000 people, and one can't help thinking back to the Gabba in 1960–61, when only a tiny crowd came to watch the final day of the first ever tied Test match, also between Australia and the West Indies.

Like that tied Test, Joseph's match really stirred the cricketing world in a way that, say, the Kolkata Knight Riders beating the Rajasthan Royals in a cliffhanger never would. Nor would we even blink if we heard that the Perth Scorchers had beaten the Hobart Hurricanes by one run off the last ball in Australia's Big Bash League. I am left with one niggling thought: how long will it be before the franchise-owners are on the telephone with a contract which may effectively rule Joseph out of playing again for the West Indies? Happily, though, Joseph himself said soon after the match that he would always be available to play Test cricket for the West Indies. I hope his bank manager agrees with him.

Now, let us nip across to Hyderabad, where, at the end of January 2024, India and England produced a first Test which will also have quickened global pulses a lot more than the efforts of our T20 franchise friends. The Indian spinners, who were always likely to make life difficult for England's batters, bowled them out on the first day for 246 before India made 436. Then Ollie Pope, fully restored to health after being injured in the recent Ashes series but with no real practice behind him after being out of the game for seven months, played a superb record-breaking innings of 196, and India were left to make 231 to win.

Left-arm spinner Tom Hartley, playing in his first Test, then took the first four Indian wickets and soon afterwards the home side found themselves at 119–7. It was now that Hartley came back and broke a dangerous eighth-wicket stand, and he took England to a 28-run victory, with the help of two fine stumpings by Ben Foakes. Hartley took 7–62 and nine wickets in the match. England had been 190 runs behind on first innings, and this was undoubtedly Bazball's most remarkable victory so far. Matches like these show that Test cricket is alive and well, even if England were then well beaten, 4–1, in the series and Bazball came home with a bloody nose, and Pope did too. Let down by his nerves, he made only 118 runs in eight innings in the last four matches.

A third piece of cheering news which burst upon the cricket world as I was nearing the end of this book is that the 2024 president of the MCC, the brilliantly capable Mark Nicholas, has inspired a long-overdue meeting between the leaders of the different facets of the modern game, an event billed as 'World Cricket Connects'. It is shameful that the ICC did not set up a meeting like this long ago. After the 2024 T20 World Cup final in Barbados, the MCC hosted this meeting between the leading protagonists of the T20 franchise game and their rivals from the world of Test cricket, at Lord's later that same week, on 5 July.

The chair of the ICC, Greg Barclay, from New Zealand, was one of the main speakers and had the chance to explain why both he and the ICC have maintained such a deafening silence. He was joined by the redoubtable Manoj Badale, effectively an immensely plausible spokesperson for the IPL. It was interesting to hear how he reacted to the BCCI's views about the need to show concern for Test cricket. We also heard from former South African captain Graeme Smith, who put together his country's T20 competition and is the shrewdest of observers (and one of the best summarisers I commentated with, although it was only briefly and right at the end of my time in the box). Then it was the turn of former Indian opening batter Ravi Shastri, a most influential and articulate figure who was a highly successful television commentator before becoming the coach of the Indian side and who has had a foot in both the Test and T20 camps. Although he felt that T20 would be the principal component of cricket in the future, he was also anxious to preserve Test cricket, in which he made his name.

The England coach Brendon McCullum, architect of Bazball, was there, as was Clare Connor, a former captain of England's women and former president of MCC, who is now deputy chief executive of the ECB, along with Richard Thompson, chair of the ECB. There was an important contribution from the game's leading writer and commentator, former England captain Michael Atherton, whose views are always highly relevant. I shall discuss the huge importance of this meeting more fully in the final chapter.

Cricket South Africa were roundly condemned for protecting their T20 competition at the expense of Test cricket, but as they are almost certainly being steered by their effective paymasters, the IPL, they surely have to do what they are told. Smith should have had plenty to say about this rather disturbing precedent. There is another serious issue here too, which is the financial plight of CSA. It is a coincidence that the full-strength South African side and India should have been playing a two-match Test series in South Africa – they won one match each – in the weeks before this massively depleted South African touring party went to New Zealand. The second of these Tests, which India won by seven wickets, was the shortest in the history of Test cricket. It was played at Newlands, in Cape Town, and was finished in less than five sessions, which will hardly have helped CSA pay even its smallest bills.

It must have been a terrible surface, for the ball moved extravagantly off the seam from the start and the pitch had a most uneven bounce. Twenty-three wickets fell on the first day and, in all, only 642 legitimate balls were needed. Bazball may have virtually eliminated draws in games unaffected by the weather, but a finish in one and a half days is ridiculous and no help to anyone. In South

Africa's second innings of 176, opener Aiden Markram made 106 off 103 balls – and the next highest score was 12. This match looked like another example of how the attacking needs of T20 are making batters less able to cope with difficult conditions where a good defensive technique is the essential requirement. Afterwards, Rohit Sharma, the Indian captain, was critical of what he called the double standards of the ICC when it comes to the pitch reports made by match referees, but, strangely, he stopped short of specifically criticising this pitch at Newlands, where they are no longer able to employ a full-time groundsman.

Among the chorus of criticism of CSA's decision to send such a poor side to New Zealand, no one's voice has been louder than that of former Australian captain Steve Waugh, who won 41 Tests while he was in charge, which makes him one of the most successful Test captains ever. Waugh said, 'Surely the ICC, along with the cricket boards of India, England and Australia must step in to protect the purest form of the game. A premium, equal match fee for all Test players might be a good starting point – something that I hope will have been discussed during that get-together at Lord's. History and tradition must count for something. If we stand by and allow profits to be the defining criteria, the legacy of Bradman, Grace, Sobers and all the others will be irrelevant.' He also said that the game's governing bodies 'obviously don't care', and that interest in major cricketing events will fall away if franchise leagues continue to consume the calendar. Wise words, indeed.

It is therefore excellent that we have all been given reason to hope that, even at this late stage, the two sides of the argument may be able to work out a reasonable compromise now that Mark Nicholas and the MCC executive has answered Waugh's heartfelt plea and organised this meeting at Lord's. And better still that the BCCI are themselves beginning to think in terms of compromise, something that should also have had a big effect on this meeting. Surely, even now, the two sides can work out a way of living together in some sort of harmony.

The first part of this book looks at the gentle, relaxed scenario of the game I fell in love with sixty years ago and the comfortable, easy-paced way of life that went on around it. All that we loved and cherished about the game seemed secure and unshakable, and nothing was too confused, complicated or hurried. Sixty years later, like the world around it, the game we knew and loved is changing at high speed and the future is gripped by an ominous uncertainty as its two halves battle for supremacy and, as far as Test cricket is concerned, for relevance in this fast-moving world with its ever-shortening attention span.

The two major divisions in the game are being driven further and further apart. On the one hand, we have those full-house crowds at the 2023 Ashes, which must be put alongside the more-than-half-empty stadiums for other Test matches; and on the other, the showbiz entertainment of the T20 franchise world, to say nothing of The Hundred, which are playing to full-house crowds everywhere. These new forms of the game are making it harder for Test cricket to survive – in the mainstream, at any rate – and it comes down to what the world wants. The evidence at the moment shows that the game of non-stop sixes is exactly what it does want and is prepared to pay for, but how long can this go on for? T20 franchises sprout up like mushrooms, while, for all its popularity in England, Test cricket no longer fits in anything like as comfortably into the world that is now around it. Although Bazball is reshaping and streamlining Test cricket, it is tempting to say it is the same game, but without the draw, which is important. Groucho certainly thought it was now very different. The same skills apply but everything has quickened up, and these days Test matches seldom go the full distance. There have been many exciting new inventions along the way, like the ramp and all the other improvised strokes, inspired maybe by T20, but now put thrillingly into the equation of Test cricket and

Bazball. These added extras may have old-timers scratching their heads, if not turning in their graves, but they have come to stay and Zak Crawley's Bazball cover drive for four off the first ball of the series at Edgbaston will be talked about for longer than anything the franchise world can produce. Many will say that is the wishful thinking of a died-in-the-wool oldie, but is it really? It is worth remembering that only the best players can pull off a stroke like this or any of the extravagant additions to a batter's repertoire which have come rushing across from the shorter form of the game.

It is difficult to believe that some of the great skills of a game developed over such a long time are in danger of being jettisoned, but this is what is happening. I repeat that in my view, a game without the late cut or the leg glance could hardly be considered to be better. But having shown myself to be an old square, the game that has been taken to new frontiers by the IPL has a good range of exciting new skills of its own. If we now live in a world which wants to see only an unending stream of sixes, the T20 franchise world is the place to be. But it is worth considering for a moment what the cricket might come to if Test and two-innings cricket were to disappear, leaving us only with one-day and predominantly T20 cricket. Bowling and fielding skills would perhaps not be appreciated as they once were, the game becoming lop-sided as the balance between bat and ball which has given cricket its structure, its character and its fascination, completely disappears. It would become an exhibition of sophisticated slogging. For how long would that hold the world's attention, and might not people soon think they were not getting value for money? It has all become too obvious. Before long they will want more than this.

Of course, the modern game has sprouted new skills of its own. If looked at without hanging on to the handrail of the past, it provides contemporary audiences with the product they want, just as the game back in the fifties and sixties satisfied what were then our needs. There is more aggression in the game today, just as there is in the world around us. It is fascinating to watch the present generation of batters develop new techniques to get on top of the modern bowlers who have tried to develop their own methods of containment, but from the way T20 is developing, bowlers are becoming little more than supporting actors whose job it is to be hit for endless sixes. New strokes raise eyebrows just as the first of them all, the reverse sweep, once did. I was in the commentary box at the World Cup final at Eden Gardens in Kolkata in 1987 when Mike Gatting was out to a reverse sweep at a crucial moment in the final, which was won by Australia. There were shrieks of horror that such a rough-hewn, unchristian stroke should have been used on such an important occasion – and by the England captain too. The reverse sweep is now so respectable it has found its way into most coaching books and has become an essential part of a batsman's armoury in all forms of the game.

Let's have a look at Joe Root's three ramp shots in the opening overs of the second day in the Edgbaston Test. At first, it was a shock that anyone should attempt something so cheeky, so dangerous and so absurd to the first ball of the day in a Test match and against such a fine fast bowler as Pat Cummins. Maybe because Root got that first one all wrong, made it look an insult to Test cricket, let alone the Ashes, and yet when the same stroke succeeded a moment or two later against Scott Boland, Root's execution was so smooth and skilful that not only did it fit in with the pursuit of excellence required by Test cricket, it also became for me one of the most memorable moments of that amazing series. It was the dramatic product of a remarkably complicated manoeuvre to get everything – feet, hands, bat and head – into the right positions so quickly. If there had been any error, it would have looked an unjustifiable risk. It was the ease, almost the simplicity, with which it was played that allowed something that had at first seemed an outrageous white-ball excess to be seen not just as a product of respectability, but as a demonstration of genius.

It was a stroke that contained everything: real humour, high skill and a remarkable nerve, and had us all looking at each other in disbelief. It was something that only a great player could have perfected. How many times have I heard it said that Geoffrey Boycott could never have played Bazball? That is nonsense, for technically Boycott was a brilliant batter and more than good enough to hit sixes over backward point or anywhere else and to play the ramp – if he had chosen to, which is another question altogether. He would have been able to fulfil all the technical needs of Bazball, although I am not sure if he would have been able to put quite the same cheeky humour into the stroke as Root. But I think he would have enjoyed it – as long as it came off.

Although Test cricket may remain as the gold standard where all the skills of the game are shown off at their best, it is not difficult to enjoy the brazen audacity of the T20 game, even if it does have a meretricious tinge to it. This is not just moving with the times; it is continuing to do what we have always done, which is to appreciate excellence, even if it is displayed in a different context and may take a little time to get used to. It is so important that we doubters should learn to relax and enjoy this modern interpretation of cricket – as long as we are allowed to enjoy both forms of the game. For me, cricket has always been the best game in the world and this is cricket in its twenty-first-century incarnation. It is the same game W.G. Grace once played, and I am sure, being the man he was, he would, after raising an initial eyebrow or two, have adapted his game to Bazball and T20 as well, and would somehow have turned both to his personal advantage. It is not all that easy to imagine him with his flowing beard playing the ramp, but I like to think he would have given it a go, and almost certainly he would have come up with a few ideas of his own.

The Ashes in 2023 demonstrated the intrinsic value of Test and two-innings cricket, something the one-innings game can never compete with, because it can never offer the same wide variety and mixture of skills as fortunes ebb and flow in a game which can go on for five days. The full-house crowds, the television figures and the all-consuming interest around the cricket-playing world were evidence that support for Bazball-inspired Test cricket is alive and well. Only the most stony-hearted would have turned a blind eye to this, but even so, did this extraordinary series really do anything to check the relentless advance of the T20 franchise world which was elbowing it out of the way? It would be good to think that it had made some people, and especially the game's administrators, realise that the two forms of the game can and should still peacefully coexist, which is why Mark Nicholas's initiative at Lord's is so important as the first stepping stone on a slippery path, even if this initial step proved to be a little more slippery than was hoped.

I have pointed a finger at the IPL for their determination to promote and expand the T20 game without any apparent consideration for Test cricket and its requirements. I have linked the IPL and the BCCI together because they live in the same nest, but the BCCI must be congratulated for their continuing support of Test cricket. After playing that strange two-Test series in South Africa, India went back home to take on England in an ultra-modern series with no other games apart from the five Test matches, and although the matches were not played in front of IPL-like crowds, the series generated huge attention which suggests that interest in Test cricket is far from dead on the Subcontinent.

The BCCI must have been pleased that the country's supreme cricketing hero, Virat Kohli, has spoken out so strongly on the continuing importance of Test and two-innings cricket. We have not yet heard Mr Badale's views about the series, and it would be interesting to know if he is now thinking Test cricket should be something rather more than an annual one-off event like Wimbledon.

Kohli's backing of Test cricket, and that of other well-known players such as the South African Kagiso Rabada and the

Australians Steve Smith and Marnus Labuschagne, is important, and Test cricket has no bigger supporter than Ben Stokes. Their voices must carry weight with both the public and with those who run the game, especially in the parts of the world where support for Test cricket is not as strong as it is in England. It is important that players such as these who are the best in the world, should continue to be part of Test cricket. For if they are, it surely won't be allowed to die.

In England and Australia, the boards of control have enough money to offer their leading players sufficiently large contracts to keep hold of them. In India the BCCI, which receives an annual handout from the ICC that comes to nearly 40 per cent of its distributable income of around $600m, is similarly placed. It would be lovely to think Kohli's stated passion for Test cricket resonates with the Indian public and even more so with those who run the game there, but the T20 franchise world has been so brilliantly marketed that it seemed to have the country in its grip, but after thrashing England in the recent series, maybe that grip is now a little looser.

I am writing like this in the hope that a formula will be found that will allow the two different forms of the game to exist along-side each other. As it is, the T20 franchise wagon has built up such a speed that it will be hard to stop, but with the BCCI look-ing as if it may be prepared to stand on the brakes, the hope must be not only that Test cricket will continue to be fitted into the calendar, but also that the world's best players will be given leave of absence to go back and play Test matches for their countries when the fixtures overlap.

To enable a satisfactory compromise to be found, it is impor-tant that Test cricket keeps hold of the Bazball approach and continues to show that it is also aware of the needs of the modern world. I believe that the two forms of the game can then only complement each other, although the dramatic expansion of the T20 franchise world has made it inevitable that fewer Test matches will be played in the future. Some people will be delighted to see *Hamlet* one night and *The Rocky Horror Show* the next, and happily go along to both; others will be love one but wouldn't be seen dead at the other. It may be stretching a point to suggest that Laurence Olivier himself might have turned swiftly from Hamlet to none other than the flamboyant Rocky, the invention of the mad scientist.

Inevitably, the modern form of the game will mean that those of us who learned and played it in a different era will be left with certain regrets. For me, one of these is that there will be less opportunity to watch the wonderful spectacle of a genuine fast bowler racing up to the wicket with perhaps four slips, two gullies and a couple of short legs perched round the bat. It is a great spectacle and one of the reasons I am always in my seat well before the start on the first morning. The opening overs are always exciting and I also like to be there when the umpires first come down the pavilion steps in their white coats and anticipation turns into reality.

Fast bowlers can leak runs which is why you seldom see them in limited-over cricket. It may seem surprising, then, to find that Australia's two opening bowlers, Pat Cummins and Mitchell Starc, were both signed up for the 2024 IPL, with Starc ($2.35m) becoming the first player in the IPL to be bought for over $2m and Cummins ($1.95m) narrowly failing to be the second. But, after winning the World Cup and hanging on to the Ashes in England, they are very much the two fast bowlers of the moment, which is always what the IPL wants. These prices give an idea of the sums of money that may be waiting round the corner. Starc is effectively being paid just over £7,000 for every ball he bowls.

I would love to be within earshot if news of what must be a financial triumph for these two Australians ever got back to dear old Fred Trueman, my *TMS* colleague and good friend, wherever he or his spirit may be. Fred had surely the best action of any fast bowler. He was also the first bowler to take 300 Test wickets and, in comparison with today, he was paid peanuts for what he did. His comments on air were nothing if not delightfully pithy and to the point, blended with a lovely earthy Yorkshire sense of humour. I would have loved to have heard his comments if Starc's rate of pay had filtered through to him for they would have been even more to the point. I shall never forget turning to him in the middle of one spell of commentary at Headingley when nothing much was happening. 'Now, Fred, what do you think of this?' I asked him. 'Can't watch this rubbish,' came back the reply, spoken with great emphasis, and that was all I got. Seven thousand pounds a ball would have stuck in his throat, and not without reason.

Cummins and Starc will not have many fielders round the bat when they ply their trade in the IPL. Spectators at these matches are not going to worry too much about whether it was a googly or a leg-break, or whether it swung in or out. On the other hand, if it goes for one of Groucho's homers, we then get the DJ at full throttle, followed by a few seconds of blaring music and the rest. If a wicket falls, interviewers race out to meet the defeated batter and dancing girls, all frills and thighs, cavort about. The DJ is off his longest possible run, fireworks go off, the crowd goes mad and the new batter comes briskly to the crease – and all the while the fast-food outlets and bars dispense their offerings, some of which would be unlikely to form part of a health diet.

Over the years the game has seen all manner of changes, but it is interesting that it was only relatively recently that one aspect of the weather's influence was taken out of the game, bringing an important improvement for spectators, but perhaps to the detriment of the game itself. Pitches used to be uncovered, and rain followed by a hot sun, particularly in the tropics, could produce surfaces on which it was almost impossible to bat. The ball would turn fiercely, spit and jump and suddenly shoot through and these conditions made batting a lottery for any but the best. But these drying conditions produced wonderfully entertaining and extremely skilful cricket.

I had one extraordinary experience of this. In the sixties I toured Barbados with E.W. Swanton's club, the Arabs. We played a three-day game against Everton Weekes's XI at Kensington Oval in Bridgetown. On the second day, when Everton's side was batting, there was a sudden, violent storm. A hot sun followed the rain and it was not long before the ball began to behave with remarkable extravagance, which, as I was keeping wicket, was greatly to my cost. Our off-spinner, Dan Piachaud, who bowled for both Oxford University and Sri Lanka, was almost unplayable and wickets began to fall. Everton Weekes himself, now well into his forties and long since retired, had put himself in at number eight. He came in and for the next thirty minutes of his innings I kept wicket to the most incredible display of batsmanship I have ever seen at close quarters.

Everton played nearly every ball from two paces down the pitch. His judgement of length was extraordinary, as was the power and authority of his strokes. He scarcely played a defensive stroke and made 40 runs in this time, driving powerfully through the off side, laying back and cutting, and then dispatching a ball to the midwicket boundary and driving another back over Piachaud's head for four. It was amazing to watch and was put into perspective when his partner was on strike and batting was again made to seem impossible. Everton then declared, so that his bowlers, led by West Indies Test umpire Cortez Jordan, who took the new ball, could have a go at us before the surface dried. Everton would have played the ramp at least as well as Joe Root, but they had no need to think of such things in those days.

I must end this chapter with a good old moan brought on by The Hundred and its T20 relations. The full scorecards of these games are not always provided in newspapers and other media outlets.

Scorecards have long fascinated me and I can think of nothing that irritates me more than an abbreviated scorecard, unless it is no scorecard at all. I want to know who scored the runs and who did not, and I want to see the bowling figures too. The full score-card is an obsession I am sure I share with many cricket lovers. Even at my vast age, my eyes are instantly drawn to any scorecard when I open the sports pages. It doesn't matter how unimportant the match is or how small the print at the bottom of the page, I have to examine it in detail.

This all began in 1947. At my prep school little boys were not allowed newspapers at breakfast, but the moment I came across one later in the day, all I wanted to know was if Denis Compton had scored more runs for Middlesex than Len Hutton had for Yorkshire. This gave me my initial taste for scorecards, and it has never left me. That year, I was on to a good thing, for Compton and his partner in arms for Middlesex and England, Bill Edrich, both made more than 3,500 runs. Bill was born in Norfolk near South Walsham, a village which was only about five miles away from where we lived at Hoveton. I always asked my mother to slow down when we drove past the large house in which the great man had lived when he was a child. I later had the luck to play under him when, in his forties, he came back to captain Norfolk in the Minor Counties Championship. As always, he fielded at first slip and caught most things and I kept wicket. We never stopped talking and what fun it was.

17

AN UNEXPECTED LIFELINE

'Can T20 and Tests live happily together?'

O<small>UR</small> old friend Manoj Badale will have been the most important man in the room on that all-important day at Lord's in
July 2024. As owner of the Rajasthan Royals, he was now the
voice of the Indian Premier League and it will have been hoped
that he will have been prepared to give more ground than anyone
if this get-together has managed to move international cricket in
the direction of a fruitful compromise. A while back now, Mr
Badale made his position clear when he said that Test cricket
should be played, like Wimbledon, in a restricted period each
year. If this meeting was to have achieved anything, he would
certainly have had to rethink that unhelpful suggestion. Recent
events on the field of play will, I hope, have made him see reason.
The next problem to be sorted out is the thorny issue of money,
which seems to have been his priority. Now, Mr Badale will have
been joined in the spotlight by Greg Barclay, the chair of the ICC,
who will also have had to deal with the accusation that the ICC
is effectively controlled by India and, as a result, has never raised
its head above the parapet. Why else would the ICC have remained
silent while there has been so much disruption in the world it is
meant to preside over?

There are twelve Full Member countries and just over ninety
Associate Members and they all receive a handout from the ICC

which, at the moment, has about $600m to distribute each year. The ICC's present financial model, approved by the ICC board, will, from 2024 to 2027, hand over no less than 38.5 per cent of their annual distributable income of $600m to the BCCI, while all other Full Member countries will each receive less than 10 per cent. This means that India will pick up approximately $230m for each of these four years. Their huge take of nearly 40 per cent is because about 80 per cent of the ICC's annual income comes from India.

The two principal Indians at this meeting at Lord's will have been Mr Badale and Ravi Shastri, and both will have presumably defended the BCCI's remuneration. They will have argued that the ICC are giving well over half of the payment they receive from India to the rest of the cricket-playing world. Will they then have been prepared to accept that it is important to keep a balance in the game between Test and T20 cricket? They must realise that India is the only country with the money to enable this to happen, but will they be prepared to receive a smaller amount from the ICC to try and help most of the other Test-playing countries or help to try and find another way round this problem? Or will they simply shrug their shoulders and say that what is happening is the way of the world? Shastri will surely appreciate the importance of maintaining Test cricket and preventing it from becoming an irrelevant sideshow, though he strongly implied that he was happy with the ICC as it was. Or did the Indians think that as they now effectively own the game after decades of being told what to do by Lord's, they are in a position to do what they want and will enjoy showing it is they who are in control?

My fear is that they may come up with a financial gesture which will not be enough to make the necessary changes and will leave England and Australia to stretch themselves to the limit to try and save Test cricket from tottering down a path which may one day lead to extinction. This would mean that the IPL and company will continue to have every chance of buying the services of any player they want and the situation will not significantly change. Have the

Indians appreciated the importance of giving more money to the less fortunate of the Full Members so they will be able to compete once again on a level playing field? Shastri and Mr Badale will have been under considerable pressure to see that India does all it can to rebalance the game – on the field and off it. It is impossible to second-guess the outcome and nothing will be decided in a hurry, but I cannot believe a serious cricket lover, which Shastri is, would have turned his back on Test cricket. And although Mr Badale professes a great love of it, I am not sure I would want to bet on where his vote would go, but as I have not met him, it may be unfair of me to say this, and when faced with the stark reality of it all, it may have helped him to change his mind, but it is not easy for rich and successful men to ignore the call of money.

Wouldn't it be wonderful if India said they would be willing to give up enough money to make all this happen? But even so, this would only help solve half the problem. The IPL must then promise to leave a big enough gap in the calendar so that Test tours, in their present abbreviated form, can be fitted in even if there are fewer of them. Another way of achieving this would of course be for the franchises to agree to release their players for a certain number of Test matches each year, although this would mean they would come back to Test cricket without any appropriate preparation. For all that, this would be far better than nothing, but it would be another huge ask for Mr Badale, who would surely not be able to agree to that decision without going to India and talking it over with the IPL's other franchise investors.

It is unreasonable to think that we are going to get anything from Mark Nicholas's brainwave other than a statement of intent, but I was confident that this would come with a serious promise to try and make things work. The Indians will have to give a lot if this is to happen, and I hope fervently that everyone else will do their best to help them make these difficult decisions and not put unnecessary obstacles in their way. This is a wonderful chance to get the whole cricket family to come together again and to help each other. How appropriate it was that this meeting was held at Lord's. The participants will only have had to look out of the windows around them to see the glories of Lord's, which represent everything that needs to be saved. Or will the T20 protagonists be militant, as Kerry Packer once was in the same room – and, remember, Packer went on to win his argument with the game?

The present disorganised financial arrangements of international cricket were well illustrated by Johnny Grave, the chief executive of Cricket West Indies, and Mike Baird, the chair of Cricket Australia. Talking about the present financial plight of the West Indies, Grave said in January 2024, 'The revenue-share model is completely broken. As an example, Cricket West Indies has spent over $2 million sending teams to Australia in the past four months, and while Cricket Australia has seen all the economic benefits from those series, we have seen nothing back. Is that really fair, reasonable and sustainable? If we really want to operate as a cricket community, we are only as strong as the weakest team and we have got to change the mindset of bilateral cricket.'

Baird was sympathetic: 'If national teams are not being prioritised then we have a lot of work to do. There is undoubtedly an economic element, but there is also a common-sense element in terms of the way we schedule and the way we collectively as members prioritise. So there is strong resolve, but we need to move at a much quicker pace.'

This leads on to the next issue, which is the seeming impotence of the game's governing body, the International Cricket Council. It is nominally presided over by Greg Barclay, but does he really have the power to do what he thinks is best for the game, or does he have to make sure of Indian approval before he says anything? There has not, for example, been a satisfactory answer from the ICC about the way in which the Indians were allowed, at the last moment, to change the designated pitch for their semi-final of the recent World Cup when they played New Zealand at the Wankhede Stadium in Mumbai. The game was moved at the last minute from a new pitch to one that had already been used, a decision which called for a more extensive inquiry than it received. The silence of the ICC's leadership over this has been remarkable and gives the impression that it is not much more than a rubber stamp. It will be interesting to hear how Barclay dealt with this charge. There are times when the ICC seems little more than the branch of a bank which has its head office in Kolkata or Mumbai.

The others at Lord's will all have had their chance to contribute. Graeme Smith will, I am sure, have emphasised Cricket South Africa's lack of money and how important it is that they should be given a larger share of the handout if the game there is to survive at the top level. He will have stressed that CSA's decision not to send their best players to New Zealand was forced upon them by the need to raise money from their T20 franchise. Clare Connor will have argued the need for more money in the women's game and maybe she will have stressed the importance of not allowing women's Test cricket to be put under similar pressure by the women's T20 franchise world, although their schedule is much less congested than the men's. Richard Thompson may have had to explain the importance of The Hundred to English cricket and how, with private investment about to happen, it will greatly improve the finances of the game here. Michael Atherton will have made a typically level-headed and instructive contribution, and all the others will have made their points.

One danger was always that the Indians might be made to think they were under all-round attack, which would only be counter-productive and have made them dig their heels in deeper and form their own corral to protect the present state of affairs. This meeting will have needed the most careful handling and that touch of humour, which can be such a help at times like these, but can also be most elusive.

These words are being written before the meeting at Lord's takes place and my fear is that having been thrown an unexpected lifeline just as Test cricket began to be in danger of sinking below the waves, it will be allowed to slip through their fingers. I hope that all those there will have shown a serious determination to do the best for the game of cricket rather than only to care for their own vested interests.

While this T20 franchise world has been gaining momentum, Test cricket has been allowed to plod along without help in the vague hope that something might turn up. Two years ago, in 2022, something did turn up. As we have seen, Brendon McCullum and Ben Stokes were then brought together as coach and captain of the England Test side. The two of them developed Bazball in their determination to make Test cricket faster and more appealing. They have also eliminated those boring drawn matches, which should reach out and appeal to the contemporary world. After a heady start in 2022, the following year it again exceeded expectations and produced one of the best Ashes series ever which mesmerised the entire cricket-playing world. After that, Bazball had its most triumphant moment when England won the first Test of their series in India in spectacular fashion. Then it all went badly wrong, to show that nothing in this crazy world is perfect, but better Bazball than 229–3 on a full first day. But Bazball has suddenly made it seem possible that Test cricket might have a reasonable future after all alongside the brasher and more outrageous T20 franchise version of the game. Before this could happen, this new twenty-first-century invention had to be pulled back, but no one seemed quite sure how that could be done. Then, thanks to Mark Nicholas and the MCC executive, the first opportunity to do that came when this get-together was organised at Lord's.

This is a meeting which takes me back again to 1977 when I well remember Kerry Packer coming to Lord's to meet the ICC in the Pavilion to try and convince the game's authorities that his invention of World Series Cricket was not a hideous revolution aimed at the game's establishment. Packer, brilliantly described by Ian Wooldridge in the *Daily Mail* as 'the man in the stocking mask', was accompanied that day by, among others, his chief cricketing officer, who was none other than Richie Benaud. Packer tried to be conciliatory, but only on his own terms, and when he refused to give up his demand to be granted exclusive television rights for Channel Nine to cover international cricket in Australia – which it was not in the ICC's remit to give – he led his team out of the Pavilion.

I would like to think this book gives a good idea of the contrasting worlds of cricket at the start and the finish of my seventy-odd years of involvement on the edge of the game. I am reasonably confident, too, that my prediction of a happy future for the two vastly different formats we now live with will eventually turn out to be right and we will all still have our own special game to love and enjoy.

PICTURE
ACKNOWLEDGEMENTS

Page 1 bottom © Topical Press/Getty Images

Page 2 top Public domain/Wikimedia Commons

Page 3 top left © PA Images/Alamy Stock Photo

Page 3 top right © Chronicle/Alamy Stock Photo

Page 3 bottom © Mirrorpix/Getty Images

Page 4 top © John Sherbourne/ANL/Shutterstock

Page 4 bottom © Popperfoto via Getty Images/Getty Images

Page 5 top © Patrick Eagar/Popperfoto via Getty Images/Getty Images

Page 6 top © Patrick Eagar/Popperfoto via Getty Images/Getty Images

Page 7 top © The Times/News Licensing

Page 7 bottom © Ivan Vdovin/Alamy Stock Photo

Page 9 top left © Dave J Hogan/Getty Images

Page 9 top right © ZUMA Press, Inc./Alamy Stock Photo

Page 9 bottom © Philip Brown/Getty Images

Page 10 © Stu Forster/Getty Images

Page 11 top left © Ryan Pierse/Getty Images

Page 11 top right © James Worsfold – CA/Cricket Australia via Getty
Images

Page 12 top © Gareth Copley – ECB/ECB via Getty Images

Page 13 top © Graham Chadwick/ANL/Shutterstock

Page 13 bottom © Matthew Lewis/Getty Images

Page 14 top left © Stu Forster/Getty Images

Page 14 top right © Philip Brown/Popperfoto/Popperfoto via Getty
Images

Page 14 bottom © Stu Forster/Getty Images

INDEX

Abu Dhabi, UAE 190
Abu Dhabi Knight Riders 192
Afghanistan 80–3, 85–91, 208
  v England (2023) 174
Afridi, Shaheen 189, 190
Agar's Plough, Eton 11
Agnew, Jonathan 'Aggers' 28, 139,
  141
Akram, Wasim 189
Albanese, Anthony 129
Alexander, Bob 64
Ali, Moeen 121, 138, 144, 148, 160
Allen, David 150
Allen, Finn 189
Allen, Gubby 131, 136, 150–1
Ames, Les 50
Ancient Mariner 125–31
Anderson, Jimmy 116, 145, 148,
  159
Ankara, Turkey 74–7
Arabs, the 15, 221
Archie MacLaren's XI
  v Australia (1921) 9, 53
Argentina 50, 52–5
Arlott, John
  Bazball 143–4

filling moments 42
Headingley 34
TMS lynchpin 1, 23, 25–8
wine break 22
Armstrong, Warwick 9
Arthur, Mark 196
Arun Jaitley Stadium, Delhi 35
Ashes series *see* Australia; England
Ashley, Mike 204
Ashton, Malcolm 44, 45, 46
Asians, British 199–200
Atherton, Michael 211, 227
Athey, Bill 53
Australia
  MLC and 181
  North American tour (1932)
    182–3
  WSC and 64–5, 66
  v Archie MacLaren's XI (1921)
    9, 53
  v England (1902) 141
  v England (1926) 6
  v England (1936–37) 136
  v England (1946–47) 60–1
  v England (1948) 117
  v England (1950–51) 148

v England (1956) 6
v England (1965–66) 146
v England (1971) 62
v England (1972) 15, 25, 41
v England (1976–77) 2, 179
v England (1981) 140
v England (1986–87) 157, 200
v England (1987) 215
v England (2005) 147, 157, 179
v England (2013) 44
v England (2015) 159
v England (2023) 113–14,
    116–17, 121–33, 195, 215–16
v India (2023) 179
v Pakistan (2023) 117
v Pakistan (2023–24) 189
v West Indies (1960–61) 209
v West Indies (1975) 62, 71
v West Indies (1977) 68–9
v West Indies (2024) 188, 208
Australian Cricket Board 63, 68,
    187, 218
Australian, The 200–2
Ayesha, Rajmata of Jaipur 96

Badale, Manoj
    Ashes and 111
    on Test cricket 102–3, 217, 225
    'World Cricket Connects' 210,
        223, 224
Bailey, Trevor 22, 23, 32
Baird, Mike 226
Bairstow, Jonny 122–3, 127–8,
    140–1
    Bazball 115, 116, 159
    form 114, 177

Test innings 148
    wicketkeeper 124, 151, 158, 160
Bakht, Sikander 31
Ballance, Gary 196
Bangladesh 208
v Sri Lanka (2023) 176–7
Barbados 39, 210, 221
Barber, Bob 146
Barclay, Greg 210, 223, 226
Barnes, Sydney 10
Baroda Cricket Association 97, 98
Baroda, Maharajah of 95, 98
Bat and Ball Ground, Gravesend
    13–14
Baxter, Peter 1, 22, 23, 32, 40, 197
Bazball 111–19, 121–31, 213–14
    approach 108, 156, 163, 169, 210
    Arlott and 27, 143–4
    Australians and 136
    Bairstow and 115, 116, 159
    Boycott and 216
    Grace and 216
    Khawaja and 158
    McCullum and 2, 169, 194, 228
    Root and 114, 116
    Stokes and 2, 139–40, 169, 194,
        228
BBC 23–5, 31–2, 40, 42, 179
Bedser, Alec 60
Belmont Cricket Club,
    Philadelphia 183
Benaud, Richie 64, 229
Bennett, Michael 72–84, 85–99
Benson & Hedges Cup 62
Bhutto, Zulfikar Ali 68
Big Bash (T20) 181, 209

Blast (T20) 4, 164, 166, 170, 187
Board of Control for Cricket in
    India (BCCI)
    ICC and 187, 218, 224
    IPL and 193, 208, 210, 217
    Saudi Arabia and 191–2
    Test cricket and 217
    'World Cricket Connects'
    212–13
Bodyline series (1932–33) 60, 131,
    177
Bombay, India 93
Booth, Lawrence 118–19
Borwick, George 60
Botham, Ian 68, 143
Boult, Trent 186
Boycott, Geoffrey 31, 68, 157, 158,
    216
Bradman, Don 6, 60–1, 117, 130,
    177, 182
Brand, Neil 187
Bray, Charlie 16, 17–18
Brazil 55–8
Brearley, Mike 31, 68
Bresnan, Tim 196
Briffa, Joanna 97
Bright, Ray 140
British High Commission, Iran 80
Broad, Chris 158–9
Broad, Stuart 46, 116, 129–31, 140,
    145, 158–61
Brook, Harry 116, 126, 144–5, 148,
    156
Brown, Freddie 41, 148
Brownlow, Claude and Morag 97
Bruno (German hotel manager) 81

Buenos Aires, Argentina 52–5
bullying 197, 202
Burnham, Forbes 69
butterflies 36
Butts, Cindy 195, 203, 204, 205

Cambridge University Cricket
    Club 11–13, 30, 198–9
Cambridgeshire CCC 10
Cardiff 35–6
Carey, Alex 127, 128, 131, 142,
    160, 177
Carnegie-Brown, Bruce 150
Casey, Judy 71–84, 85–99
Champions Trophy 176
Chapman, Brian 16, 17–18
Chile 51–2
Church Street Park, North
    Carolina 184, 185, 186
Clarke, Giles 166, 205
Clarke, John 14
class-based discrimination 198–9
Collingwood, Paul 112
commentary boxes 32–5
Compton, Denis 1, 5–6, 10, 13,
    222
Connor, Clare 211, 227
Cook, Alastair 46
Copacabana, Rio de Janeiro 55, 56,
    57
County Championship 1, 155, 164,
    168–9, 173
Coventry City FC 49, 58
Coward, Noël 13, 18
Cowdrey, Chris 50
Cowdrey, Colin 11–12, 150

Cozier, Tony 39
Crawley, Zak
    fielding 140, 142
    Test innings 113–14, 121, 122,
        144, 145, 146–8, 156, 159
Cricket Australia 226
Cricket New South Wales 181
Cricket New Zealand 187
Cricket South Africa (CSA)
        104–5, 187–8, 207–8, 211,
        227
Cricket Victoria 181
Cricket West Indies 226
Croft, Colin 201
Crouch, Maurice 10
Cummins, Pat
    captain 116, 139, 179, 186
    fast bowler 121, 122, 147, 156,
        214, 215
    IPL contract 219, 220
    Test innings 123, 143, 160

D. H. Robins' cricket team
    v New Zealand (1979–80) 50
Darling, Joe 147
Davies, Dai 12
de Kock, Quinton 186
Dean's Hotel, Peshawar 91–2
Decision Review System (DRS)
        178
DeFreitas, Phil 200
Dexter, Ted 11–12, 151, 198
Dietrich, Marlene 176
Dinenage, Dame Caroline 204
du Plessis, Faf 186

Dubai, UAE 44, 192
Duckett, Ben 114, 122, 126, 127,
        144, 156, 159
Duckworth Lewis Method, 'It's
    Just Not Cricket' 44–5

Ecuador 51
Eden Gardens, Kolkata 184, 215
Edgbaston, Birmingham 15, 25,
        117, 121–4, 151, 156, 179, 215
Edrich, Bill 1, 10–11, 61, 222
Eisenhower Park, Long Island 185
elitism 198–9
England
    Pakistan (2022–23) 115
    Test selectors 23
    v Afghanistan (2023) 174
    v Australia (1902) 141
    v Australia (1926) 6
    v Australia (1936–37) 136
    v Australia (1946–47) 60–1
    v Australia (1948) 117
    v Australia (1950–51) 148
    v Australia (1956) 6
    v Australia (1965–66) 146
    v Australia (1971) 62
    v Australia (1972) 15, 25, 41
    v Australia (1976–77) 2, 179
    v Australia (1981) 140
    v Australia (1986–87) 157, 200
    v Australia (1987) 215
    v Australia (2005) 147, 157, 179
    v Australia (2013) 44
    v Australia (2015) 159
    v Australia (2023) 113–14,
        116–17, 121–33, 195, 215–16

v India (1951–52) 97
v India (1963–64) 67
v India (1974) 26
v India (1976) 2
v India (2023–24) 193
v India (2024) 209–10, 217
v Ireland (2023) 172
v New Zealand (1929–30) 46
v New Zealand (1977–78) 68
v New Zealand (2022) 114–15
v New Zealand (2023) 115–16,
    172–3
v Pakistan (1977–78) 31, 65, 68
v Pakistan (1987–88) 202
v Pakistan (2020) 205
v Pakistan (2023) 176
v South Africa (1889) 131
v South Africa (1956–57) 6, 15
v South Africa (1994) 200
v South Africa (2015–2016)
    45–6
v West Indies (1929–30) 6
v West Indies (1963) 150
v West Indies (1967–68) 2–3
v West Indies (1984) 200
v West Indies (1997–98) 39, 40
v West Indies (2021–22) 112
England and Wales Cricket Board
    (ECB) 106–7, 163–4, 169–72,
    202–5
CSA and 187
Gould and 202
Graves and 163, 166
Harrison and 137
The Hundred and 117, 167
players' contracts 175, 218

South American tour 49
staff 205, 211
Thompson and 149, 163
Watmore and 195
Yorkshire and 137
See also ICEC
equity, diversity and inclusion
    (EDI) 195
Erasmus, Marais 127, 176–7
Essex CCC 16–17, 25, 137–8
Eton College 11, 15, 50, 198, 199
Eton Eleven 5–6, 53
Evita (musical) 52

Falcon, Mike 9–10, 53
Fayed (Ady's friend) 79–80
Fenner's Cricket Ground,
    Cambridge 11, 12
Finch, Aaron 186
Fingleton, Jack 15
Fleming, Ian 13
Flintoff, Freddie 179–80
Floyd, George 4, 195
Flying Scotsman 28
Foakes, Ben 210
Forty Club 5
France Cricket 178–9
Frindall, Bill 22, 43–4

Gabba, Brisbane 188, 208–9
Gaffaney, Chris 127
Gatting, Mike 200, 202, 215
Gibbs, Lance 3
Gibson, Alan 19, 43
Gibson, Clem 53
Gibson, Clem (Snr) 53

Gillette Cup 62
Goodall, Fred 200–1
Gough, Darren 203–4
Gould, Richard 169–71, 202
Gower, David 200
Grace, W.G. 216
Grand Prairie Stadium, Texas 184, 185, 186
Grave, Johnny 226
Graves, Colin 163, 166, 203, 204, 205
Graves Family Trust 204
Green, Cameron 123, 127, 140
Greenidge, Gordon 68, 143, 200
Greig, Tony 2, 64, 179
Guha, Isa 41
Gymkhana Club, Karachi 31

Hadlee, Richard 201
Hall, Wes 150
Hammond, Walter 60
Hannon, Neil 44
Harrison, Tom 137, 163, 166, 172, 195, 205
Harrods 52, 55
Harrow School 50, 199
Hartley, Tom 209
Harvey, Bagenal 62
Hazare, Vijay 97
Hazlewood, Josh 156, 160
Head, Travis 125, 140, 142, 160, 179, 186
Headingley Cricket Ground, Leeds 34, 35, 136–45, 152, 172
Hemingway, Ernest 176

Hemmings, Eddie 202
Henderson, Matthew 46
Heyhoe Flint, Rachael 197–8
Higg, Ken 12
Hill, David 66
Hira, Fanos 172
Hobart Hurricanes 209
Hoggard, Matthew 196
Holding, Michael 201
Holmes, Percy 16
Hoveton, Norfolk 8, 135–6
Hudson, Robert 24, 25
Hundred, The (T20) 103, 117–18, 163–72
    affording players 4
    impact of 186–7, 213, 227
    men's and women's 155
    scorecards 222
    setting up 205
    style of play 109, 192
Hurlingham Club, Buenos Aires 52–3
Hutton, Len 222
Hutton, Roger 137, 196

Ikin, Jack 60, 61
ILT20 192–3
In Town Tonight (BBC Radio) 28
Independent Commission for Equity in Cricket (ICEC) 4, 195–7, 199, 202, 203, 205–6
India 92–9, 208, 223–5
    v Australia (2023) 179
    v England (1951–52) 97
    v England (1963–64) 67
    v England (1974) 26

v England (1976) 2
v England (2023–24) 193,
    209–10, 217
v New Zealand (2023) 227
v South Africa (2024) 211–12
Indian Premier League (IPL)
    102–3, 165–6, 189–93
    BCCI and 193, 208, 210, 217
    contracts 107, 219–20
    CSA and 188, 211
    expansion 167, 181, 224
    MLC and 3, 183
    popularity 214
    Yorkshire CCC and 204
Ingleby-Mackenzie, Colin 16
Ingram-Johnson, Colonel 8
International Cricket Council
    (ICC) 178–9, 192–3, 207–8,
    223–4, 226–7
    BCCI and 187, 218, 224
    lack of leadership 4, 210, 227
    Packer and 228–9
    schedules 149
International League T20 (ILT20)
    192–3
International Management Group
    205
Iran 79–80
Ireland
    v England (2023) 172
Istanbul, Turkey 73–4

Jaipur, India 96–7
Jardine, Douglas 177
John Player League 62
Johnston, Brian

butterflies 36
Frindall and 22, 43
India 67, 71
Mosey and 30
TMS lynchpin 1, 22, 23, 24,
    25–8, 43
Jones, Jeff 3
Jordan, Cortez 221
Joseph, Shamar 208–9

Kabul, Afghanistan 90–1
Kandahar, Afghanistan 88–91
Karloff, Boris 131
Kensington Oval, Bridgetown 221
Kent CCC 11, 13–14
Key, Rob 112, 175–6
Khan, Rashid 186
Khawaja, Usman 123, 129, 140,
    144, 157–8, 159, 160
Khyber Pass 91
King, Barton 182–3
Kohli, Virat 105, 217, 218
Kolkata Knight Riders 192, 209
Kumar, Ashwini 94–5

Labuschagne, Marnus
    on form 116, 138, 146, 148, 158,
    160, 179
    Test cricket supporter 218
Lakenham Cricket Ground,
    Norwich 9
Lancashire CCC 12
Lancashire Second XI 11
Langar Hall Hotel,
    Nottinghamshire 33–4
Larwood, Harold 60

Lauderhill, Florida 185
Leach, Jack 130
Lee, Brett 179
Leyton Cricket Ground, London
    16–17
Liddell, Adrian 'Ady' 71–84, 85–99
limited-over cricket 2, 6, 19, 62–3,
    110, 188, 219
Lloyd, Clive 68, 69
Long John Scotch Whisky 72, 77,
    78, 82, 84, 92, 94, 96
Lord, Thomas 50, 199
Lord's Cricket Ground 124–31
    fixtures at 25, 41, 50, 150, 165,
        172, 199, 200
    Nursery End 35
    Nursery Ground 117
    Pavilion 21
    Pavilion End 150
    Warner Stand 21, 150
    'World Cricket Connects' (2024
        event) 4, 189, 210, 212, 226,
        228
Lord's Taverners 44
Lotbiniere, Seymour de 'Lobby' 42
Luckhoo, Sir Lionel 69
Lyon, Nathan 116, 122, 125, 126,
    158

McCormack, Mark 205
McCosker, Rick 65
McCullum, Brendon 112–14,
    115–16
    Bairstow and 128
    Bazball and 2, 169, 194, 228
    Blofeld on 156

Crawley and 146
'World Cricket Connects' 211
Mackay, Ken 'Slasher' 158
Mailey, Arthur 130, 182–3
Major League Cricket (MLC),
    USA 3, 181–7, 189, 191
Malcolm, Devon 200
Markram, Aiden 212
Marsh, Mitchell 140, 141–2, 144,
    146, 148, 160
Marsh, Rod 141
Martin-Jenkins, Christopher
    (CMJ) 23, 29–30
Marx, Groucho 3, 119, 121–31,
    145
Marylebone Cricket Club (MCC)
    debacle in the Lord's Pavilion
        129
    executive/committee 199, 212,
        228
    fixtures at 13
    life memberships 26
    presidents 210
    TMS and 23
    tours and 49, 52
    'World Cricket Connects' 4
Mashhad, Afghanistan 80–1
Mathews, Angelo 176–8
Maxwell, Glenn 186
Maxwell, Jim 45
Melford, Michael 71
Metro Bank One-Day Cup 118,
    163–4
Middlesex CCC 5–6, 10, 222
Midway House Hotel, Karachi 31
Milburn, Colin 34

Miller, Keith 12–13
Minor Counties Championship 9, 11, 61
Mitchell, Alison 40–1
Moeran, Henry 45
Morgan, Eoin 190
Morris, Arthur 60
Mosey, Don 'Alderman' 30–2
Mosey, Stuart 30, 68
Mountford, Adam 40, 45, 47
Moxon, Martyn 203
Mumbai Indians New York 185
Murdoch, Rupert 200, 201
Murphy, Todd 143, 158, 160

Nancy (Lord's dining rooms) 23
Narendra Modi Stadium, Ahmedabad 184
Narine, Sunil 186
Nepal 193
Netherlands, the 174
Nevill Ground, Tunbridge Wells 56
New Delhi, India 93–6
New Road ground, Worcester 117
New Zealand
    v D. H. Robins' cricket team (1979–80) 50
    v England (1929–30) 46
    v England (1977–78) 68
    v England (2022) 114–15
    v England (2023) 115–16, 172–3
    v India (2023) 227
    v Pakistan (1976–77) 91
    v Pakistan (2024) 189
    v South Africa (2024) 104, 187–8
    v West Indies (1971–72) 25
    v West Indies (1979–80) 200–1
Newlands, Cape Town 211–12
Nicholas, Mark 210, 212, 217, 225, 228
Norfolk, Bernard, Duke of 16
Norfolk CCC 9–11, 61, 222
Nottinghamshire CCC 12

Old Trafford, Manchester 26, 114, 141, 145–50, 151, 153
Olympic Games 190
Oval, The 155–62
    Concorde over 36
    fixtures at 6, 108, 113, 151, 200
    Harleyford Road 35
    'leg over' moment 28
    press box 14
    TMS and 24
Oxford University Cricket Club 198, 199

Packer, Kerry 19, 63–6, 68–70, 226, 228–9
Pakistan 208
    v Australia (2023) 117
    v Australia (2023–24) 189
    v England (1977–78) 31, 65, 68
    v England (1987–88) 202
    v England (2020) 205
    v England (2022–23) 115, 176
    v New Zealand (1976–77) 91
    v New Zealand (2024) 189

v Sri Lanka (2009) 205
v West Indies (1987–88) 40
Pakistan Super League (PSL) 193
Parfitt, Peter 50, 54, 55
Parker, John 201
Pataudi, Nawab of 198
Patel, Lord 137, 196
Paterson, Miss 8
Peebles, Ian 11
Perth Scorchers 209
Peru 51
Petherick, Peter 91
Piachaud, Dan 221
Plunkett, Liam 186
Pollard, Kieron 186
Pope, Ollie 126, 138, 209, 210
Professional Cricketers'
    Association (PCA) 173

Rabada, Kagiso 217
racism 136–8, 195–7, 199–203, 205
Radcliffe Road End, Trent Bridge
    34
Rafiq, Azeem 4, 136–7, 196,
    203–4, 205
Rainford-Brent, Ebony 41
Rajasthan Royals 102, 103, 111,
    209, 223
ramp shots 8, 122, 213–14, 215–16,
    221
Rana, Shakoor 202
Raza, Ahsan 127
Reddy, Santosh 199
Rest of the World XI 64
Rhodes, Wilfred 6
Richards, Alan 25

Richards, Viv 68, 143, 158
Richardson, Garry 29
Riddell, Henry 24, 36, 41
Rio de Janeiro 55, 56–8
Roberts, Andy 65
Robertson, Austin 69
Robins, Derrick 2, 49–58
Robins, Walter 5
Robinson, Ollie 140
Rolls-Royce/Rover adventure
    (1976) 2, 49, 71–84, 85–99
Root, Joe 141–2, 156–7
    Bazball and 114, 116
    character 115
    England captain 112
    on daily overs 149
    declines number three 144
    ramp shot 214, 215–16
    in the slips 160
    Test innings 122–3, 126, 148,
    159, 175
Rose Bowl (T20) 157
Rought-Rought, Rodney, Basil and
    Desmond 9
Roy, Jason 186
Russell, Andre 186
Ruth, George Herman 'Babe' 122,
    126, 130

SA20 (T20) 104
Samson, Andrew 45–6
São Paulo, Brazil 55–6
Saudi Arabia 3–4, 187, 191–2
scorecards 147, 156, 178–9, 222
scorers 22, 43–4
seagulls 35–6

Seattle Orcas 185
Sehwag, Virender 190
Seymour, Kelly 50, 51, 55
Shackleton, Derek 150
Shakib Al Hasan 176–7
Sharma, Rohit 212
Shastri, Ravi 210–11, 224, 225
Simpson, Bobby 68
Simpson, Reg 12
Singh, Himmet 96
Singh, 'Pissy' 85, 92
Sivas, Turkey 77–8
Skirving, Imogen 33
Sky Television 166, 170
Smith, Ed 159
Smith, Graeme 210, 211, 227
Smith, Sir Aubrey 'Round-the-
    Corner' 131
Smith, Steve 116, 125, 138, 158,
    160, 186, 218
Sobers, Garry 158
Somerset CCC 13–14
Sophia Gardens, Cardiff 35
South Africa 104–5, 208
    v England (1889) 131
    v England (1956–57) 6, 15
    v England (1994) 200
    v England (2015–2016) 45–6
    v India (2024) 211–12
    v New Zealand (2024) 104,
        187–8
South American tour (1979)
    49–58
Sri Lanka 190, 208
    v Bangladesh (2023) 176–7
    v Pakistan (2009) 205

Staffordshire CCC 10, 61
Starc, Mitchell
    bowler 44, 143, 145, 159, 208
    IPL contract 219, 220
    Test innings 160
Statham, Brian 12
Stevenson, Graham 53–4
Stoinis, Marcus 186
Stokes, Ben
    Bazball and 2, 139–40, 169, 194,
        228
    contracts 175
    England captain 113, 122, 142,
        143, 146
    fielding 160
    McCullum and 112, 115–16
    Test cricket supporter 105, 218
    Test innings 126–7, 130–1, 148,
        159
summarisers 41–3
Sunak, Rishi 129
Sunningdale School, Ascot 7–8
Surrey CCC 24
Sutcliffe, Herbert 16–17
Swanton, Ann 16
Swanton, E.W. ('Jim') 15–16, 221
Symmonds, Donna 39–40

T10 competitions 190, 193
T20 competitions 3–4, 102–7,
        109–10, 190–3, 213–14
    Big Bash 181, 209
    Blast 4, 164, 166, 170, 187
    ILT20 192–3
    India and 2
    MJC 3, 181–2

popularity 139, 188, 218
Rose Bowl 157
SA20 104
World Cup 3, 174, 184–6
  See also Hundred, The
Taylor, Claude 11
Tehran, Iran 79–80
Test and County Cricket Board
    (TCCB) 49
Test Match Special (*TMS*) 39–47
  Arlott and Johnston 1, 25–8
  best cricket teas 33
  cakes and champagne 32–3
  current 135, 141
  early days 15, 21–5
  hotel bedroom commentary
    157
  Lord's Pavilion 21, 23
  'View from the Boundary' slot
    44
Test matches 102–10
  See also individual Tests
Thompson, Richard 149, 169–71,
    211, 227
Thompson, Wilfrid 9
Times, The 2, 13–14
Tink, Arthur and Mona 8–9
Today (BBC R4) 149
Tongue, Josh 138
Trent Bridge, Nottinghamshire 12,
    33–4, 44, 159
Trenton Cricket Club,
    Philadelphia 183
Trueman, Fred 9, 12, 23, 219–20
Trumper, Victor 141
Tufnell, Phil 44–5, 143

Tuke-Hastings, Michael 23
Turkey 73–9

United Arab Emirates (UAE) 192,
    193
United States 3, 174, 181–6,
    189–90

Van Cortlandt Park, New York
    City 185
Varsity Match 11, 50
Vaughan, Michael 147, 196
Venezuela 50
Viljoen, Hardus 46
Voce, Bill 60

Walcott, Sir Clyde 39, 201
Walsh, Tom 44
Wankhede Stadium, Mumbai 227
Ward, Brian 54
Warner, David 129, 140, 158, 159,
    160
Warner, Sir Pelham 'Plum' 10, 150
Watmore, Ian 195, 204–5
Waugh, Steve 151, 187, 212
Webber, Roy 43
Weekes, Sir Everton 39, 221
Wellings, Evelyn ('Lyn') 14–15
West Indians, British 200
West Indies
  T20 competitions 190
  T20 World Cup 3, 174, 185–6
  WSC and 64–5, 66
  v Australia (1960–61) 209
  v Australia (1975) 62, 71
  v Australia (1977) 68–9

v Australia (2024) 188, 208
v England (1929–30) 6
v England (1963) 150
v England (1967–68) 2–3
v England (1984) 200
v England (1997–98) 39, 40
v England (2021–22) 112
v New Zealand (1971–72) 25
v New Zealand (1979–80)
    200–1
v Pakistan (1987–88) 40
White, Crawford 16, 17–18
Whiteley, Peter 51
Willey, David 139
Willey, Peter 139
Williamson, Kane 115, 188
Willis, Bob 140
Wisden Cricketers' Almanack
    118–19, 124
Woakes, Chris
    Test bowler 138, 141–2, 144,
        145, 146, 158, 160
    Test innings 156
women commentators 39–41
Women's Ashes 155
women's cricket 164–5, 170, 178,
    197–8, 227
Wood, Mark
    Test bowler 138–40, 142, 143,
        146, 148, 159–60
    Test innings 156
Woodcock, John
    character 18–19

Packer and 65
Rolls-Royce/Rover adventure 2,
    49, 71–84, 85–99
Times cricket correspondent
    13–14
Wooldridge, Ian 229
Worcestershire CCC 108, 117,
    172
'World Cricket Connects' (2024
    event) 210, 212, 226, 228
World Cup
    first 62
    format 118
    India (1987) 215
    India (2023) 139, 155, 164, 166,
        173–5, 178–80, 227
World Cup (T20) 3, 174, 184–6
World Series Cricket (WSC) 19,
    63–6, 68–70, 229
World Test Championship (ICC)
    104, 117, 187
Worrell, Sir Frank 39
Wrigley, Arthur 43
Wroxham, Norfolk 8

Yardley, Norman 41
Yorkshire CCC 16–17, 136–7, 196,
    203–6, 222
Younis, Waqar 189

Zaltzman, Andy 46–7
Zimbabwe 190, 208